may the 5th

Revelations:

LORD has given me conviction

you that — TONGUES are the

AUDIBLE SPOKEN WORD of God !!

Echoes from What else

HEAVEN can the

Holy Spirit utter ?

Blessings, Love in

our Wonderful

Jesus

Grace McGonigle

Echoes from
HEAVEN

Grace McGonigle

TATE PUBLISHING & Enterprises

Published by Tate Publishing & Enterprises, LLC
127 E. Trade Center Terrace | Mustang, Oklahoma 73064 USA
1.888.361.9473 | www.tatepublishing.com

Tate Publishing is committed to excellence in the publishing industry. The company reflects the philosophy established by the founders, based on Psalms 68:11,
"The Lord gave the word and great was the company of those who published it."

Book design copyright © 2007 by Tate Publishing, LLC. All rights reserved.
Cover design by Sommer Buss
Interior design by Lynly D. Taylor

Published in the United States of America

ISBN: 978–1–5988623–9–1

07.08.28

Dedication

It is with joy that I dedicate this book to my sister, Reverend Carly Cheney. Through the years, she has been the source of my greatest encouragement. She has prayed for me, cried with me, and gone to bat for me in every instance. She sponsored my third Bible smuggling trip into Russia and fasted during my entire trip. She bought recording equipment for our first radio broadcasts and gave me a mobile home that was used as a Hospitality House for our 'Living Waters, The Fountain of Israel Ministries'. A combination Christian Book Store and Hair Styling Shop we owned and operated together was such fun! We saw God answer many prayers as we ministered to our customers in our "Prayer Room," a converted mop and broom closet!

Carly, born a "preemie" of two pounds, was "tossed aside" on a table, considered dead! A nurse came into the room, took one look, let out a stream of expletives in German, picked her up and swatted her. Carly let out a tiny sound. She was immediately put into a "preemie" ward, where she stayed for five months. I am eternally grateful to that unknown nurse, and the God in Heaven who had her life spared and gave her to me for a sister! Thank You Lord! How could I not succeed, with so much dedicated love flowing my way!

Acknowledgments

Thank you my dear husband Larry for the many ministry trips you have sponsored and for your patience as I have spent hours working on this book. Glenn, Amy, Jennifer and Rebecca, thank you for the joy you have brought into our lives. Cathy, Georgie, Autumn and Mike you have filled our lives with love and delight, and Georgie you have especially blessed me by saying: "Grandma, my buddies here at College really 'dig' your booklets!" They especially like the story of how you put the Psychoanalyst through deliverance!

Ruth Heflin and her wonderful family, all in heaven now, have been such blessings since first we met in 1972. Their Ministry at Calvary Pentecostal Campground in Ashland, Virginia, now under the able direction of Jane Lowder, has successfully led so many into trusting for the 'faith walk'. The 'House of Prayer' in Jerusalem, led by Ruth for 25 years, was initially, my 'way' to be able to live in Israel! It had blessed so many in the same manner. Its value was beyond measure!

Rev. Gwen Shaw, twenty-three years as a missionary in China and the establishment of 'End-Time Handmaidens and Servants International' have been a shining example to so many, of what just one life totally 'sold out' to our Lord, can accomplish! I'm so grateful to be a part of this wonderful group of missionary encouragers! Rev. Doris Swartz, having credentials with, 'International Ministers Forum' is a privilege and I have been so pleased to hear you say: "I always take time to read your booklets, I enjoy them!"

Rev. Mertis Stamps, thank you for introducing me to Mexico. You privileged me to preach for many years in some of the 29 Churches you have established there! Rev. Anna Mae Strausser, you and your late husband Charles granted me my first Ministerial credentials in 1973, through your wonderful School of Ministry, there in Coatesville, Pennsylvania. You have been instrumental in establishing Churches and Schools of Ministry throughout the earth.

Rev. Dr. Billy Graham, thank you for the life-changing statement I found in your book, 'Peace with God'. It turned my world around and returned me to the path of Life! Frances Gardner Hunter, thank you for the lessons I first learned, on how to lead others to Christ through your book, 'God Is Fabulous'! Your sense of humor is so refreshing! Rev. Pat Robertson, your 700 Club has been my T.V. mentor since 1978! Thank you for showing us the practical ways of putting Christ first—in everything!

Alice Twitchell's fine art (she is in heaven now) has filled many of my booklets. She deftly sketched while I played my autoharp and sang the 45 songs that the Lord had given me. Thank You Lord for those 'Echoes from Heaven' given while I worshipped You with Song in the Spirit. Alice presented the drawings of each of these songs as a love gift! They may be interspersed throughout this book. Her son Larry and his wife Cass blessed me with their friendship, living quarters and hilarious events while this artwork was taking place. Thank you both so much.

Thank you God for the Ministry of precious 'Prayer Warriors'; Carly and Max Cheney, Lila Aldenderfer, Gerry Yusko, Fay Montgomery, Ken Barker, Michelle Peace, and cousin Patty Cimador. The love and encouragement of Betty and Mack Peace and family, especially daughters, Melissa, Marlene and Mary have blessed me continually. How could we ever do without Christian brothers and sisters!

Rev. James and Alma Gilliam and your lovely congregation at Shiloh Baptist, here in the South Hills of Pittsburgh, have encouraged me all through the years. As well, have the members of the congregations of Peters Creek Baptist and the South Hills Assembly of God. Christian Pastors and friends are one of the sweetest of God's blessings!

Thank you to so many who have accompanied and blessed me on Mission trips: Shirley Smith, Anita Christopher, Rev. Thelma Oney, Beverly Ramer, Kathy Kuntzelman, and others. Lillian Righi as well as the little North Apollo Branch of E.T.H. surprised me—while I was living in Israel—with a timely e-mail stating that they were paying the airfare of my first trip to Honduras.

Dianne Landis graciously decided to help me financially the whole time of my stay in Ofakim, Israel in 1979–1980, and did so! During my 1998–99 stay in Bethany, Israel, You Lord, always had a check from Rebecca Rose Rodgers and others, turn up just when needed! Our parents and Godly Grandparents have blessed Carly and I all of our lives with their love and encouragement. Thank you Lord for the privilege of the gift of writing—may this book be pleasing to You and Yours!

Table of Contents

A Foreword to this book—and
a portrayal of its author!

My experience of receiving the Baptism of the Holy Spirit was a wonderful surprise! Along with this Baptism, came a revelation concerning speaking in Tongues. As a Baptist I 'fought' this truth, before the reality of the experience took place in my life! Afterward, my fervent prayer became, "Oh Lord God, please help my sisters and brothers in Christ to understand and enter into this wonderful 'Realm' of Your Spirit!" Thus, 'Living Waters Flow' was born. And concerning this book, I remember a comment made by Pastor Marcos Demendreoff of Argentina. He had invited me to preach in his Country and just after interpreting for me the first time, he said: "Sister Grace, you squeeze me like a lemon!"

When we arrived in Chile a few days later for a Pastor's Conference I was privileged to preach, sharing my little 'portion' of the Lord's Vineyard concerning Worship and Singing in the Spirit. This was received and acted upon wholeheartedly! But I left unsaid a few of the visions I had shared in Argentina, in an effort to avoid exhausting him. Brother Marcos corrected me.

He said: "Sister Grace, pay no attention to my complaints. You must not leave out the visions that the Lord has given you! They are the wonderful affirmations of your message, especially the ones concerning worship with Song in the Spirit!" You will find *all of these visions* in this volume.

(This Ministry with Pastor Demendreoff took place in 1985. An earthquake took place in Mendoza just before our plane landed, and then again in Valparaiso off of the Coast of Chili four days later! We were in the midst of this devastation, but were guarded by the Lord.

In Chile, the Area of the Church in which we preached had been hit by the 'quake'. This happened during the Sunday night Service. Many people fled in fear, but a huge angel was seen holding up the corner of this Church by those who stayed in the Church praying! But the façade of another Church had been demolished. At night, it was strange seeing the ceilings in the Pastors home in which we stayed. My room had cracks at the juncture of all four walls with the ceiling!)

Along with this Baptism came a new, deep love for the people of my Savior-Bridegroom! I wanted to go to Israel to meet His ethnic 'family members'; to see the Land where He was born and walk on the hills of the Galilee where He preached. God let me have this privilege. I wrote of this journey. The resulting booklet, 'Window Washing in Israel' is a favorite of many. It speaks of my experience of working as a volunteer with Moroccan Jewish children in Ofakim, a little development town in the Negev. *This booklet is not in this volume* but the fact that God called me to this land and allowed me to visit and spend much time in Israel over the next 34 years contributes to the writing of 'A Call to Sanity' 'The Birth-Right of Ishmael'.

While noting the brilliance and the courage and the endurance of the Jewish people in spite of all 'odds against them'—I wrote: "An American Christian speaks out on Behalf of Israel!" This is encapsulated in my booklet, "Israel, a True 'Time-Line' concerning 'His Land'. This is a compilation expressing my love for the Jewish people! I wrote of their *new beginnings.* After the almost two thousand years of the dispersion that took place *from* the Land of Israel, as they were scattered to the 'ends of the earth'—late in the eighteen hundreds—*long before their* official birth date of 1948—the Jews once more began settlement in their *Promised Land!*

I have written in an attempt to help others realize that it was the Jew who restored this *desecrated, neglected, forgotten piece of property.* It was the Jew, the pioneer, the halutzeem who married the land—dug her soil—planted the seed and brought her back to life! Even while others, at the same time, not only neglected but tried to 'undo' her. The Jewish people have *'homesteading rights'* to their land, as well as Biblical! This booklet helps one to realize truth—as opposed to the lies that have been parading as such—for far too many years! It will appear in my next book with Tate Publishing, along with another little booklet I speak of just a bit later!

My first trip to Russia began as an answer to the tears I shed as I read 'Tortured for Christ' by Richard Wurmbrand. This pastor's imprisonment and agony lasted for 14 years! This was the result of this Romanian Jew's response and faithfulness to the Gospel of Christ. My prayer as I wept was: "O God—how do you get Bibles to these suffering people?" The Answer: Six weeks later I was flying into Russia from Finland, where I had received the sixteen Bibles that were hidden in the pockets that had been sewn into my mouton fur coat.

While not delivering all of these 'Gifts' when in Leningrad, we took a 'night-train' to Moscow, still concealing our 'Treasures'! Once in Moscow, an assignment to deliver one of Ruth Heflin's personal letters to 'The Social Secretary of 'His Excellency Brezhnev' became 'my job'! Delivering this letter, this 'credo' demanding the release of Russian Jews for the privilege of 'going home to Israel' was one of my 'scariest' of experiences that year. I go into this *escapade, in this volume* along with my *forays into China* that took place in later of my 'missionary journeys'. All of these 'Ministry Trips' began after a Prophet laid his hand on my forehead and said: "Lord, send her as a Missionary into many lands!"

And, 'Oh, yes—as I was walking out of the Baptist Church in Moscow on my second trip to Russia, (when I was not allowed to take Bibles in this year because of the difficulties we had experienced on this first trip) a young man approached me and quickly whispered: "Bibles, you have Bibles?" As I sadly said "No.", I could see in my 'mind's eye' the 250 Russian Gospel's of Matthew, Mark, Luke, and John that I had left behind in America. I said within: "Lord, how should I know if this is a Russian spy or not?" He answered: "If I send them to you, it will be of Me, fear not!" I vowed on the spot! "Lord, if You ever get me into Russia again, I will not come without Bibles!" "New Freedom—Stay Free!" is the story of this vow fulfilled and 'Gifts' delivered in my little booklet telling of my 3rd trip to Russia for 'Bible Smuggling' purposes. I had to do this alone, and the wonderful ways in which God led each step, is to me a memory of sweetness; of encouragement and strength.

During certain times, a wonderful anointing comes upon our minds and spirits. Worshipping and singing in the Spirit with uplifted hands signifying surrender of heart, soul and being, to the Magnificence and rule of our Awesome God results in 'Echoes from Heaven'. I learned years ago, that as we lift our hands and bless our God in worship, He in turn, blesses us abundantly 'out of Zion' far beyond, what we have ever given to Him. This results in a time of incomparable *mutual blessings* with our Lord

(The above mentioned booklets that are not found in this volume are available. Write me!)

(Or, look for my next book with Tate Publishing. It will probably contain those above, plus a few more surprises!)

I pray that the length of my dissertations do not exhaust but rather excite and encourage my readers to want to enter, and live in—on a day to day basis—the new realms of the Wonderful Holy Spirit that He has provided for each of us who hunger for such! This reminds me of a song that came to me as I awakened for my nightly Bible Study. I heard out loud, as though I had a radio on my bed-bar, a wonderful melody. I ran to my piano and sounded the first note, then went to my kitchen to write down the song. This took no more than 15 minutes. No sooner had I scored the notes, than the following words flowed out!

'Dispelling the Gloom'

"In the evening hours I come to you, when the night is calm and still.
Listen while I teach you patiently and your understanding I fill.

I will take your minds and lead you free, if you will but come to me.
I delight in filling 'hungry hearts'! Listen and learn of me, my loved ones".

And then the melody repeated itself. I was thrilled to hear Him call us: His loved ones, even as He called Daniel a man greatly beloved! This must have been so wonderful for Daniel to hear! I was given to know that this was a song that David played when the evil spirit vexed Saul and so I named it: 'Dispelling the Gloom'! Many find that when this song is sung, it lifts heavy hearts and brings joy along with it! In fact, one friend takes it along to a sanitarium and says that singing it causes peace and serenity. When my sister Carly had 'wiggling' youths in her Barber Chair, she began humming 'that song'. She soon found her little customers pacified—to the surprise of their mothers! Since then, when the Holy Spirit brings one especially for me to witness to, I know that they have a 'hungry heart'! What a blessing! We thank You Father, for heavenly Music and Words. These are surely—Your 'Echoes from Heaven'!

'Living Waters Flow'

This is a handbook on 'walking in the Realm of the Spirit'. The Visions and Revelations shared encourage us to desire to Worship our Lord, singing in the Language of the Spirit, the Unknown Tongue!'

Table of Contents for 'Living Waters Flow'

Introduction

I have earnestly tried to help others understand the reality and importance of Tongues. The revelation that I have on this subject, was given me by the Word of Wisdom! This is just a Word out of God's vast amount of wisdom. It was given as visions were shown to me. And then, through the previous and further study of the Bible, with the leading of the Holy Spirit, these visions were confirmed and enlarged upon. I didn't even know what the Gift of the Word of Wisdom was before I received a portion of it from the Lord, *through* these visions! I received them, shortly after receiving the Baptism in the Holy Spirit! Until this time, I was 'in the dark' concerning so many spiritual realities, especially regarding the subject of Tongues.

I believe that it is vitally important that we begin to speak and sing in the Spirit, much more than we are presently doing! This is a Key that unlocks so many Doors to the 'Spiritual Realm'! These, we are invited to enter, explore and live in daily! Please take this journey with me now, with the prayer that the Holy Spirit guides us into *all* Truth. We know that we can trust Him to answer this cry of our 'hungry hearts'!

I have called this booklet '*Living Waters Flow*' because of the importance of the revelations that are contained in these few Precious Words—*Living Waters*, the *Fountain* of Israel. Jeremiah 2:13 tells us that the Lord God is this Fountain! And a portion of this fountain is *within us!* "Christ in us, the hope of Glory", this is the mystery spoken of by Paul in Colossians 1:27. Oh may we, the Church, the Body of the Living Christ, understand and *act* upon these revelations, enabling us to more fully bring forth—out of *our* 'bellies'—the Living Waters residing there!

These 'Wonderful Waters' were spoken of by our Lord on that last day of the Feast of Tabernacles. John 7:37-39, "On the last day, the climax of the festival, Jesus stood and shouted to the crowd, "If you are thirsty, come to me! If you believe in me, come and drink! For the Scriptures declare that *rivers of living water will flow out from within*." (When he said "living water," he was speaking of the Spirit, who would be given to everyone believing in him. But the Spirit had *not yet been given*, because Jesus had not yet entered into his glory.)" (NLT) While in Argentina, preaching on this passage, the Lord brought a deeper understanding of this scripture to me.

Yes, of course, the Holy Spirit had been present and moving in power since the beginning. We see Him in Genesis named as the very *Spirit of God,* hovering over the face of the waters. And yes, He has been busy anointing and directing all through the Bible! But Saint John tells us that He—the Spirit—*had not yet been given as the Gift of God,* in the whole new way now possible since the Crucifixion, death and Resurrection of our Lord! He is received *into us,* through the 'born-again' experience. And then He is poured out *upon us,* and thereby received in a further, way, on *our* special 'Day of Pentecost'! And as this takes place—'we *are changed into another man'*—as was Saul when the Holy Oil was poured out *upon* him by the Prophet Samuel. The pouring out of this cruse of oil brought the Presence of the Holy Spirit upon Saul in a wonderful new way!!

Yes—the Holy Spirit is given *within us, when* we are 'born again' but then—He is given *upon* us, as we are baptized—anointed *from on high*—with the invisible 'Holy Oil' of His Spirit!

This Baptism of the Holy Spirit has to do with a pouring out of *Holy Oil* upon the believer! This is not an immersion in water, as is the Baptism of Repentance taught by John the Baptist. Obedient devoted followers of Christ enter into this 'water baptism' as an outward expression of their burial of the old man—being buried with Christ in His death. This signifies a resurrection of the new man that they have now become in Him! O Glory!

Then, the Baptism of the Holy Spirit is not of water, but rather of an *invisible oil* that is poured out *upon* believers who desire 'more of Jesus'—even as was a *'horn of oil'* poured out upon those who would be dedicated as priests and kings and prophets in the time of the Old Testament! We *need* this *'anointment-appointment'* from on High—for does not I Peter 2:9 (a) tell us that, "we are a chosen generation—a royal priesthood—a holy nation". (NKJV) And further, Revelation 1:6 reveals, "And hath made us kings and priests unto God and his Father; to him be glory and dominion for ever and ever. Amen." How marvelous, that we are become a *Nation* of Kings and Priests unto our God!

There are powerful verses surrounding this verse and the Word tells us that there is a special blessing in their reading, so I have included them!

Rev. 1:4, "John to the seven churches which are in Asia: Grace be unto you, and peace, from him which is, and which was, and which is to come; and from the seven Spirits which are before his throne; Rev. 1:5, "And from Jesus Christ, who is the faithful witness, and the first begotten of the dead, and the prince of the kings of the earth. Unto him that loved us, and washed us from our sins in his own blood. Rev. 1:7, "Behold, he cometh with clouds; and every eye shall see him, and they also which pierced him: and all kindred's of the earth shall wail because of him. Even so, A-men" (KJV)

(Isn't this really important powerful "stuff" that we become a part of, *when we become children* and then *Sons* of the Living God, our Father, the Creator of the Universe? No wonder we cry: "Glory Hallelujah!")

Our God who is a Consuming Fire comes ***upon*** us in this Baptism We are immersed, encompassed about with *'Holy Oil'*—taken *into the Holy Spirit* as He comes *upon us* completely, and we are *completed!* We are *energized* by a 'Baptism of Love!' We are empowered and can now go forth with a new greater boldness, witnessing to *His Marvelous Love* which is the *'true essence'* of Life!

Right along with the 'pouring out of this Holy Oil', a Tongue of Fire for the 'lighting' of the Oil is given! This Warm 'Oil of Love' begins to burn and our vessels become filled with His Power! This Power makes of us fervent witnesses! We become witnesses, because of this 'Bath of Love'—for our God *is Love!* And being inundated with His Spirit, we are filled with a greater desire to share the Love of Christ with others! The Words of Christ to His disciples become a new reality in our lives! Acts 1:8 says, "But you shall receive power—ability, efficiency and might—when the Holy Spirit has come *upon* you; and you *shall* be My witnesses in Jerusalem and all Judea and Samaria and to the ends—the very bounds of the earth." (Amplified Bible-TAB)

Later, as we learn to 'light' this oil that stays upon us, through using the 'Tongue of Fire'—given in part for this very purpose—we become 'filled' over and over! A new anointing, of warm oil, power and love flows through us! We are inundated with the new joy of this *new dimension* of our God that we have entered into! The 'unknown tongue' is no longer unknown to us. We begin to realize that its use is a 'Life-line of Love', straight from our Heavenly Father! And that it has been given to us to equip us to be capable of praying—in the Spirit—in the Holy Spirit of our Living Almighty God—*using His Words!*

And note here, the Word of God does *not say* in Acts 1:8, "You shall speak in unknown Tongues—and be My Witnesses." But rather it says, "You shall *receive power—when* the Holy Spirit has come *upon* you, and *you shall be witnesses to Me.*" Again, even as Saul was said to be changed into another man when the Holy Spirit came *upon* him as related in I Samuel 10: 6, "At that time the Spirit of the Lord will *come upon you with power,* and you will prophesy with them. You will be *changed into a different person."*(NLT) Even so, are we *changed into different persons* when the Holy Spirit comes *upon us with power;* as was Peter on that Day of Pentecost. When the Holy Spirit came upon him, he was changed into a powerful fearless orator—from a cringing fearful coward.

"Lord God, if in any way there is error or misrepresentation of the Truths that I feel are from You—forgive and correct—that none be led in any way, other than 'Your Perfect Way'—the clean *'Holy Path of Truth'.*

A 'Sampling' of Holy Spirit Disclosure

A Startling Revelation—a 'Word of God'—
given to one of His Prayer Warriors!

In 1938, a Revelation concerning 'Tongues' was given to a faithful 'prayer-warrior,' named Navetta Rexroad. A student at Elim Bible Seminary, she was deeply grieved when she heard another say "Tongues are satanic." Her Father, a Pentecostal Pastor, assured her that such statements are inspired by Satan!

He said, "Forgive them daughter, and pray for those who make such remarks. They are ignorant of the Truth concerning Tongues!"

Navetta went to her prayer closet and travailed and cried and prayed for hours getting no release from this burden.

Suddenly the Holy Spirit said within: *If you will be faithful in prayer concerning this matter, I will use your prayer to release from the Body of Christ—the poison that is in it. For, said He—a body cannot get well as long as poison is in it, and the 'misconception' concerning Tongues is a poison in My Living Body!*

When Navetta shared this Word with me—33 years later in 1971—she told me that she had *never shared this* with anyone before, lest she call attention to herself!

But, said she, "The Holy Spirit has directed me to share this with you just now!"

I leaped in my spirit in Joy! Certainly not because of the *condition of the Church* that had just been shown me, but rather that the Holy Spirit had just moments before, spoken to me and said:

"Be still now and listen, I want to show you something."

Her words, immediately following His direction to me, confirmed what He had been teaching me about Tongues, with this added perilous dimension—that the misconception concerning Tongues was *causing* a poison to be present in His Church!

"Poison, I questioned...Lord, is it possible that such a damaging condition exists in your precious Body of Believers? Misconception concerning Tongues has become a poison? Poison is venom! Venom is that which comes out of the mouth and off of the tongue of a snake, or out of the mouth of one being used by Satan—even when they are unaware that they are being used as a puppet. Can this be so Lord?"

Peter we know was once guilty of being used by Satan to contradict our Lord Jesus as stated in Matthew 16:23 and Mark 8:33, "Jesus turned and looked at his disciples and then said to Peter very sternly, "Get away from me, Satan! You are seeing things merely from a human point of view, not from God's."(NLT) (This scripture 'clues' us that Jesus is not pleased when we speak thoughtlessly and only in the natural and can thereby be motivated by Satan to use his damaging words!)

Poison is a toxin that brings destruction! It causes contamination and brings weakness and disability! It incapacitates and leads to apathy, lethargy, indifference and even death!

"Lord, can it really be that there existed in Your Church this condition—and that it still exists?"

The confirming answer came that very evening! The 'key-note' address brought by Harold Hill was: "The Tongue, a Small Member Capable of POISON!" James 3:8 says, *"But no man can tame the tongue. It is an unruly evil, full of deadly poison"*. NKJV

All of this took place at the Full Gospel Businessmen's Fellowship International in the Sheraton Hotel in *Syracuse,* N.Y., where I feel that God brought about the ability to *'sear-the-accuser'! We may do this* as we begin to more fully understand this Revelation, and learn of *our ability,* through *the proper and proficient use of* the Holy Spirit's Language and His Power—to *drain this 'poison' out* of the Living Body of Christ, His Church! Hallelujah!

The Antidote!

Oh 'sleeping Church'—listen! The Spirit is giving us the *antidote!* Let us *wake-up* and use our voices to speak forth pure, undefiled Holy Words! Words that are the utterance of the Holy Spirit given straight from Heaven especially for such a time as this! These Words, in the Bible are called Unknown Tongues! They are *unknown and unable to be uttered* by those who do not know the Lord our God! 1Cor. 2:14, "But people who aren't Christians can't understand these truths from God's Spirit. It all sounds foolish to them because only those who have the Spirit can understand what the Spirit means." (NLT)

But we, who have Christ in us and the Holy Spirit *upon us,* can and should and must begin to inundate the air waves with these Holy Words! These are the Words of God that can absolutely cleanse our atmosphere—at least the atmosphere in our immediate vicinities—of the filthy words that are presently inundating us as in a quagmire of garbage!

Unholy words of filth and profanity and blasphemy—words that take the Name of our God in vain—shouted daily from our televisions and radios and other technical devises, are Satan's *un*holy gifts—his contributions in an effort to bring about the destruction of humanity! We need to take our Holy Ghost 'Fire-Powered-Hoses' out of our mouths and cleanse away the mud of corruption with which our air-waves are polluted—even as our Firemen use great streams of water from their hoses to cleanse away the ravages of natural floods!

The evil one, the Great Imitator has brought forth this 'flood of filth' giving his imitation of God's flood in the days of Noah. Especially has he delighted to organize this at the very time that the Lord uses the Flood of Noah as a prophetic 'sign' of the 'time of the end'!

Or is this—flood of filth instigated by Satan—exactly what our Lord was speaking of in His great discourse of end-time happenings in the 24th Chapter of Matthew and verse 37?

Oh are we now living in that time related in Luke 17:26–30, "When the Son of Man returns, the world will be like the people were in Noah's day. In those days before the flood, the people enjoyed banquets and parties and weddings right up to the time Noah entered his boat and the flood came to destroy them all. And the world will be as it was in the days of Lot. People went about their daily business—eating and drinking, buying and selling, farming and building—until the morning Lot left Sodom. Then fire and burning sulfur rained down from heaven and destroyed them all. Yes, it will be 'business as usual' right up to the hour when the Son of Man returns." (NLT)

Yes most probably, *we are now living in that very hour!* Oh, *it is 'High-Time'*, for the Body of Christ to open their mouths and *speak* the **'Antidote'**! (A friend just asked me what the word antidote means. It means a cure, a remedy, a solution!) Let us begin to use this method of healing and deliverance!

The Great Disappointment!

When first I wrote—'Living Waters Flow'—in 1974, I couldn't *wait* to share it! I rushed off to a conference being held in New York City, expecting that someone was going to come up to me and say, "I know you have a manuscript concerning *tongues* and *worship* and the Lord told me to publish it!" My first book had been placed on the shelf; surely this would not be the destiny of this second one! Thus, my hopes were high and I couldn't wait to see how things would transpire! During the first morning class, Rev. James Beale gave a message that began, "When God wants to use a man or a woman, He *gets them all excited;* He *gives them a vision* and then He says, *'Wait'!*"

Upon hearing those words, I cried within, "No Lord!" This book was surely not to go on the shelf along with the first?"

Beale continued, "Take Abraham for instance. God gave him a Word, told him He was going to make his seed as numerous as the sands on the seashore. Then he had to *wait* twenty-five years for Isaac to be born. Then he had to *wait* fourteen years for him to grow up."

With each word that Beale spoke, I realized that the book 'Living Waters Flow'—the first of a Mini-Anthology was not to be published at that time. My

tears and argument did not change the mind of the Lord. (Thankfully, I have just learned that in the Hebrew Language, 'wait' means: to be entwined with! And what better position could we be in than to be 'wrapped up' 'tied up' 'and tangled up' with Jesus! A beloved song I first learned while in the Rev. Gerald Derstine 'Ten Week School of Ministry' in Bradenton, Florida!)

When my first book was put on the shelf it was as a desert experience. I had never had such before and was literally 'numb' with misunderstanding. (This is when I learned of 'Picking the Fruit of the Holy Spirit'; found in Chapter Ten of this book.)

On Sunday morning, Pastor Mouton called for a three day fast. My response was, "Lord, I don't know if I can do this, but I'll try." By the second day my head felt as though it would burst with pain and I cried,

"Oh Lord, I have to break this fast!" Immediately, the pain left! I said, "Lord, you must really want me in this fast...alright." I committed to it and continued fasting.

On Wednesday evening, no sooner had I entered the Church than a visiting Pastor; (one who had met me previously) began to prophesy. As I listened, tears began to stream down my face and within I said,

"Lord, this sounds like an exact answer to my dilemma."

The Pastor's wife then spoke and said: "Oh, this is so wonderful, often when my husband prophesies; I have a vision. "I saw someone in a desert place, but there is cause for rejoicing for I see a *new Stream* coming down from Heaven!"

Immediately the Pastor pointed to me and said,

"Sister Grace, you're the one. I have seen this since you walked in the door. Now something has been wrong in your life for the past two to two and a half weeks (the exact time). Satan has been trying to pull you in another direction, but you stand still and see the Salvation of the Lord."

He then began to sing another prophecy; part of it was this: "Precious in the sight of the Lord is the death of the saints, that thou die, not only in the natural, but also in thy thoughts, and in thy will, and in thy life, yea, the Lord has laid aside, that He might bring forth His Purposes in thee *in the Fullness of God, at the End of the Age!*"

This prophecy of many pages was caught on tape, and has been a portion of guidance for my life all of these many years. I share this now, for I feel that this, finally, may be the time for that Prophecy to be completed and I believe that these *Revelations concerning Tongues* and the marvelous joy of the anointing that comes when we—alone or corporately—Worship the Lord with *Song in the Spirit,* are all part of the fulfillment of that Word!

"Oh, may this be so, Lord!"

Chapter One

The Doorway This Baptist Almost Missed Entering!

"**W**ell, you *do know* about the Baptism of the Holy Spirit?" questioned this lovely red-haired woman.

I thought to myself: "Here is that expression again! Well, this is my opportunity to *set at least one person straight* on this subject!"

"Do I know about the baptism of the Holy Spirit? I *certainly* do! I know that it is the same thing as being born again and I wish people would stop confusing others by referring to the 'born again experience' as a *'Baptism of the Holy Spirit!'*"

I answered her self-assuredly and ready to prove my argument and do battle with any who disagreed with my conclusions. After all, I was a Baptist who had studied the Word of God for eight years and I certainly *knew* what the Bible had to say about baptisms!

"No dear," she replied lovingly, "it's not the same as being born again. It is receiving the Holy Spirit in a whole new way!" She then walked off to help others, seeking to know their prayer needs.

She returned to me after awhile and smiled. Wanting to help her to understand that she was confused, I said:

"Look!" I said adamantly, "When I asked Jesus Christ to come into my heart, He came in! And it is His Holy Spirit that came in, so I already have the Holy Spirit in me!"

"Yes, of course," she softly replied. "You must have Christ in you before you can be baptized in His Spirit. There just is *more of Jesus* that you may have." And again she returned to the crowd to help them. When later she returned, in exasperation, I asked:

"How can I possibly have any more of Him?" I tried to explain my position to her. "When Jesus came into my heart and life, He didn't put in just an arm or a leg. His whole Spirit *came into me!*" I thought that statement would surly straighten out her thinking! I wanted her to realize that she was talking about being born again and that therefore, she had received all of Jesus that she needed, and there was no more of Him that she *could* receive!

She smiled sweetly and said, "There *is* more of Jesus that you may have." She continued on, "I understand what you are expressing, for I was 'born again' when I was twelve, even as you have told me that you were 'born again' at twelve, but last year I received the wonderful experience of being baptized with the Holy Spirit." "I received more of Jesus!"

I attempted once more to clear things up for her.

"Look, in Ephesians 5:18 it says, We are to be filled with the Spirit, speaking to ourselves in psalms and hymns and spiritual songs, singing and making melody in our hearts to the Lord. He has promised never to leave us, so if I want to be filled with more of Jesus, I just have to pray and read my Bible more and I will draw closer to Him. He never goes away, though I may draw away from Him. I *have* the Holy Spirit *in* me!"

"Yes, I believe you," she replied, "but there *is* more of Him that you may receive!"

I took my Sword out of its sheath once more and spoke the Scripture that *I was sure* would make her see the *light!*

"Ephesians chapter four says, "There is *one* Lord, *one* faith and *one* baptism." Now, if there is one, there can't be two as you are suggesting. I have already been baptized, twice in fact. I was sprinkled when I was a baby in Dad's Methodist Church, and again, immersed as a Baptist, after I was born again!"

"Wonderful" she replied, "but there *is more* of Jesus that you may receive!" She said this with such warmth and love and kindness and assurance, that finally, I had nothing more to add to my 'one-sided argument' except to wonderingly state:

"If there is more of Jesus that I may have, I want it, because I like what I have of Him already."

"Well, you go home and read I Corinthians chapters twelve and fourteen."

"I've just read them," I responded in surprise, "I'm trying to figure them out! In fact, my friend Joyce and I sat on her swing just last week discussing those very chapters! We said: 'Wouldn't it be nice, if we could figure out all of this business in the Bible about Tongues. If only God would show us one way or another. If they are for us today, how do we get them? If they were just for the early Church, we can put the subject away from us and forget about them.'"

Now she broke out into laughter, "Oh, you are ready now, to pray!"

She said, "You don't like the expression 'Baptism of the Holy Spirit,' but you trust Jesus don't you?"

"I trust Him with my life!" I exclaimed.

"Well then, ask Him just as you said it to me. Tell Him you want more of Him!"

"Right now" I asked

"Why not," she replied, "you're not ashamed of Him are you?"

"Of course not, I know that if we are ashamed of Him before men down here, He will be ashamed of us before His Father in Heaven!"

At last I was ready to pray, and ask Jesus for more of Himself!

The Pouring Out of Heavenly Water and Oil—in a Bath of Love!

As I closed my eyes to pray, Velma laid her hand on me gently. As her hand touched my shoulder, I felt an unusual sensation. It was as a 'sting of fire,' but without the hurt. That is a strange statement, isn't it? It is difficult to explain the moving of the Holy Spirit. The natural mind can only wonder concerning these things.

I bowed my head and prayed, "Jesus, if there is more of you that I may have I want it!"

Can I ever forget the marvelous experience of love that followed? Never! I get thrilled over and over again each time I tell it. Let me try to share it with you! A complete reversal took place as the love of God poured over me. My hands could not seem to reach high enough and I stood exclaiming over and over,

"Praise You, Lord. I love You, Lord Jesus!"

The more I expressed praise, the more I experienced that waves of love were pouring upon and over me. I began to realize that this praise and thanksgiving was the language of those who were wearing '*Praise Garments*'!'

Tears of happiness and joy streamed from my eyes. I almost could not stand upright. In fact, I had fallen into the arms of a friend who was holding me up! Perhaps this explains in part why those first baptized on that Wonderful Day of Pentecost were accused of being drunk!

When I could finally stand upright, still lost in praise and thanksgiving, my new friend, the lovely redhead said:

"Now, not in English dear, praise the Lord in a Heavenly Language." She began to pray in the Spirit.

I had no idea of what she was talking about, nor speaking, and furthermore, I could care less. I didn't mean to be ungrateful, but I was having the time of my life telling the Lord how much I loved him in my own language, and I didn't want to be interrupted! I must have stood there for over an hour, lost in worship. I had never before felt such capacity for love.

When I finally could think in the natural again, I said to the Lord,

"Lord, I don't want to read a book on this subject, or hear a tape. Lord, the book of Ephesians says that there is One Lord, One Faith, and One Baptism. This experience that I have just had is as marvelous as the one I had the day I asked you into my heart and had a vision of Jesus. Velma is telling me that this is called the 'Baptism of the Holy Spirit' Lord, please help me to understand! If there is just one Baptism, and it is the one that I had already received, affirming my salvation experience in normal water after I was saved, how can there now be a Baptism in the Holy Spirit? That would make *two* baptisms!"

God was so gracious to me. On the way out of the Church door, He spoke in my heart, and said: *"The Jew says the Lord our God is One Lord—and He is! But they miss—the Father, the Son and the Holy Spirit!"* Oh Lord, yes, One Lord, but three, Father ,Son, and the Holy Spirit, One, but Three Oh, that made me so happy to have this understanding of the Scripture. It made me realize that there could be more than one Baptism! And that this Baptism that I had just received was not just marvelous and wonderful but more importantly—valid according to the Word of God!

All of the above took place because of the following:

Going to the basement of the Presbyterian Church here in Pittsburgh, Pennsylvania, that day, I had joined the overflow crowd of those attending the Friday morning "Miracle Service" led by Kathryn Kuhlman. I had been going to these "Miracle Services" ever since Kathryn came to town in 1947 and began her meetings in the old Carnegie Music Hall. I was 14 at the time, had been saved for two years, when my Grandfather, Jacob Edward Steffen said to me:

"Gracie, there is a women in town having Miracle Meetings. I want you to go to them." I loved my grand pap and so off I went. At the very first meeting I was standing next to a woman with a huge goiter on her neck. That day I saw this goiter disappear! Miss Kuhlman hadn't even laid hands on her. Needless to say I continued going to these meetings. I listened to Kathryn on the radio during my teen-age years, and followed her ministry all through the years.

Now I was 37 years old. The year was 1970. Lately I had been hearing Kathryn speak of a Baptism in the Holy Spirit, and wondered why she was doing so. It seemed to me she hadn't been preaching about this before, and wondered why she was giving the 'born again experience' another name.

It was August and summer was almost over. This would be my last chance to get to a Miracle Service before school began. I asked Amy, my oldest daughter to watch Jenny, now four years old, and Becky the two-year old. Amy loved her little sisters and graciously agreed.

Stepping into Church, I spied a friend of mine who was a "worker" there.

"Oh, Marie, Hi there, it's so nice to see you! We haven't gotten together in ages!"

"Grace, I'm so glad to see you, I hear that you're having weekly Bible Studies in your home and you aren't praying for Miracles!"

"Aw, Marie, one can't 'con' God, I don't have the faith to believe for miracles. I asked for a miracle and look!" I pointed to the scar of my recent Thyroid operation.

"Well, you should be praying for miracles," Marie replied adamantly.

"Now Marie, you come to my Bible Study and you pray for the miracles. I will lead the study. Kathryn laid her hand on me two years ago, and since then, I seem to have a greater understanding of the Bible. I see into the Word of God with new eyes. Then you can do the praying for miracles!"

"Sounds great," she agreed!

Just then Velma Clate, another "helper" working for Kathryn came by and Marie introduced us. I smiled, we hugged in greeting and Marie invited Velma to our (now mutual) Bible Study!

As shown in what took place at the beginning of this Chapter, this meeting was a "Divine Appointment"—arranged by the Holy Spirit! I have been and will always be, grateful for this occurrence that 'Energized and Changed' my life and my walk in the Lord—forever!

Seated in a trolley on the way home that day, I felt such love that I wanted to put my arms around everybody and tell them that Jesus loved them! I restrained myself, but when I was almost home, I caught sight of a young neighbor. He was a little boy of five who was mentally retarded. I rushed over, caught him up in my arms and hugged and kissed him, delighted to be able to express this new-found love. Before this baptism I knew that as a Christian, I should be very loving with this little boy, but he had a catarrhal condition that resulted in a constant runny nose! I would pat him at arms length, lest, perish the thought; I would get some of it on me! But this day, I cared not if I should get tangled up with that runny nose and its results. *Comparing me now, with me* before this experience, I had an abundance of love to express in a measure that I had not had before. Such a wonderful experience! I ran to the home of my best friend and shared with her everything that had just happened. She wanted to meet my new friend and learn more about this special baptism of love!

My understanding now is that having the Holy Spirit come upon one can be likened to being surrounded by and encompassed in an immersion of *liquid love*. God is Love and His Presence in this pouring out of Himself renders one almost incapable of giving a written description. The Garment of Praise, a lovely wedding garment, is placed upon us. From the top of our head it is extended down to the soles of our feet. This was the manner of the marriage ceremony in the Old Testament. A man took off his cloak and cast it over his bride covering her completely. This act meant, "She is mine!"

This garment replaces the hard yoke of bondage that the evil one has managed to place around our necks. And as this broken yoke slides off, the burden of the spirit of heaviness slips off of our shoulders right along with it! Isaiah 10:27 is taking place! The anointing has broken the yoke! (I felt this snap of the breaking, the moment I received this Baptism.) It was a 'snap' on the back of my neck! I immediately lifted my hands in thanksgiving. This is something that I *had not wanted to do, and resisted,* up until this very moment! Up until this time, *I never really wanted to lift my hands unto the Lord.* I felt that raising my hands was being unnecessarily demonstrative. I would resist Kathryn's admonition to, "Lift your hands unto God and Worship Him!" Through the years as I sat in her meetings I would lift my hands partially and say within, "This is not necessary, please let's get on with the meeting!"

Also, I did not like to hear the expression, "Praise the Lord!" when stated with explosive exuberance. I thought within, some people get so noisy, but I like things to be dignified. Also, I said within, just how many times can one say, 'praise the Lord', 'praise the Lord'? David's Psalms get a little boring with that repetitive phrase. And what's all this business about lifting up the hands? I did know that the Bible said to lift up holy hands and bless the Lord, and He would bless us 'out of Zion'! But I didn't understand any of that either, so I disregarded it.

I blush now with shame to think how blind and ignorant I had been in my limited conception of what was pleasing to the Lord, though I really was not more than vaguely aware that I was guilty of all of the things I have just admitted to. This had been my inner attitude. Was it because of the yoke? Surely! I know now that these attitudes were a demonstration of *my* proud flesh and possibly a 'religious spirit'! This is a spirit and an attitude, which causes one to be proud of their Church attendance and service, rather than having a spirit of humility which creates emotions of thanksgiving and praise, and a desire to glorify God in which ever way He leads us to behave. "Lord, forgive me for my inward criticism. Help me to see my own faults, rather than those of others."

I loved seeing and feeling the Presence of God as the miracles took place in those Miracle Services. In fact, after being in one of those services it took me three days to recover from the weight of the Glory! But before this day I was completely unaware concerning this Baptism of the Holy Spirit; nor did I understand *the word anointing and its meaning!* I just knew that to sit in those Miracle Meetings for four hours was heavenly! I hadn't realized that we all were being bathed in the warm oil of the Holy Spirit's Presence!

It took me a year to see this in the Scripture, but when I read, Isaiah 10:27, "And it shall come to pass in that day, that his burden shall be taken away from off thy shoulder, and his yoke (of the Assyrian, who is a type of Satan) from off thy neck, and the yoke *shall be destroyed* because of the *anointing!*" (KJV) I knew that this is what the Holy Spirit had allowed me to witness and discern in my very own vessel on that Wonderful Day!

The Oil of Joy was poured upon my head and the spirit of mourning had to leave! Sorrow and heaviness had to vacate with it! In the raising of my hands in thanksgiving and praise and worship, I found a joy that I had never known before! Truly it was as unspeakable, for I knew not how to express it except to say over and over again, "Oh, I love You Lord!" I actually took upon myself the spiritual yoke of Jesus, which is easy, and His burden, which is Light. Light has little weight. It has power to illuminate!

With this power now generating and flowing out of my being, I was given the ability to become a light house with new boldness and new light! I didn't realize it then, but I became as a high tower with the ability to broadcast in a whole new way! We are to be cities set upon a hill. Is this not what the Word is referring to when we are told that we shall be witnesses? Suddenly I had not only the ability and knowledge that I should witness to others about Christ; I now had an even *greater desire* to tell everyone of this marvelous experience! I discovered that very day, even on the way home after the meeting that not only was I supposed to witness to others about Jesus, I now could almost not keep from 'shouting' about His Goodness and Mercy and Love! I had been *anointed by the very Spirit of God!* If we could see this anointing it would probably be as the halo of light painted by artists of old! I had indeed been changed as though into another person!

Because I was free of a heavy yoke, I could now lift my hands way up high in the air towards our God, and because I was wearing a garment of praise, my heart was flooded with praise and I could praise and adore, magnify and glorify our wonderful Lord in a way and with a 'will-to' that I had never experienced before in all of my years of following Jesus!

I became a witness to the reality of how He can take a handful of ashes, my clay vessel, 'burned out' in part, and put new beautiful clothing upon me, His 'Garment of Praise', clothing me with His Beauty.

Isaiah 61:3 says, "To appoint unto them that mourn in Zion, to give unto them beauty for ashes, the oil of joy for mourning, the garment of praise for the spirit of heaviness; that they might be called trees of righteousness, the planting of the Lord, that He might be glorified." (KJV)

I think of this experience as though I, who had Christ in me, had been completely engulfed in or encompassed about, as though I had been taken into *His* Heart! I think of this Baptism of the Holy Spirit as being the oil of joy poured out upon me, and the 'garment of Praise' as being His Wedding

Garment wherein we become His Brides! And I think of this experience as now, being truly or fully—*in* Christ Jesus!

II Corinthians 5:17 says, "Therefore if anyone is *in Christ,* he is a new creation; old things have passed away; behold, all things have become new." This Scripture had new meaning to me. The 'all things' being *a new appreciation of the Holy Spirit and a new ability to believe for taking part in those signs spoken of by Jesus* in Mark 16:17 and18 such as the *casting out of demons, speaking with new tongues* and *laying hands on the sick and seeing them healed!* All of these happenings are to bring glory to God! (More will be written of, on these miraculous happenings in later Chapters.)

Fear…is this really of God?

Just four days following my baptism in the Holy Spirit, I began to have fears and doubts concerning the validity of this new baptism. I had invited Velma Clate, the woman who had led me into this experience, to come to our weekly Bible study, that others might receive this Baptism in the Holy Spirit. As the day of the study approached, I began to get unnerved! My stove had broken down. I had a tremendous headache. Pressure and tension were wearing me out. I was fearful that perhaps I was opening our group up to something strange and perhaps *not* of the Holy Spirit. I shared with my dear friend Joyce, who normally was very cautious concerning such matters. I thought that she would agree that we should cancel the meeting. She surprised me. She said, "We know that Jesus is with us and will protect us. If anything wrong takes place, we will not invite this woman back. But Grace, do you remember how filled with love you were last Friday just after she prayed with you? I have *never* known you to be so filled with love!" She was right. The reminder of that love-filled day of my Baptism in the Holy Spirit took away all of my fears.

I am reminded of something else that Joyce shared with me. I thought it strange at the time. She told me a story that seemed to be secondary to what we were discussing, but since then, I realize the significance.

She said: "For some reason I am remembering a story that I read years ago. There was a tremendous storm brewing out on the waters of a lake by the home of the man who told this story. Hurricane warnings were announced, and he did all that he knew to do before retiring for the night. During his sleep, he dreamed that he walked out onto the beach just in front of his home and told the storm to cease! When he awakened in the morning, he remembered his dream, and walking to the place where he had stood in the dream, was utterly amazed! Wreckage and ruin was everywhere, up to that point. All else behind him was safe and secure."

I see now that the Holy Spirit was telling me that my fears and doubts were even as the storm that was raging in the story. The words that Joyce spoke to me were as commands to the enemy of our souls, or reminders that it was Satan who wanted this proposed meeting to cease or be cancelled, even before it took place. I praise the Lord for His goodness and revelation to listening ears.

We had the meeting and it was marvelous! Thirteen women asked Jesus to baptize them with the Holy Spirit. Many began to speak in Tongues and one began to sing in the Spirit. I did neither. I experienced a tremendous anointing of fresh oil and was led of the Spirit to *minister in the Word of Knowledge and in the discerning and casting out of spirits.* I, who up until that time had said, "One can't 'con' God; He knows that I don't have the faith to pray for healing," was *immediately given the Word of Knowledge and the Gift of Faith* and had no qualms at all in obeying the Holy Spirit and praying for healing.

The one prayed for was healed of a whip-lash injury that had happened to her sixteen years before. She, who could not raise her hands over her head after the accident that caused the injury, went home that very day and rejoiced in being able to lift her arms and wash her windows by herself for the first time in sixteen years; something that she had been unable to do because of the injury to her neck!

We left the meeting that day with a sense that truly it had been a very special day! We realized anew the importance of gathering together, rather than forsaking the assembling of ourselves. A tribute to that meeting might be that three Churches, a Christian grade school, a School of Ministry, Missionary trips in many lands, a Radio Ministry and later a Television Ministry, and this book, came indirectly out of that *first* of many such marvelous meetings!

After this first meeting, I walked around for two weeks with the sense of a heavy anointing upon me. The moment it lifted, I was so tired I could hardly move. During this time, I was taught concerning wonderful things that could take place *while the anointing was present in fullness.* I was asked to go to hospitals and pray for the sick. A friend of mine who had begun to sing in Tongues that first day at the meeting went along with me and prayed in the Spirit. I could feel the Presence of the Holy Spirit as a new strength or power, 'welling up' in my arms and hands as I heard those Tongues being spoken. This was one of my first lessons in the Spirit. The Lord was teaching me part of what Tongues were all about. (The *anointing was teaching me* concerning *the anointing!*)

We went into the Intensive Care Unit. I asked the woman who had stomach cancer: "Do you really want to be healed? You are sixty-some years old and the only way to see Jesus is to go to Heaven?" She assured me that she wanted to live and serve Jesus. So I said: "Nancy, speak some of those tongues." Nancy did so, and as the Tongues were spoken, I *felt* the Spirit of God welling up in my hands and arms. My Lord was teaching me through this experience, that speaking in Tongues actually causes the Spirit of the Lord to respond in such a manner that He (who is the anointing) *can actually be felt in our physical beings,* as in this case, the power of God filled our arms and hands with His Power! We laid those 'power-filled' hands on her and she was actually up and eating solid food the next day. She had been healed!

A few days later when the report of this healing was 'spread around' we were asked to go to another hospital and pray for another who was ill. We went and once more as my friend spoke in Tongues, the Power of the Holy Spirit 'welled up' in my arms. As we laid our hands on this one, I actually felt the 'presence' of a tremendous 'spirit of tension' lift and release her. She was soon discharged from the hospital! Together, during those next two weeks, we saw the Lord do more wonderful healings.

I bring forth the Tongues!

With my limited understanding of the Bible concerning speaking in Tongues, (remember, I had not yet spoken in Tongues, rather I had received a baptismal pouring out of *love* and *power*) I decided that this was how body ministry was carried out. But after a few times of having to depend on others to speak in those Tongues in order for the anointing to be brought forth, I finally had a talk with the Lord.

"Lord, I recognize that those who speak in Tongues seem to be happier than I have ever known them to be. Lord, I feel such joy in my heart when I hear Nancy singing in the Spirit; it is as though I can almost see 'heavenly' notes on a staff in the air. Lord, I am the one leading the Bible study; I need to understand concerning Tongues. Please Sir, give *me* these Tongues."

I then opened my Bible and my eyes fell on the words, "Living Water" in John 4: 10, which says, "Jesus answered and said unto her, 'If you knew the *gift* of God, and who it is that says to you, Give Me to drink; you would have asked of Him, and He would have given you Living Water!'"

I felt a slight movement as though a finger brushed against my throat, and the sound, *ohr,* with a rolling 'r' came to me. I immediately went to my car that I might be alone, and as I spoke that one sound, for that is all it was to me at the time, a sound, many more sounds came to me and were articulated through my lips.

My first reaction was, "I am making this up," for strangely, I had no aware-ness of the Presence of the Anointing as I had received when others spoke in Tongues. Then I said to myself, "No way, I asked the Lord, and He gave me my request. Thank You, Jesus." I continued speaking many words for over an hour.

I was afraid that if I stopped speaking, I would lose the Tongues. (See in a later Chapter: '*Speaking in Tongues Can Be Stolen, Beware*'.) I'm glad now that I spoke for a long time until the flow got steady and sure. Upon awakening the next morning, I was delighted to discover that I could still speak in this Heavenly Language.

Note: I did not ask Jesus to baptize me in the Holy Spirit; I *knew* that He had already done so! I asked Him to give me the Tongues. I was really asking Him to help me to bring these words forth out of (my belly, my spirit). These words of the Christ within me, which were already in residence!

I certainly was *already* baptized in the Holy Spirit *before* I asked for the Tongues! The *Gifts of the Holy Spirit* such as *discerning of spirits,* and the *casting out of them;* and the *Gifts of Healing* and the *Gift of Faith*…not only the measure of faith, but the Gift of Faith which had been *absent in my life before this experience,* was now present. This is so important, because many *mistakenly* (I believe) insist that if one does *not* speak in Tongues, they have not yet been baptized in the Spirit! I know that this causes many to have a sense of defeat. I have seen the reaction of these ones. It causes them to feel that they are somehow lacking, or must do something worthy of being baptized, which is in error! The *only factor necessary* for this Baptism is that one be born again; and then truly and sincerely desire to receive this Baptism and *ask* for it. The Rushing Mighty Wind came, and then the Tongues of Fire were seen and used. And then, (many times) for Tongues to come forth, one must *desire and seek them further!* I am sharing all of this from personal experience and from the testimonies of others…not from unfounded information!

I have learned that sometimes, the Tongues cannot come forth until one has first been delivered from the spirit of fear concerning them! Or if one is holding un-forgiveness, one must forgive. At other times, spirits such as the spirit of pride, must first be recognized and cast out! And then again, I have witnessed some, who have asked for the Baptism years before, receive the tongues as they hear the Song in the Spirit and begin to repeat some of the words they hear. This is as a 'priming of the pump' with the 'Holy waters' that are springing forth. This causes a release of the 'waters' that are already within a Christian!

Back to my experience of receiving Tongues; I discovered later when studying Hebrew in Israel that the word "*ohr*" means *light!* The second word that the Lord gave to me was "*ahhrecka,*" again with the rolling 'r.' It seemed that the interpretation of that word was, *"I will give. I will give light!"* I believe this is exactly what the Lord has done, especially concerning Tongues! This is one of the main reasons for the writing of this book.

More and more I have come to realize that the one doing the speaking of these Heavenly Words is the Spirit of the Lord Jesus Christ within me, through the Power of His Holy Spirit. I am actually participating with Christ to speak forth His Words when I open my mouth and give my lips and vocal chords over to His speaking. He is such a Gentleman, that most of the time He allows me the privilege of deciding when His Words will come forth.

Just now I am reminded of a Word that came forth that seemed so *strong* and almost something which I would not want to repeat, but I realize now that it was given to show forth what the Lord God thinks of the *untrue dastardly opinion that unthinking ones are expressing when they attribute speaking in Tongues to Satan.* The Word given by prophetic utterance was this: "Would you ask of Me *bread and living water* and would I then give instead *vomit and filth?*" This is such a stern word given by the Spirit of One who loves us so much that He died for us! It should warn us to be *very careful concerning the subject of speaking in Tongues* and perhaps giving a stern warning against grieving the Holy Spirit of the Living God, by and from whom all blessings flow, including the *Tongues!*

Your Spirit was *in me already!* How is this Baptism different?

UPON in Golden Letters appeared!

A few days later, while sitting in my rocking chair pondering all of this, (for I *knew* that before this Baptism, I had the Holy Spirit *in* me) I was asking the Lord, "Lord, what is this difference?" *Suddenly, I had a vision!* In large neon lights, in the air above my head, I saw, in huge letters about a foot high each, the letters: *U-P-O-N!* "Upon, Lord, what are You saying?" I got into my concordance and discovered Acts 1:8, "You shall receive power after that the Holy Spirit is come *upon you.*" (Emphasis mine!) Yes, Lord, thank You that is what happened in this baptism, the Holy Spirit came *upon* me!

The Last Adam, Jesus Christ, had become a *quickening spirit* as in I Corinthians 15:45. When I asked Him into my heart, I received Christ, the Passover Lamb *into* my spirit, by the power of His Holy Spirit, Christ, the Holy Spirit of God, *in me,* the hope of glory as in Colossians 1:27.

Now I had received this same Christ, the Holy Pentecostal Dove, the Holy Spirit *upon me!* Glory! This was the same baptism that Jesus had after that He was baptized in the material water of the river Jordan, to fulfill all righteousness as in Matthew 3:15.

We then, the first fruits, along with Jesus, *the* First Fruit, and all who through the years have received from Him the Gift of Salvation and then the Baptism in His Holy Spirit, have also experienced our Pentecost, and have had the privilege of having the Spirit of God descend *upon* us!

Do you get it? The Golden Letters I saw in my vision, at least a foot high—

UPON—are the important revelation that can lead one to truly understand the experience of this Baptism!

Before that 'Special Day of Pentecost', when it was possible for the Holy Spirit to be poured out *upon all flesh,* He came *upon* just kings, priests and prophets, and then *upon just certain* men and women in order that they speak, write, bear children, dance, judge, rule, and prophesy! His coming was always, *upon!* He came *upon them. Scripture never states that the Holy Spirit came within them!* He came upon Mary the Mother of Christ, and John the Baptist and his mother Elizabeth, at which time they *experienced the Presence of* the Holy Spirit! In this day we now have the privilege, because of Christ's Presence *within us,* of *asking for this precious anointing,* and then it is the promise of the Father, and the intention of Jesus, to baptize us by sending the 'Oil' of the Holy Spirit to come down *upon* us!

It is up to the Bride to make herself ready now, thorough leaning on Christ's strength to do so! Most certainly now many things have become new. They are an addition to my life! I have received a new boldness and power to witness; a new Language with which to express Heavenly Worship; new spiritual eyes to see into the Realm of the Spirit! The Gift of Discerning of spirits and along with this sight, the Gift of Tongues, is also a weapon with which to battle the enemy. I am now capable of believing for and seeing signs taking place, with the casting out of demons; the speaking with new tongues; and the laying on of hands for the recovery of the sick! These are the signs capable of being used in Mark 16:17–18, for those who believe!

I know that personally, before the Baptism of the Holy Spirit, I had trouble even believing for miracles even though I had seen with my own eyes many miracles of healing taking place. And I wasn't sure that I even believed there were demons, even though the Bible verified their existence, and I certainly had not ever cast one out of a poor struggling inhabitant of such, until—the Lord opened my eyes and let me see—a demon! More on this later!

Chapter Two

Astounding Results—Witnessing with New Power!

B efore this experience, I desired to lead others to Christ. In an effort to learn how to do so, I became a counselor in the 'Billy Graham Crusade' that was being held in Pittsburgh in 1968. This was a first-class training period, and through it I learned how to memorize Scripture.

In particular I memorized the book of Romans the 'Roman Road' Plan of Salvation: [Romans 3:23, "For all have sinned and come short of the glory of God."—Romans 6: 23, "For the wages of sin are death; but the gift of God is eternal life through Jesus Christ our Lord."—Romans 5:8, "But God commended his love toward us, in that, while we were yet sinners, Christ died for us."—Romans 5:12, "Wherefore, as by one man sin entered into the world, and death by sin; and so death passed upon all men, for that all have sinned:"—Romans 10: 8–10, "But what does it say? The word is near you, in your mouth, and in your heart (that is, the word of faith, which we preach). That if you shall confess with your mouth the Lord Jesus, and believe in your heart that God has raised him from the dead, you will be saved. For with the heart one believes unto righteousness; and with the mouth confession is made unto salvation."]

[Then I always added: Revelation 3:20, "Behold, I stand at the door and knock; if any man hear my voice, and open the door, I will come in to him, and will sup with him, and he with me." And John 3: 3–8, "Jesus answered and said unto him, most assuredly, I say unto you, unless a man is born again, he cannot see the kingdom of God. Nicodemus said to him, "How can a man be born when he is old? Can he enter a second time into his mother's womb, and be born?" Jesus answered; most assuredly, I say unto you, unless a man is born of water and of the Spirit, he cannot enter into the kingdom of God. That which is born of the flesh is flesh; and that which is born of the Spirit is spirit. Do not marvel that I said to you: You must be born again. The wind blows where it wishes and you hear the sound of it, but cannot tell where it comes from and where it goes, so is everyone who is born of the Spirit.] Later, I saw that quoting the 'Great White Throne Judgment' found in Revelation 20: 11–15 concerning the books that God is keeping and the *second death* that results in being cast into the lake of fire, really makes people get sober and want to know how to become 'born again'!

The Graham Team challenged—and shamed us—concerning Scripture memorization: They said: "If we gave you $100 for every scripture you learned, how many do you think you could learn?" They then encouraged us that if we had learned the 'Lord's Prayer', we could memorize. And so I did! So can you dear reader is my prayer for you.

While nine months pregnant with my youngest daughter, Becky, and praying that she wouldn't arrive on the scene until the Crusade was over, I was blessed to lead others into a prayer for salvation. But it was Dr. Graham who led them to the Lord. I wanted to learn how to lead others to Jesus when Dr. Graham was not available.

The Lord led me to a book about soul-winning by Francis Gardner called *God Is Fabulous.* It was written before she married Charles Hunter. It was a marvelous book containing a four-step plan for soul-winning. I laughed and cried and rejoiced as I read that book, and finally got up enough courage to go out and lead a soul to the Lord! [As I remember, the simplicity of this plan was something like this: A. All have sinned and come short of the Glory of God! B. Believe on the Lord Jesus Christ and be saved! C. Receive Christ Jesus into your heart!]

Leading a soul to the Lord made me so happy that when I learned of a Church that was involved in weekly soul-winning, I joined it. (It was a struggle and a sacrifice to leave the dear Baptist Church that I had attended and loved for years, but they did not teach 'soul-winning'!) I began to go out with these new church members into the neighborhood to share the Good News of Jesus Christ. In the *two years* that I was involved with that church, I had the privilege of leading *four people* into the experience of being Born Again!

I remember a prayer in that church during a New Years Eve 'Watch-Night' service. I asked the Holy Spirit to help me to lead sixty people to the Lord that next year! Then I received the Baptism of the Holy Spirit—probably in answer to that 'Watch Night' prayer. Of course, when my Pastor heard that I had received the Baptism of the Holy Spirit, he came to my home and brought Matthew the Deacon with him. To my great surprise he said to me: "Grace, you are almost like an assistant Pastor to me. You lead the people to the Lord at the altar, and you supervised the Vacation Bible School. You have been such a blessing, but I can't even let you continue your Sunday school class, if you don't stop going to these Pentecostal Meetings!"

I replied: "Pastor, I have never been to a Pentecostal meeting, but I will have to stop reading the Bible, if I am not to speak of this Baptism!"

Matthew the Deacon was 'hanging on every word' as I began to explain about the Baptism. Pastor John took one look at his Deacon, and put his hand to my mouth and said: "No, don't say anymore! C'mon Matt, we have to leave." I am still praying that he will see the light! In fact my latest prayer is that he will burst forth in Tongues from the pulpit one day!

One month later I took a trip to California to be with my mother who was having an operation. The operation was a success. On my way back to Pittsburgh, I sat on the plane and marveled over what had taken place in just *two short weeks!*

"Lord," I prayed, "I have led *eleven people* to you on this trip! The cab driver taking me to the airport, the woman sitting next to me on the plane, a 'hippie' on the highway, my own father, my cousin, a customer having a haircut in my sister's barber shop, and others! Lord, they all received You as Savior and Baptizer!" As I remembered and reflected on such a miracle as this, I inquired, "Lord, how come? I'm sharing the same scriptures as before, the same Gospel, but somehow, they seem locked into what I am saying and are receiving in a way that I have never seen happen before! Lord, what is the difference?" His reply, "You shall receive power after the Holy Spirit is come *upon* you, and *you shall be my witnesses.*" Acts 1:8!

I could only surmise that this power has to do with the Joy of the Lord, which is our strength! I was so filled with the *Joy* of the marvelous experience of being baptized with His Spirit, of having Love poured down *upon* me, that I was sharing my testimony and the scriptures with the love that a new bride expresses when speaking of her Bridegroom. Or as one who learns of a wonderful secret and wants to share it with others that they may be a part of it!

Learning How to Share with the Brethren!

I wanted so much to be able to explain to my brothers and sisters in the Lord the difference between being *born* of the Spirit and being *baptized* in the Spirit. I asked the Lord to teach me how to do this. He gave me the eleventh chapter of Luke.

The disciples came to Jesus and asked Him to teach them how to pray. He gave them the Lord's Prayer. Then He gave them a parable extolling persistence. Then He admonished them to ask, seek, and knock, confirming that the request would be given, found and opened. He then reminded them of their *earthly parental love* whereby they desired to give good gifts to their *children.* Romans 8:15 speaks of having received a spirit of adoption whereby *we cry,*

"Abba, Father!" And Galatians 4:6 says that, "God has sent forth the Spirit of His Son into your hearts, crying, *"Abba, Father!"* We know that *only the born again are considered children of God* with the right to call Him 'Father'! So we see in the following statement of Jesus that He is encouraging the *children* of God, (those who are Born Again *and have received the Spirit of Christ in them) to ask* from the Father for the *Promise of the Father.*

He said this to them in Luke 11:13, *"If ye, being evil know how to give good gifts to your children, how much more shall your Heavenly Father give the Holy Spirit to them who ask Him?"* (KJV) This scripture helped me to see that the Lord wasn't saying that we had to be all cleaned up and perfect before we asked for 'more of Himself', (in fact we can't be cleansed really…without His strengthening help) and further, he was saying in essence, "My *Children,* you who (are or will be born again): ask for "More of Me!"

This word *shall,* in the preceding scripture, given by Jesus, was projecting into the future of what could take place after His Resurrection…when they could then be born again…and then later, after His Ascension…when on the Day of Pentecost, they could receive this Promise…the Baptism in and of, the Holy Spirit!

Luke 24:49, "Behold, I send the *Promise* of My Father *upon* you; but tarry in the city of Jerusalem until you are endued with power from on high." NKJV This *Promise of the Father* is found in Isaiah 44:3, "For, I will pour water *upon* him that is thirsty, and floods *upon* the dry ground; I will pour My Spirit *upon* your descendents and My Blessing *upon* your offspring." NKJV Joel 2:28–29 reads, "And it shall come to pass afterward, that I will pour out My Spirit *upon* all flesh, and your sons and your daughters, shall prophesy, your old men shall dream dreams, your young men shall see visions. And, also *upon* the servants and *upon* the handmaids in those days will I pour out of My Spirit!"

This would result in the pouring out of Holy Water upon them. This admonition was given them on the very day of His Resurrection after He appeared to the two on the Road to Emmaus. This account is found in Luke 24:13–49. These two returned to Jerusalem and told the disciples of their encounter with Jesus. Jesus appeared unto them; showed them the wounds in His hands and feet; ate a piece of broiled fish and a honey comb and opened the scripture unto their understanding, of what was written in the law of Moses, and in the prophets and in the psalms concerning Him, that they might understand the scriptures.

Luke didn't mention the account of the disciple's new birth that very day but John did! In John 20:22, *"Then he breathed on them and said to them, "Receive the Holy Spirit."* (NLT)

We see that Jesus re-birthed the disciples breathing into them! Thereby,

He put the Holy Spirit *in* them on the Day of His Resurrection, when for the very first time this experience was possible!

A Trinity in the One!

I have already shared that the very day I received the Baptism of the Holy Spirit, the Lord gave me the revelation concerning the Trinity in the phrase, one Lord! Later, *because of this revelation,* I could see and understand the Trinity in the words, *one faith* and *one baptism.* I think this is so important to clarify and enlarge upon here, because so many are *stumbled by a surface understanding* of the Scripture, even as was I.

Ephesians 4:4–5, "*There is* one body and one Spirit, just as you are called in one hope of your calling: *one* Lord, *one* faith, *one* baptism."

In the beginning of my conversation with Velma, this was my main argument. My thinking was this. If the Bible says that there is one, then there can't be another. That would make two, and those who speak of the Baptism of the Holy Spirit are in error. Also, when she said "There is more of Jesus that you may receive," I knew that I already had Christ in me, and I 'hadn't a clue' that He also wanted to come *upon* me!

After the Lord reminded me of the truth concerning the Trinity of one Lord, (one, but three, Father, Son and Holy Spirit) I went on to discover the Trinity in the words, *one faith* and *one Baptism!*

I read Romans 1:17 which says, "Herein is the righteousness of God revealed in that *the just shall live, from* faith, *to* faith and *by* faith." Here was a trinity in the word 'faith.' I wasn't *living* it then, but I could see a trinity concerning the word, 'faith!' And then *in all four Gospels,* though I had read them many times before, I had *never realized* that John the Baptist in Matt. 3:11 had said, "I indeed baptize you with water unto repentance, but when He is come whose shoes I am not worthy to unloose, *He will baptize you* with the Holy Ghost and Fire!"

Fire Power!

Even so with this second Baptism…one, but three; a baptism in normal water, and then a baptism in the Holy Spirit, and a baptism in Fire. These are now invisible but accompanied with such power that I was almost knocked off of my feet on the day of my Baptism in the Holy Spirit, even as a mighty wind was experienced on that first Pentecostal Day!

A physical sign of this Fire; the Tongue of Fire was visible! No longer is this sign visible! Do we ever say that because the Tongue is no longer visible, that it has not been given? Of course not! But neither should we say that because it is not instantly heard, that it has not been given. We certainly can feel the fire. This is what the Tongue does. It 'heats' us up! The Tongue is given, in part, to light up the oil of the Spirit which is in the anointing! This sets us ablaze with the Presence of Himself!

We are Wells!

Jesus told the disciples that they would be baptized with the Holy Ghost and Fire. Both are given at the same time. This 'Fire Power' (dynamos) is the dynamite needed to break open our *shallow* wells! We are already wells that have water in us, (the Living Water of the Christ within us who are born again). But we need this dynamite 'Fire-Power' of the Holy Spirit to make of us 'Artesian Wells'! Because the 'dynamite' is not set off instantly, it doesn't mean that it has not yet been given!

I think also that there is a Spiritual mystery concerning wells and water and song, in the Scripture found in Numbers 21:16–18, "From there they went to Beer, which is the well where the Lord said to Moses, 'Gather the people together, and I will give them water.' Then Israel sang this song: 'Spring up, O well! All of you sing to it.' The well the leaders sank, dug by the nation's nobles, by the lawgiver, with their staves." NKJV I believe that we can bring forth this Living Water within us, by singing in the Spirit. And doing this together with our leaders and our nations nobles brings a special blessing of unity and love! We need to 'sing' to the well that is within us!

Chapter Three

Revelation! A Vision of Worship and Song in the Spirit!

M y dear Pastor Mouton, who is with the Lord now, had a beautiful sensitivity to the leading of the Holy Spirit. He had been baptized in the Spirit for the last twelve years and exhibited extreme patience with those in the congregation who were resisting this 'move' of God. There were not many in this Church who had received this wonderful experience. He began his message by reading from Jeremiah 33:3, "Call unto me, and I will answer thee, and show thee great and mighty things, which you know not." (KJV) He then began to call out to the Lord! "Oh God, send down the anointing." He repeated this several times. "Oh Lord, send down the anointing!"

As he was speaking this request, the Lord spoke in my heart and said, "I said: *Call!*"

Now the Baptist church in which this was taking place was a body of believers who knew how to dance and clap unto the Lord, and they had just done this for over an hour. But the anointing that the Pastor was calling for had obviously not taken place. The people had been ministering in the outer courts. *There had been no song in the Spirit.*

Each time the Pastor implored, "Lord, send your anointing" I heard within the same word, "*Call!*" I knew immediately what the Lord was expressing. He was urging me to arise to my feet and *Call* by singing a love song of worship *in the Spirit!*

God let me know that just above our heads there was 'as it were' a thin pane of glass (the windows of heaven)? And that if I would stand and *Call* unto Him, through a Song of Worship in the Spirit—using the Language of Tongues—the glass would shatter and the Holy Oil, the anointing that the Pastor was calling for, would flow down upon us. The fear of man which brings a snare (Proverbs 29:25) made me hesitate. I had shared before concerning the Lord's desire for Worship Songs in the Spirit and felt that many did not understand its importance.

This was a divided congregation of those who had the baptism and those who did not. I finally rebuked the spirit of fear that keeps our lips from speaking, our feet from dancing, our hands from clapping, and our mouths from witnessing, and as I did so, the fear left. I arose to my *feet*, closed my eyes, thought only of my Lord and His Goodness, lifted my hands and heart and spirit and voice and worshipped Him with song in the Spirit!

No sooner had I begun the song than the panes of glass above us were shattered and the Holy Oil, the anointing of God, the blessing out of Zion, flowed down upon our heads. I knew this was happening because I not only felt the anointing, but I heard my Pastor begin to thank the Lord. He was worshipping and crooning to the Lord words of thanksgiving and adoration, "Oh Hallelujah, Hallelujah!" The Mind of his understanding - the Mind of Christ - had been put on and had enlightened the Pastor to the awareness of the anointing flowing upon us!

I was so thankful and happy that I had indeed understood what the Lord was saying and had been obedient. Tears of joy were streaming down my face and then the vision began.

I saw just the Form of the Lord standing high above us in a majestic attitude of giving, with His Hands held palms upward at His side. I wanted to kiss those palms that I knew were nail-scarred for me, but I felt unworthy to do so. I thought to prostrate myself before Him to kiss His Feet, but again felt unworthy of the privilege.

Just then the vision changed. No longer was Jesus standing, He was seated on the Church platform. His face was filled with laughter and happiness. My two youngest daughters were with Him. The youngest, Becky, was sitting on His lap and the older, Jenny, was standing, leaning on His shoulder. (Later, I realized that He had let me see their nearness to Him because of the times I had to leave them to share the message of this vision). His left Hand was outstretched toward me as though beckoning me to come nearer—that I need not hold Him at arm's length, reasoning myself unworthy. At His Feet, just below the platform were a myriad of young faces. I couldn't tell whether they were children or cherubs. They had adoring expressions as they gazed up at Jesus. It was as though He wanted me to be at ease in His Presence and had put aside His Majesty for a time, that I might relate to and respond to His Personableness, His Sweet humility that the children understand and love so. Suddenly, behind Him, I saw a Golden Light and in that Light there was a choir of angels standing in the form of a triangle-like arch. They had their wings folded at their sides and were standing with their right sides forward so that all that I could see of them was their wings, which were like golden shafts of light.

All of this vision was taking place as the Pastor was ecstatically praising the Lord. I began to have the realization of that burning within the heart, that unspeakable joy that one feels during those blessed times when we lead one to the Lord, or do a deed of Mercy unto Him! It was as though, the Oil of the Spirit's Anointing had flowed first upon the head—as the Pastor was displaying the results of ecstasy—and then the oil flowed down onto the heart and we felt Jesus Joy rejoicing in us—in our obedience of Worship. And just then, a woman beside me began to play her tambourine, as though the oil had flowed down upon her hands, and as she did, the angel choir began to move in unison back and forth, keeping perfect time to the music we were singing and in rhythm with her tambourine. This was thrilling! Then as though the oil had flowed down to the skirts of the garment, a young woman leaped to her feet and began to dance unto the Lord, while others were clapping and shouting Hallelujahs!

Before the Song in the Spirit and this Vision took place, the saints had spent almost two hours singing and dancing and clapping and praising in the Outer Courts! There had been no Tongues neither spoken nor sung! Therefore, the Anointing that the Pastor was pleading for *had not taken place.*

After the Song in the Spirit and the Vision, the *Joy* of the Lord was present in new fullness and the playing of the tambourine and the clapping of hands and the dancing were done in the *Throne Room,* in the very *Holy of Holies* that we are privileged to enter with boldness because of the Blood and the Torn Flesh of Jesus making that provision for us, mentioned in Hebrews 10:19–20.

The first time that I shared this vision, the Word came forth, "The little ones at the Feet of Jesus were those who would receive this Word as little children, and act upon it!"

Another word concerning this vision was, "If my people will worship me with the high praises of God in their mouth, I will go forth as a Mighty Man, bringing salvation, and restoration to the backslider, and healing and deliverance!"

Just days after this word was given, I found the essence of it in Isaiah 42:8–18. This passage mentions, "Sing a New Song unto the Lord" and "Let the inhabitants of the Rock sing!" And then it goes on to tell how He (our *Rock*) will respond! I believe that this *song—a song in the Spirit singing in Tongues—is* so new that it has never been sung before in just this way, and so rare that it will never be sung again identically, as are most songs in a known language. This takes place when we are using Song in the Spirit to Worship our Lord and Master!

This Vision, given in 1970 concerning Worship and Song in the Spirit, took place after a 'Call in the Spirit.' I believe the Lord showed me in this Vision a 'Perfect Order of Worship'! We are to Feed Him a 'Little Cake' *First!* We are to sing a 'New Song' unto the Lord. Again, a Song so new, it has never been sung before! A Song so rare, it will never be sung in just this way again! This takes place when we are using Song in the Spirit to Worship! This song can be sung when alone, or with another or when gathered together. I find that it does and would bring multitudes of blessing if we would offer it up on every occasion. We just can't give to God without His Wonderful Anointed Presence responding in Showers of Blessings upon us!

Through this vision the Lord showed me a *Perfect* order of praising in His Sight. First of all, the Lord was worshipped. Lifting our hearts and hands and spirits and songs unto Him, with the highest praises, the exalted songs of worship through singing in the Spirit with the Tongues, the Words that the Spirit supplies, is worshipping Him in the beauty of holiness. This is a way of entering into His Holiness. Using His language is the way to be in *One Accord*. (How else can we, who have such diversities of thoughts, be in perfect unity in any other way?) It is like the precious ointment upon the head.

Our minds, in 'putting-on' Christ by using His Words, are the first to be aware of this anointing. This anointing is even as that given in Psalm 133, "Behold, how good and how pleasant it is for brethren to dwell together in unity! It is like the precious oil upon the head that ran down on the beard even Aaron's beard: that went down to the skirts of his garments. As the dew of Hermon, and as the dew that descended upon the mountains of Zion: for there the Lord commanded the blessing, even life forevermore." (KJV)

That oil which ran down on Aaron's beard, (is as a smile on the Face of Jesus, reflecting this anointing.) This oil ran down to the skirts of Aaron's garments. Even so, this anointing (the 'oil of joy') runs down over us, from the top of our head to the soles of our feet. On the way down we can *feel* the joy of the Lord rejoicing in our hearts. The oil of the Spirit is invisible—but more real than anything visible! (Again, this is that unspeakable joy that one feels on occasion when one is witnessing or doing something that is really pleasing to our Lord.) And then as the oil flows onto our hands, we just have to clap them unto the Lord and play instruments that then play anointed music. The 'Oil of Joy' (can't buy it in any store) flows clear down to the feet, and those feet can't stand still but must dance unto Him!

God is uplifted, glorified, exalted, honored, magnified, worshipped and adored perfectly as the Holy Spirit leads the Hosannas! Though we must not put God into a box of our own making, He has shown this Perfect Order and over and over has responded to this way of worship by pouring down the anointing. The lifting of our whole selves in worship is as 'feeding Him a little cake' *first, that is we give to the Lord first, before all else, an offering of worship!* It expresses our joy rejoicing in Him, and He allows us to feel that 'burning heart of love' (that experience shared by the two on the way to Emmaus), His joy rejoicing in us. And then the clapping and dancing and singing express our joy rejoicing once more in our Lord and His anointing. This is a beautiful circle of love being manifested!

We have been spending much time in the outer gates and courts, thinking that this is necessary before entering the Holy of Holies. And then once in the Holy of Holies, we spend just moments singing in the Spirit. We have it backwards. Though many and maybe even most come to a service with the soil of the world on their feet, we have only to 'wash their feet' and they will be ready to enter fully into worship. Jesus washed the feet and told Peter it was enough. We need to bring forth the Living Waters that the feet may be washed. The Lord showed me through this vision that it only took *one* to 'break the windows' of Heaven!

Let us, the Bride of Christ, give to our Beloved—a 'Love Song!'

A Song in the Spirit using the unknown Tongues, first of all, brings the whole Body of those singing into a Perfect Unity The whole of psalm 133, expresses this thought of the joy of the Lord as we praise and worship Him and then speaks of His response in blessing to us! How better to be unified as the Body of Christ than to be Worshipping in the Spirit using Perfect Words, His Words, the Words of the Spirit coming forth from our lips. Do we really understand just what Living Water is? It's Creator and substance is identified in Jeremiah 2:13, "For My people have committed two evils: They have forsaken *Me, the fountain of living waters,* And hewn themselves cisterns-broken cisterns that can hold no water." (NKJV) God identifies Himself as the *Fountain* of Living Waters!

We are admonished to offer God the sacrifice of praise, which is the fruit of our lips. Hebrews 13:15, " Therefore by Him let us continually offer the sacrifice of praise to God, that is, the fruit of our lips, giving thanks to His name."

I asked Him, "Lord, what is the Fruit of our lips?"

His answer was: Isaiah 57:19, "I create the fruit of the lips; Peace, peace to him that is far off, and to him that is near," says the Lord "And I will heal him." (He even gives us the interpretation!)

(And then God calls for the *Voice!*) The Lord gave me Jeremiah 33:11, 'The *voice* of joy, and the *voice* of gladness, the *voice* of the bridegroom, and the *voice* of the bride, the *voice* of them that shall say, Praise the Lord of hosts: for the Lord is good; for his mercy endureth for ever: and of them that shall bring the sacrifice of praise into the house of the Lord. For I will cause to return the captivity of the land, as at the first, saith the Lord." (KJV) We give Him our *Voice,* ahhh, the voice is only a sound—and then He gives us His Words!

The little woman in Scripture fed Elijah *first* - before she fed herself and her son - and the reward was all of the OIL she needed…plus! Even so does the Lord want to supply us with fullness of Oil, the Oil of the Holy Spirit of the Living God! Remember, the wise virgins had oil—but then, *all of the virgins were sleeping*—it was the Bride that went forth proclaiming His coming!

Jesus Christ is the Great High Priest of the profession of our mouths. Hebrew 3:1, "Wherefore, holy brethren, partakers of the heavenly calling, consider the Apostle and High Priest of our profession, Christ Jesus." (KJV) Let us profess in song our adoration, our worship. Let us thereby bring forth the Scripture Hebrews 2:11–12 that tells us, "For both he that sanctifies and they who are sanctified are all of one: for which cause he is not ashamed to call them brethren, Saying, I will declare thy name unto my brethren, in the midst of the church will I sing praise unto thee." (KJV)

Think of it, He is not ashamed to call us brethren. He says He will sing in the midst of the Congregation. This is a direct quote of Psalm 22:22, the Psalm that speaks of our Lord's agony during the crucifixion in the first 21 verses, but the very next verse, Psalm 22:22 tells us of His desire! Psalm 22:22, "I will declare Thy Name unto My brethren; in the midst of the congregation I will praise Thee." Is this not part of the joy He saw as He despised the shame of the Cross, for the joy that was set before Him! He saw us—blessed and healed and delivered—because of what He was going through on our behalf!

We are then blessed to be part of the bringing about of the Ministry of Jesus that is His more excellent Ministry in Hebrews 8:6, "But now hath he obtained a more excellent ministry, by how much also he is the mediator of a better covenant, which was established upon better promises." He said we would do greater things than Him because He went to the Father. Are the greater things only those acts concerning healings and miracles and raising of the dead that He did in abundance while here on Earth? Rather, they are all of these acts along with the ability now given to us to lead others into Salvation and the Baptism of the Holy Spirit and speaking in Heavenly Tongues, and thereby being capable of joining together with Jesus in Worshipping the Father in Spirit and in Truth!

Because of the Word of Wisdom vision given me; I feel that the desire of our Lord, is that we begin with a Song of Worship in the Spirit, every gathering that is in His Name; every meeting, whether it is during our Sunday Worship Service or a business meeting in the Church or just a meeting of two or three, or just our private morning meeting with the Lord as we begin our day. The Lord is saying through this Vision that we are to lift our hands and hearts and spirits unto Him and Worship Him with Song in the Spirit and in Truth—that is with minds concentrating upon Him—feeding Him just a 'Little Cake'—

First! The Anointing oil will then flow down *upon* our heads and the Mind of our spirits will be made aware of the Holy Oil pouring down upon us. Our lips will be kissed by the Spirit, enabling us to speak His Words afresh, and songs with our understanding will have the sweetness of the spices of the Garden of Solomon permeating them.

This Oil will flow down upon our hearts, enrapturing us with the Glow of His Love. The Oil will then pour onto our hands, enabling them to be His Instruments of touching others with His Love. Our hands will be equipped to be more readily used of Him - to clap with joy or to smite evil spirits.

Our feet will have the washing of Living Water by the Word, removing the cares of our daily walk, equipping us to dance unto the Lord with renewed joy, thereby also trampling upon serpents and other demonic influences.

Sadly, many are lagging behind in this Marvelous Revelation of Spiritual Song!

This experience took place in a Baptist Church where just few in the congregation (along with the Pastor) had been baptized in the Holy Spirit, so up to that point, only songs with our understanding had been offered. Sadly, I find that this is even being done in churches that understand and embrace the Baptism in the Holy Spirit. Tongues, for the most part, are *misunderstood* and in large part, *ignored!*

The Body of Christ generally has been taught to come together, enter His gates with thanksgiving–singing fast songs with words of *thanks giving* - and then to proceed into His Courts with Praise–singing fast songs with words of praise - they are then to increase into worship - singing slower songs with words of *adoration,* magnifying the Lord.

All of this is to be done with words of our understanding. If ever the congregation has been led to sing in Tongues, the instruction more than likely has been that Songs in the Spirit are to be done only in evening meetings, where the 'faithful' are gathered, in order that any 'newcomers' to the Church will not be filled with fear because of their misunderstanding of the Language. Paul only admonished in this way concerning *speaking* in Tongues; this has *nothing* to do with the beautiful *Song* in Tongues (singing in the Spirit).

And then if Tongues are sung, for most congregations, it has been for just a very short time, and if the Lord is gracious and begins to take the Body into the Glory, it is more often than not cut short or quenched with sudden changes in the order of service by ones who don't understand or appreciate that a Worship Service is akin to 'love-making' by our Bridegroom, with His Bride! Or by announcements having little or nothing to do with this Glory, or a passing of the offering plate with words that tell us that this is part of Worship.

Of course we are being obedient when we give tithes and offering—and we don't normally do this unless we do worship the Lord—but the Lord led one Pastor in Malaysia—Mel Tari who wrote: 'Like a Mighty Wind'—to put the offering plate next to the door and not even mention an offering! He did so continually, and they had no lack! Those in his congregation were blessed to be a part of seeing the Lord raise the dead many times and have the water turned to wine over 30 times! He walked on the water through rain swollen rivers of 30 foot depth, to reach the lost, and each step he took had his feet stepping on (as it were, smooth stepping-stones).

A woman in his congregation fed and give drink to a number of pastors during a meal when her husband surprised her by bringing home the visiting pastors and wives and families. After prayer she fed this group, with just one cake of rice and one pitcher of water…with crumbs and drink left over! The Lord told her to take just the little flour she had and make a cake out of it and bake it. This she did. When baked, the Lord instructed her to break it in half. She did so and placed the broken piece in a plate for a serving, the other half grew whole again. This continued until all were served, and then the water pitcher just continued to pour until everyone had drink! (I think that these testimonies confirm the place that the offering has during services.) I believe that the Lord is also showing us *in these incidents* how we can survive during great need—such as following earthquake or hurricane or such as would be the case *if* we are still around—when buying and selling are issues of life and death!

Forgive me, Lord, if I sound critical, I think that I am only relating 'things as they are' in many churches. I speak these things, longing for the congregations to 'get it,' for I have been in marvelous, awesome meetings that have been such, because those present gave the Holy Spirit *first place* through worship leaders who know to sing songs that are filled with adoration and worship directed, preferably in the First Person, to God!

And then as they lead into Song in the Spirit, they *stay* in the *Same Chord*—very important, enabling all gathered to sing their individual Song in the Spirit. They just *Stay there in that same Chord*, with minds and hearts and spirits uncaring of time, until the Lord is blessed, and being blessed, He blesses out of Zion with the Anointing of His Spirit, and everyone participating experiences that most wonderful of blessings of being uplifted right into the courts of our Heavenly Father! Oh, such bliss, such ecstasy, such Heavenly awareness of what it will be like in Eternity even before we are there!

I remember once while being in this awesome state saying to the Lord, "Oh Lord, I am in Your Presence!"

He replied, "You are always in my Presence; *you are not always in my Courts!*"

When I ponder this Word in my heart, it gives me the sense of meaning:

being 'up so close to Him' as though I am pressed to His Heart, not in outer courts of a His Palace, but right there in the Holy of Holies, which, when I think of it, His Heart really is the Holy of Holies! Isn't it?

O God, May Your Precious Body read of these words concerning Worship and begin to respond, even as little children, worshipping at Your Feet! May we then through these experiences be filled with the Beauty of Holiness, that we might go forth as lights shining with Your Light, that others may be drawn to You and Your Precious Bleeding Side!

If King David, who appointed myriads of musicians and singers, had been given the privilege of entering the Holy of Holies, I am sure that he would have gone right in boldly and then danced and skipped happily out into the Outer Gates and Outer Courts to minister to the people, which is what we become capable of doing after the Holy Anointing Oil is poured out on us afresh and anew. We become, over and over, His Oil Lamps, burning with His Love, having our batteries charged, as it were, and desiring to run to others with the Light that we have, to share our Pearls - our revelations of Him!

I remember sharing all of this with the Pastor of my Church Home. He didn't 'get it'. I told him that hearing Living Water doesn't frighten, but rather gives one 'thirst', even as when one walks in the woods and hears the gurgle of a brook. There is something in hearing the sound of water gurgling that gives us a longing to reach down and scoop a drink into our mouths; if only we knew that the water were pure. (As any of you 'nature lovers' out there can attest to!) Even so does Living Water in the Form of Song in the Spirit. The sound, gives us a thirst for more Living Water! When I 'sprinkle' my conversation with Tongues (believing the Lord to give me the interpretation in words to use for witnessing) I find others receptive and wanting to hear more of the Tongues! After all, they are a sign for the unbeliever; why not let them hear them?

After writing this pastor a nine page letter after the manner I have just written, he still refused to lead the congregation into morning Songs in the Spirit. I began to become angry with him. While playing my piano one day, which is close to my living room door, and thinking about this Pastor's refusal to heed my advice, the Holy Spirit said to me: "If a blind brother came in your door and bumped into your piano, would you get angry with him?" I said: "Oh no, Lord!" He replied: "I have not given your pastor the same light that I have given you on that subject - pray for him!"

Oh, this understanding made me so happy and I did pray for him and was thrilled when one year later - because of traveling, I hadn't been to this Church - I turned on the radio and heard this congregation singing in the Spirit in the *Sunday morning Service!* The congregation swelled and they had to build a new Church!

O Lord, teach us to do this. Teach us to 'Feed You a Little Cake' *First!* You are so gracious to ask so little. But we do remember that the Word has told us that You are a Spirit and You are seeking for those who will worship You in Spirit and in Truth. (This means, in part, that as we sing in the Spirit, we are truthfully thinking about God and not other things that can turn even this Lovely Song into just noise and emptiness.)

‡

Chapter Four

Wonderful Results of Singing in the Spirit!

W hile we were gathered on the tenth floor of the Sheraton Hotel for prayer a Word of Prophecy came: "Worship me in the Spirit!" The group then began to sing in English. Inwardly I rebuked the 'fear of man', gathered up courage, arose to my feet and said, "Excuse me, but the Lord has just asked us to sing *in the Spirit.*" One little black sister understood and began singing in Tongues. One by one others joined her and the music became glorious, as though the Holy Spirit had taken the baton and led the singing.

When we finished singing in the Spirit, a gentleman arose and began speaking by the Word of Knowledge. He said, "The Lord would have us to know, that while we were singing in the Spirit, a six-year-old in another city has been cured of blindness." Though I can't remember the other healings that he said had taken place, there were about five other miracles of healing and deliverance spoken! All of these were not coincidence, but rather co-*incidents!*

I thanked the Lord that He was confirming that as we sing in the Spirit in Worship and Adoration, as a Bride ought, He goes forth like a Mighty Man doing what He alone can do in response! He heals, and delivers and restores poor fallen mankind!

All of this reminded me of verses I had discovered in Isaiah 42:10–13–16, "Sing unto the Lord a new song and His praise from the ends of the earth, ye that go down to the sea, and all that is therein; the isles, and the inhabitants thereof. Let the wilderness and the cities thereof, lift up their voice, the villages that Kedar inhabits. *Let the inhabitants of the rock sing;* let them shout from the top of the mountains. Let them give glory to the Lord, and declare His praise in the islands. The Lord shall go forth like a mighty man; he shall stir up jealousy like a man of war: he shall cry, yea, roar; he shall prevail against His enemies." "*And I will bring the blind by a way that they knew not; I will lead them in paths that they have not known: I will make darkness light before them, and crooked things straight. These things will I do unto them, and not forsake them.*" (KJV) May we say that Jesus is the Rock, and Song in the Spirit—is a song *so new*—that it has never been sung before—so rare, that it shall never be repeated and sung in exactly this same way again!

This happening in the Sheraton Hotel also reminds me of another similar incident that took place in the Pittsburgh Theological Seminary later in 1972. It was the first time that I ever heard a very large crowd singing in the Spirit! I was seated in the balcony and the music was glorious; again sounding as though the Holy Spirit took His baton and led it! When it was finished, a Minister (Russ Bixler) stood up and gave the Word of Knowledge, saying that while we were singing in the Spirit, the Lord had been healing many! He proceeded to name about six or seven illnesses that had been healed! Again, these were not coincidences, but rather co-incidents! This is what the Holy Spirit will do as we become one in the Spirit by worshipping in His Spiritual Song! Now, back to the happening in the Sheraton Hotel

As the meeting ended, I dropped to my knees in a window well close by and with uplifted hands looked up into the sky, and thanked and worshipped the Lord for strengthening me to speak, and for all of the glorious results! The rays of the sun streamed down, covering me as in further Blessing!

Finally, I arose from my knees and turned to go. The room had emptied out quickly of those who had gathered to pray. I spied a lone elderly lady who was busily searching under the table and through the chairs for what I soon discovered was a lost treasure.

"Oh, it isn't important to anyone but me," she sighed mournfully, "it's only a hanky, but it was a gift from a dear friend." Understanding the emotional attachment of such a keepsake, I helped her search. Unable to find the hanky, we left the room together, and wanting to restore her joy, I began discussing the wonderful happenings that had just taken place in the meeting. This lifted her spirit, and by the time we had reached the elevator, our mutual sharing had somewhat dismissed the pain of her loss. As she stepped into the elevator, the Holy Spirit spoke in my heart, "Go with her. I want to show you something."

I accompanied her to the lobby. She settled into a chair and began to speak. "My name," said she, "is Navetta Rexroad. That means, 'The King's Daughter on the King's Highway'. My father was a Pentecostal minister. I belong to the Elim Prayer Group, you have heard of them?" (I replied that I had not.) She reminisced for awhile concerning life as a pastor's daughter and then spoke of the Song in the Spirit that had taken place in the morning meeting. As she enlarged a bit concerning that subject, I was responding, and we were rejoicing that we both were seeing 'eye to eye' of the subject of 'Singing in the Spirit'!

The Holy Spirit spoke to me then and said, "Be still now, and listen."

Just then she said, "My dear, I feel to share with you something that I have never before shared with anyone, lest I call attention to myself, but I feel that the Holy Spirit wants me to share it with you. Will you be my guest at lunch?" With great expectation, I joined her for lunch!

She began, "I am aware of the *power* of prayer. I know that the Lord doesn't need a large number praying before He responds. The small prayer group to which I belong has seen the Lord respond mightily through the years. He had us pray in the early 'forties' for the healing ministries to come forth and we saw the beginning of the Healing Ministries of Oral Roberts and Kathryn Kuhlman take place before that decade was over! I know that He has others praying about the same things, but He honors the prayers of each of us.

"Now," said she, "this is the thing that the Lord wants me to tell you. Years ago, when I was a young woman, the year was 1938, I heard someone saying that Unknown Tongues are satanic. I was terribly upset by this statement, I cried. I went to my father and repeated what I had heard. He told me that those who say such things are mistaken and that we are to pray for them. I went to my prayer closet in the attic and I prayed and prayed. I agonized in travail for hours, but could get no release from the anguish that I was experiencing!"

I listened to her intently, though I had no idea at that time what the word *travail,* even meant. "Suddenly," said she, "the Lord spoke in my heart." He said, "If you will be faithful in prayer concerning this matter, I will use your prayer to release from the *Body of Christ,* the poison that is in it. For, said He, a Body cannot get well as long as there is poison in it, and the *Misconception concerning Tongues is a poison in My Living Body!"*

* Note: See this in the introduction under: "A Startling Revelation"

As she made this last statement, I leaped in my spirit in joy and wonder! This joy certainly was not because of the horrible state of affairs surrounding the poisonous state of the Body of Christ, but rather, that here, through this little woman, the Lord was confirming to me, the many truths that He had shown me concerning Tongues! I marveled that I, only a handmaiden, had been shown these truths. And wondered that the one whose prayer had been used concerning this matter was sharing this with me for the first time! Again, the *Keynote Address* given that very night by Harold Hill, from James Chapter 3 verse 8: *"Though the tongue is a small member, it can poison the whole body."* confirmed to me this word of prophecy repeated to me that morning!

Brother Harold Hill's Sermon 'The Taming of the Tongue'—an excerpt

The Parable of the Unforgiving Servant: Forgive us our debts!

James 3:8, (KJV) *"But the tongue, can no man tame; It is an unruly evil, full of deadly poison."* Brother Hill gave me written permission to use the corrected copy of his message. I am including portions of it because of the clarity that it brings to this subject. I pray that it will *benefit you*, dear reader—as it did me!

"I met Jesus as Savior the night I invited Him to move inside of me and turn me on. And He did so! It was as though He opened me up, moved inside, closed me up—and He's been there ever since. Praise God! When Jesus moved in He changed my life. It's just that simple. God was in Christ and He's in us. We transport Jesus when we travel. We have this treasure in earthen vessels. Are we important people? We are 'Containers for Jesus'—'Portable Prayer Towers'."

"And ye shall receive power after you become proficient at 'Your Church's Five Point Program'." No, no! Acts: 1:8, *"And ye shall receive power after that the Holy Ghost has come upon you."* (And ye shall speak with other tongues.) No! *"Ye shall be witnesses unto me!"* This is what it's all about. So, we have received power; those of us who have met Jesus—first of all, as Savior—and then as Baptizer in the Holy Spirit. I met Him both ways seventeen years ago. *Then* I was *equipped with power.* But, *without* teaching and *without* instruction, I didn't know *the vital organ of the body that tunes up this whole body organism.* Do you know what that member is? *It is the tongue.* The tongue tunes up your whole system. If we are functioning like pagans; griping, grumbling, and gossiping, there is nothing attractive in us to draw others to our Lord. Rather—we 'turn them off'!

The third chapter of James is so important. I am becoming aware in my travels, of God's people settling for 'second best' because of the 'nit-picking' tongue. I want you to get this.

James 3: 1–2, *"My brethren, be not many masters, knowing that ye shall receive a stricter judgment. For we all stumble in many things. If anyone does not stumble in word, he is a perfect man, able also to bridle the whole body."* (NKJV) What a statement! If your tongue never offends someone, you are perfected in the spirit. The tongue is the external of the spirit, the human spirit. And if the tongue is on the loose the spirit is in rebellion. It's a direct result.

James 3:3–4, *"Indeed, we put bits in horses' mouths that they may obey us; and we turn their whole body. Look also at ships; although they are so large and are driven by fierce winds, they are turned by a very small rudder whenever the pilot desires."*

A tiny little rudder; compared with the size of the ship, the rudder is insignificant. And yet—it turns it! The captain makes the ship go where he wants it to go by turning this very small rudder. Where does that fit into the tongue in the body?

James 3: 5, *"Even so the tongue is a little member and boasts great things; see how great a forest a little fire kindles."* The tongue of a Christian can destroy!

James 3:6, *"And the tongue is a fire, a world of iniquity. The tongue is so set among our members that it defiles the whole body, and sets on fire the course of nature, and it is set on fire by hell."*

This is the organ—that tunes you 'spiritually up—or 'spiritually down'! The tongue tunes you to the left away from God or to the right down the course that He would have you travel. I know, because mine was the worst offender. I had to seek the Lord many months before I found out His method of taming the tongue. I searched these things out. The tongue is so important! James 3:7–8, *"For every kind of beast, and bird, of reptile, and creature of the sea, is tamed and has been tamed by mankind, but no man can tame the tongue. It is an unruly evil, full of deadly poison."* You can't do it. It's not a 'do-it-yourself-thing' at all!

James 3:9–10, *"With it we bless our God and Father, and with it we curse men, who have made in the similitude of God. Out of the same mouth proceed blessing and cursing. My brethren, these things ought not to be."* That is written to Christians—for Christian people!

I never used profanity. My mother taught me it was stupid. I was about five years old I think when she taught me this.

She said—"Harold, never take God's name in vain because some day you might want to call on Him in earnest and if you waste His time calling on Him in vain, when you're in trouble He might not listen, and you might be destroyed!"

I thank God for a Christian mother who taught me that. So I never used profanity. I noticed that only stupid people did—ignorant people. You have to be ignorant to take God's name—the name of the Mighty God—in vain. And so *I trained my tongue in sarcasm.* This is *much more wicked and vile and destructive* than stupid profanity. And I could cut you to ribbons. Oh, I could slice you thin.

And then I came into the Christian fellowship and tried to tame my tongue, and it got worse. I was a menace, an actual menace. I would arrive in a prayer group and in five minutes I would have the place in turmoil and I didn't want to. I couldn't open my mouth without this 'thing' squirting poison with 'nit-picking', back biting, telling about the brethren, gossiping. It got so bad I couldn't call it gossip—I called it sanctified reporting. That didn't help it a bit.

That burning down below got worse. Well you know God guarantees *a method of getting ulcers.* Did you know that? In Proverbs towards the front end He says, *"The words of a tale bearer are as wounds and they go down into the innermost parts of the belly."* And in case you miss it in the front end of Proverbs, He puts it also in the back end. It is that important! And so I was burning here in the belly, because I was burning here, with the tongue! The tongue was burning the stomach. Because when you have a tongue full of deadly poison and you swallow, it goes down into your insides. It was burning.

And then I came across the promise of a *gift of tongues.* I didn't know anything about it. Being a Southern Baptist, I had no business to. Tongues made them *"uncomfortable"* at that time, the Baptists that is. I'm glad to report now, I'm still a member of the Southern Baptist Church, and *ninety per cent of our members, including our Pastor, and his wife,* have met Jesus as Baptizer, and now you're really an odd ball if you haven't done so!

The first scripture the Lord gave me was I Th.5:16–18; *"Rejoice always, pray without ceasing, in everything give thanks; for this is the will of God in Christ Jesus for you."* And I tried it and it didn't work because of that second principle, *"Pray without ceasing."* That's another dimension of prayer.

I had prayed for the baptism and *all the other gifts* began to be manifested. But you see, I didn't know! I had no instruction. The words were there. I know I could have spoken in tongues the night Jesus baptized me. I'm sure of it. Acts 2:4 says, *"They spoke with other tongues as,* not when, but rather, because, the *spirit gave them utterance."* I almost choked to death trying to swallow the words. I didn't know they were words. No one told me. I had no way to find out until *a long time later.*

I sought the Lord for months about this tongue! One night I had just come from a prayer meeting. That night it had been a real vicious session. My tongue was the vicious part of the session and I left two or three of the brethren bleeding there! I had gossiped about everybody and I was miserable. I said, "Lord I'm either going to have to muzzle me, wear a gag to Church, or run out before the service is over—before I can even say "Good morning"—because I can't even say: "Good morning" without hurting somebody. "Lord, is there something about the gift of tongues that tames the untamable? Now, it's not fair Lord, for you to tell me that no man can tame the tongue and then leave me on the loose like this. That's not 'fair' unless you have provided a way out!" God never condemns. He reveals the state of affairs, then says; "By your permission I will change those circumstances my way." Is that right? He will change things, His way!

I have found that God can do anything, including taming my tongue, because that night I couldn't pray, I could only cut. That's all my tongue was good for. I had three words of prayer, maybe four, they went up to the ceiling, plopped on the floor and I started to criticize somebody. My tongue was a 'mess'! In extreme misery, I cried: "Lord take it, take this wicked tongue, however, and whatever. Just take it." And before I realized what was happening, I was praying in tongues! So, *desperation opened the door! I* guess *I prayed for two hours without a let up! I* began to *pray without ceasing!*

The hot line to heaven, is praying in Tongues and in everything giving thanks. Lord, we thank you for everything! 'King's kids' know where we're going. We know where we came from, that's our testimony and we know who did it, Jesus! And we know that our future is guaranteed and our present is in His hands. Is that right? Then rejoice! And again I say rejoice! Hallelujah!

A Modern Day Parable of the Unforgiving Servant—Forgive us our trespasses!

Matt. 18:31–33, *"So when his fellow servants saw what had been done, they were very grieved, and came and told their master all that had been done. Then his master, after he had called him, said to him, "You wicked servant! I forgave you all that debt because you begged me.* All you had to do was ask and I did it. *Should you not also have had compassion on your fellow servant, just as I had pity on you?"* And then the result came, the penalty. You know what the penalty was? Cast him into prison? No, No. I read it a hundred times, I guess, and read that into it. It's amazing how I can read the scripture and not see what it says because my mind has been biased by my own thinking.

Matt. 18:34(a), *"And his master was angry, and delivered him to the torturers..."* These are Demons, children! And when they get through with you, you will be delighted to forgive if there is anything left of you. Either forgive or burn.

Are you feeling heavy in the spirit? Are you feeling depressed? Leave your gift at the altar if you have anything against another. Stop acting religious and don't waste the brethren's time trying to get the demons prayed off; because when God puts them on they stay. Matt.18:34(b), *"...until he should pay all that was due him."* And what is that? *Forgiveness,* we must forgive!

This has made a tremendous difference in my praying for people. I've noticed a pattern among God's people. The first night of a week's service, Sister 'So-and-So' would come.

"Brother, I'm feeling so heavy in the spirit. I've lost my joy. Pray for me." I prayed for her. The next night she's back with the same thing. Wednesday night she hasn't gotten a bit better. Thursday night she's identical. Friday night she's back. Everybody's prayed for her. When I saw this, the next time this happened, this pattern business, I said: "How many of the saints have prayed for you for this thing, and for how long?"

Oh, she said: "I've had it for years."

I asked: "Who prayed for you?"

She replied: "Oral Roberts, Brother Duplessis, and Brother 'This one' Brother 'That one' prayed for me." She named all the great healers and the minor prophets as well, right on down the line! She never missed a one of them!

And I said: "And you are no better, not a bit?" I said, "Who do you hate?"

She jumped! "Nobody, nobody Brother—I don't hate a person in the world."

I questioned: "Who has done you a terrible wrong?"

Quickly she replied: "Oh, that 'So-and-So'!" She began to 'yak-yak' and the big mouth started and the poison! …There it was. I said, "Sister do you know what you have to do?"

She replied: "What?" She didn't want to know but she did want to know because the misery was just about total. When you get total torment from the tormentors—the demons of oppression and depression—and they force you and pound you down into the ground deep enough so that your eye balls are just about level with the sod, then you're ready for a change. And she was just about at that point. I never saw anyone more dejected.

I said: "First of all, how long has it been since you have prayed in tongues?"

She replied: "*Oh, about fifteen years!*"

I asked: "How come? Did Satan tell you the same thing he told me? 'Now you've spoken in tongues, forget it.'"

Thoughtfully she replied: "Well, yes, I believe he did."

I said: "And you *haven't used the one gift that will keep this thing tuned up* so you turned negative; and you called somebody and told them a nasty thing on the phone. Did you?"

Surprised she questioned: "How did you know that Brother?"

I said, "Because I've done it too, that's how I know. I was the worst offender. Do you know what you have to do?"

Hesitantly ponderingly she said: "Hmmm, I think so, I think so."

I said, "Go, do it *tomorrow*. Go and ask forgiveness."

She cried: "They did it to me!"

"Go and ask forgiveness. When you stand praying and think of somebody that ought against you, go."

I thought that was a misprint too, when I first read it. I thought they ought to come to me. No, you go to them. "Who's hurting? The one that's hurting had better go. The other person probably doesn't know a thing about it. They have probably forgotten all about it."

She came back the next night. We didn't have to pray for her. She was 'tuned up'. Praise God she was healed. She was delivered. She looked more like a teenager because she was delivered from the tormentors, the torturers!

Let's stand and praise Him together and be dismissed. You know if you have Spiritual Bursitis, raise your hands way up and get rid of it. It sets in the shoulder sockets of Baptists mostly, it is Spiritual Bursitis. Put them straight up in the air because that means surrender in every language, and Satan knows it and that's why he doesn't like it.

Lord we praise you. We thank You Jesus. In Your Name we pray! Amen.

[Brother Hill also gave a thrilling account of ministering in Albuquerque in spite of 'fire-bombers'. He later wrote his book 'King's Kids' and it is filled with wonderful stories.]

Chapter Five

Tongues! What is this Language?

W hat are Tongues? Where do they come from? What do we do with them? Why should I speak in a language that I do not understand? Is it really necessary that I use Tongues once I have them? Why? Are these questions that you are wondering about? Engage your spiritual antennae and see if you receive within a heavenly 'Green Light' concerning some of the answers that I have found through seeking. The Holy Spirit has promised to lead us into all Truth and to bear witness to that Truth. You will have within your spirit a sense of affirmation as you read Words of Truth.

First, very simply, speaking in an unknown Tongue is the act of speaking in a language that is unknown to the one doing the speaking! How's that for a simple explanation? Does that sound strange…hmm? This may be oversimplification, but it is basic to the beginning of an understanding of what Tongues are all about. This may be a little scary, isn't it? But let's pursue this and search it out. Perfect Love casts out fear.

Tongues may come out of one's mouth as a known language to some listener, as happened on the Day of Pentecost, recorded in Acts 2:1–11. Many present heard the disciples speak in languages that they, the hearers, understood. However, the disciples speaking the languages were unaware of what they were themselves saying. While speaking in Tongues *they could not, therefore, interfere* with the messages that the Holy Spirit was giving to the hearers. This really was the *Word of the Holy Spirit*, thus the Word of God to the listening ones. What other can the Holy Spirit utter through the lips of men, or give to the mouth of man to utter, than the *Word of God*, seeing that He is God—the Spirit of the Living God!

He uses the vocal chords and the speech faculties of the speakers for the deliverance of *His Message*. The following scripture are—(NKJV) It is recorded in the Book of Acts. 13:2 *"As they ministered to the Lord and fasted, the Holy Spirit said, "Now separate to Me Barnabas and Saul for the work to which I have called them."* Do we think that the Holy Spirit actually verbally spoke this? No, surely we do not! Rather, we realize that this was *a prophecy,* spoken by one of those present who had been fasting and praying for direction, and in all probability this—that was stated in the Word of God as a speech of direction from the Lord of the Church—came as an interpretation of Tongues! We, who understand the prophetic, realize that when a message in Tongues is spoken, we are being prompted to immediately 'stop and listen'—and to pray for an interpretation!

When this interpretation comes, it is in the Language of the hearers. Because that the tongue, the lips and minds and speech faculties of humans, are now engaged in this interpretation, the possibility of error is realized. This is not the Audible Spoken Word of God, but rather is a prophecy and it is to be judged according to the Word of God. Rightly so, for the Word tells us to do this! I Cor.14:29, *"Let two or three prophets speak, and let the others judge."*

Now concerning the Tongues used in a message in Tongues. I Cor.14:2, says *"For he who speaks in a tongue does not speak to men but to God, for no one understands him; however, in the spirit he speaks mysteries."* He (or she) is speaking Utterances of the Holy Spirit in the Language of the Spirit!

That which comes forth is the *Word of God*—Jesus Himself who is within us—in the Person of the Holy Spirit! *He—Jesus*—who is called the Word of God—speaks forth—His Heavenly Words—by using our vocal apparatus! John 1:1 says: *"In the beginning was the Word, and the Word was with God, and the Word was God."* Think deeply about what I have just written. I know that it is a new way of thinking and understanding about Tongues, but this does not make it invalid—but rather—*revelation* that brings clarity to this subject!

Can we understand that this is the *Audible Spoken Word of God, no less* than when He chose to use the pen of His messengers to deliver the Written Word of God, the Bible? Is this not so? Herein we are given the examples of God using the mouth and speech of men and women to deliver His Word. We know that He even put His Words into the mouth of a donkey. How do you think the other donkeys reacted to that! If they had the powers to reason and discuss—they would have most probably—stubbornly refused to listen or believe that such a 'new thing' could happen!

There is nothing new here then, except that in this day, when God uses so many to speak His Word as He has poured out of His Spirit in this new wonderful way, He uses Unknown Tongues! Consider this, the miraculous new Gift of Tongues, was *never ever used* in the Old Testament. *It was not given—until—* Jesus paid the price on Calvary and gained the ability to come into, and remain, and speak and move, through those of us who have wisely invited Him to come in and live His life in and through us! And then we ask Jesus to baptize us in or with His Holy Spirit! Through this miraculous act of speaking in Tongues, the speakers are *guarded from adding to, or taking from, the Word of God as they speak.* Their understanding is unfruitful, being by-passed, (I Corinthians 14:14) "For if I pray in a tongue, my spirit prays, but my understanding is unfruitful." Thus I cannot add *my own thoughts or words! Nor can I gossip nor say unholy words in this language for I do not understand how to speak it on my own!* See and understand the secret of how God guards us from improperly using His Word—or adding to—or taking from the Word of God! Men and women can go beyond the Spirits anointing and speak words from their own minds while giving a prophecy or interpretation of a message in Tongues, using their own given language, but while speaking in Tongues this is not possible. The Bible tells us that Tongues are a *manifestation of the Holy Spirit!* They are a 'giving forth'—a 'bringing forth'—a 'doing'—of the Holy Spirit—*however*—He uses our vocal apparatus! Can we not understand that this Spiritual gift which is a *manifestation* of the Holy Spirit is given to us, by the Holy Spirit—even as He had the Written Word, the Bible to be scripted through men? This is equal to what He gives further—presently—by His Holy Spirit. When we are preaching—or giving an *interpretation* of tongues—we are using our native language—therefore there is the possibility of human error. But that is the beauty of Tongues—we cannot use our own mind to express these words. *They are not ours and do not come from our minds but rather from our spirit—that is joined to the Holy Spirit—through the power of the Holy Spirit.* I Corinthians 6:17, "But he who is joined to the Lord *is one spirit* with Him." Hallelujah—this is truth!

"Did I Say That?"

Now what did I say? Did you read that right? Did I say that Tongues are the *Audible Spoken Word of God?* Are they not? Are Tongues and their use dangerous? For one thing—they are to be used—in ministry—*against* the works of darkness! I just heard Rev. Jack Hayford say—last evening on T.V.—"I could sell many more books if I would just stop speaking about Tongues!" This is the problem—and the 'poison' in the Church today—as I understand it! And I am not going to 'duck'—or avoid the subject of Tongues for supposedly monetary benefits! I am going to repeatedly 'address this issue'—in words written, even as I preach—as I have in other Nations—Chile, Mexico, Honduras—and seen stunningly good results! And I will continue to write—with the ammunition of the vision and clarity that God has given me—concerning this 'touchy' subject. Tongues ought *not to be avoided* or **'shunned'!** This is the exact Word the Holy Spirit just gave me. He interjected the word *'shunned'* as I was searching for the right word to describe the cowardly act of avoiding any of the wonderful gifts given us by the Holy Spirit! Rather we need to 'come and reason together'—until we learn *all the truth* on this very important subject! We should then be 'flooding the air-waves' with 'Song' of these 'Cauterizing-Swords' that can frustrate the 'works of darkness'! Just now, we are inundated—flooded with ugly profanity and blasphemy every day on our radios and televisions. It is 'high-time' to retaliate with these ultimate weapons given us by the Holy Spirit—*for just such a time as this! Singing in the Spirit cleanses the air-waves!* This is the reason that the Holy Spirit gave me the unique opportunity of singing in the Spirit all over the world via T.V. during the nine months that this took place while I was living in Israel! Read it again—Chapter Nine—concerning World-Wide Television!

The very first time that I shared the statement*: "**Tongues are the Audible Spoken Word of God**"*—the resulting anointing was so heavy that all of those present and listening had to place their hands on one another to *get release from* the magnitude of the anointing that fell upon us—and was filling us! We wound up staggering under this anointing. It took great effort to remain standing. Many just collapsed and lay prostrate before the Lord, while others filled up with laughter and joy! We truly had become *'drunk in the Spirit'!*

The conservative Christian market is the very one that needs to hear an enlargement of the truth concerning Tongues. For too long this group of Christians has 'come against' Tongues to the detriment of their own selves. Should we let fear of the opinion of others make us compromise? I am not speaking of the spoken word of men, but rather the **Tongue** *of the Holy Spirit!* The speech and ideas of many have been in error, speaking in their native language that which has sprung from their intellect. This is not what I am explaining here, but rather I am endeavoring to help others understand the utmost importance of the Tongue given by the Holy Spirit! *Tongues are not the speech nor creed nor understanding of any!* Rather—they are that which is given out of Heaven, through human vessels by the Holy Spirit! He uses an Unknown Tongue, (Language) so that others *will know—should know*—that this speech *is not of human origin!*

Acts: Chapter 2, verse 4 says, "And they were all filled with the Holy Spirit and began to speak with other Tongues, *as the Spirit was giving them Utterance.*" Who was giving them the Utterance of the Spoken Word? The Holy Spirit of the Living God of Israel was giving them the Words. *What other Word can the Holy Spirit give but the Word of God?* The Holy Bible is called the Word of God! II Peter Chapter 1:21, "for no prophecy was ever made by an act of *human will*. But men moved by the Holy Spirit spoke from God." This passage I quote, not to emphasize prophecy, but rather to high-light the sentence: *But men moved by the Holy Spirit spoke from God. This is what I believe Tongues are—speech from God—and the misunderstanding or 'misconception' of all of this—is the cause of the problem of 'poison' in the Body of Christ today! The opening preface of this book is not* something that I made up—it was a 'Word of God'—given and confirmed—in order that light and illumination be given to Christ's Body of believers—the Church—concerning this very subject—that healing can come forth. And that this marvelous supernatural Gift of God will begin to be used widely and comprehensively—rather than being avoided!

They were gathered together on that Day of Pentecost—as recorded in Acts 2:1–3, "When the Day of Pentecost had fully come; they were all with one accord in one place. And suddenly there came a sound from heaven, as of a rushing mighty wind, and it filled the whole house where they were sitting. Then there appeared to them divided tongues, as of fire, and one sat upon each of them. And they were all filled with the Holy Spirit and began to speak with other tongues, as the Spirit gave them utterance."

They surely felt the anointed Presence of the Spirit. And there appeared to them Tongues as of fire distributing themselves, and they rested on each one of them. The gathered ones were empowered from on High! The Winds of the Spirit, heard, and experienced by those present and the Tongues of Fire visible, were the wonderful manifestations of the Presence of the Living God of Israel!

Even as He had appeared to Moses in the burning bush that illuminated but did not consume, and even as He showed His Power and authority in the fire that consumed the sacrifice on Mt. Carmel as Elijah prayed fervently—and as He answered the prayer of Solomon and sent the fire from heaven to burn and consume the sacrifice—so now God answered the prayers of these 'waiting ones'.

He manifested Himself through Invisible wind and in a Tongue of fire! God Almighty, Creator of the universe, showed His reception of the living sacrifices, those first Christians, He *came upon them* with Holy Heavenly Fire! They had fulfilled the Word of God—even before Paul had written of such! Romans 12: 1, "I beseech you therefore, brethren, by the mercies of God, that you present your bodies a living sacrifice, holy, acceptable to God, which is your reasonable service." Father God put His Fire upon them. He used this Heavenly Fire Power as a source of electrical energy with which to draw forth, from those that had become His *wells of salvation!* Christ Jesus, the Word within them came forth as a Fountain of Living Water!

As one puts a pump down into a natural well in order to bring forth water, even so the Holy Spirit, the Mighty Wind, engulfed, immersed, and surrounded them in a baptism of Invisible liquid love and power. And heavenly words of love and truth and light came forth from these who had been anointed to be a nation of kings and priests unto our God.

Does Jesus speak in unknown Tongues? Oh glory, it is He, the Living

Word, which is speaking and coming forth as the Living Water, when we open our mouths and allow the Tongues to *gush forth!* We might say—or could we say—that our natural speech is as a 'wooden bucket' for our internal wells as compared with the 'explosive pumping power' of the Tongues in bringing forth 'Living Waters'!

The Word now becomes, not flesh, but rather Holy Breath, Holy Water! The Tongue of Fire—Heat of the Spirit—ignites the oil of the Spirit, causing the Water of Life—Christ in us—to reach boiling point, becoming steam and a Holy Cloud—in response to worship in spirit and in truth being offered up in the Holy of Holies—to which we are invited to come boldly—by His ordained priests.

A river of living water comes up out of our bellies, a Pillar of Cloud—His Presence—that ascends up into the nostrils of God. This *cloudy pillar is permeated* with the *fragrance of Christ*. The Lily of the Valley and the Rose of Sharon has become Incense through the grinding of the mortar and pestle of the Cross. It—this 'Fragrance of Christ'—is therefore received and smelled of by our Father. Remember, to Israel, when disobedient and willful He said in Amos 5:21, "I hate, I despise your feast days, and I will not smell in your solemn assemblies." Then there was the warning In Lev. 26:31, "I will not smell the savor of your sweet odors." So we see in these Scriptures, that the Lord God of Israel *receives offerings—through His nostrils!*

As we light this incense of Jesus, with the Tongue of Fire given in part for that purpose, it heats the Living Water to 'boiling point' and goes up out of our mouths as a 'Pillar of Cloud' straight into the nostrils of God the Father. He inhales and then He exhales…ahh…! And 'Essence of Christ' comes back down upon us, making of us a *fragrance of life* unto life for those who will receive and death unto death for those who will perish. II Corinthians 2: 14–16, "Now thanks be to God who always leads us to triumph in Christ, and through us, diffuses the fragrance of His knowledge in every place. For: we are to God the fragrance of Christ, among those who are being saved, and among those who are perishing. To the one *we are* the aroma of death *leading* to death, and to the other the aroma of life *leading* to life. And who is sufficient for these things?"

The Father also *condensates this pillar of cloud* and sends it back down upon us as a gentle rain, causing our desert places to blossom and bloom. I am reminded of Psalm 45:8, "All thy garments smell of myrrh and aloes and cassia out of the Ivory palaces whereby they have made Thee glad." The congregation has the 'oil of joy and gladness' to come upon them as they worship in this manner. They are strengthened, refueled, and refilled with the Spirit's anointing, enabling them to go out into the workplaces of the world and be joyous, and loving, effectual witnesses for our Lord! (Old Testament Priests were commanded to make offerings unto the Lord—by fire! Herein we see the shadow. Just written above—we see our part in the fulfillment—of that required of Priests in Leviticus Chapter 23.

And how do I have an understanding of that which I have just written? At the beginning of my 'Walk in the Spirit' in 1970 when I first received the Baptism of the Holy Spirit and was so completely new to all of the issues of the Holy Spirit, I asked questions as would a little child. When our Pastor admonished us with: "We are wells! Let's get the logs out of our wells that the Living Waters may flow!" I asked: "Father, if I am a well, I have no hands, and how do I get the logs out?" Much to my joy, God gave me *my second vision in the Spirit!*

I saw a huge pillar of cloud coming up out of the ground similar to the action of 'Old Faithful', the geyser in Yellowstone National Park. At the same time I heard the Spirit say: "Take the oil of the Spirit that I have placed upon your head and put it under the Living Water within and strike it with the Tongue of Fire!" Worship me with Song in the Spirit and this will cause the Waters to get so hot, they will come out of your vessel as this Pillar of Cloud you are seeing!" "That will push out all of the logs!"

My husband is a retired steamfitter and when I mentioned Living Waters to him, he said: "In the trade we call 'live water' steam, and almost nothing can resist steam pressure." "One can take a 50 year old pipe, discolored and soiled on the outside, but inside it is shiny-squeaky clean!" So I contend that all of the 'foregoing' shows the use of Tongues to be as an internal cleansing agent! And we are the first partakers! These logs that are dislodged are many things—memories, habits and hurts that we may not even be aware of—that the Holy Spirit, by this wonderful action, dislodges for us! And this certainly helps to build up our faith as promised in Jude verse 20, "But you beloved, building yourselves up on your most holy faith, praying in the Holy Spirit." (i.e.—in part—Tongues!) As for the idea of the Lord smelling of this Cloud, that came later, as well as the thought of the condensation of the Cloud for the dispersion on Living Waters as refreshing rain! Also, remember that the Lord spoke to Moses at the door of the Tabernacle—in a Cloud—and we are His Tabernacles and our mouths are this door!

Conclusion! This book is written in part, to help others, to realize that the admonition to pray in the Spirit—is really telling us that we are to pray using Tongues, the Language of the Holy Spirit! Are we issuing forth from our lips this Fire? Do we hear it coming forth from the airwaves? Do we hear Christians using this Marvelous Gift when teaching or sharing about this subject? No! Tongues are being spoken aloud—very sparsely. This is part of the *great misconception.* Among other things—Tongues are a sign for *unbelievers!* We are depriving them of the *sign given expressly for them*—if we never let them hear them! Because that Paul had to instruct the Corinthians concerning the *abuse* of Tongues, we have practically thrown the baby out along with the bath water! (This is a good illustration, for we were given the ability to bring forth Tongues through a Holy Ghost Baptismal Bath!) And more than likely—this abuse and misuse was done originally—because of the excitement and joy that speaking in Tongues can create!

Some state that the Bible is declaring that if we do not *immediately speak* in Tongues, we have not received this Baptism. I disagree and beg of those who hold this stance to 'hear me out'! Yes, Tongues are spoken of as being *evidence* that this Baptism has been received. But because that the evidence is not initially spoken, does this indicate that there is no evidence—that these Tongues are not there within us? I think not! What Court of Law would declare such—that because evidence is not presently available, nothing has taken place?

This is similar to the error made by critical 'fruit inspectors'. If they see or hear or suppose that a brand new baby Christian or one with little teaching is bringing forth no or little fruit, they disqualify them as being 'unsaved'. This is like chopping down a maple *sapling* because that the syrup is not yet flowing! I feel that the Holy Spirit is grieved when statements are made…especially by Christians, that can hinder new Christians.

Concerning the issue of whether one has or has not this Baptism, based solely on the evidence of Tongues being voiced—my personal experience has value that speaks to the opposite experience. When I received this Holy Spirit Baptism, an overwhelming outpouring of love such as I had never known before took place and was my blessing—as I have already related in this book! The Tongues, the Living Water of Jesus Christ speech, the utterances of the Holy Spirit, *were already resident within me!* At the time of this inundation of Love, I was *not interested* in speaking any other words than those of my own understanding—which were words of love and adoration and thanksgiving to a depth that I had *never here-to-for* known or experienced—spoken silently to God inwardly—in my native speech!

I had no interest in speaking in Tongues, even though the one who had led me into this experience of receiving 'more of Jesus' interrupted my flow of adoration to the Lord God with the statement: "Don't speak in English now dear—speak in Tongues." I hadn't a 'clue' to what she was saying and furthermore I 'could care less' I was not interested! I just wanted to continue worshiping and thanking God for this marvelous here-to-fore unknown experience and expression of love that I was responding to!

In the next two weeks—*before these Tongues*—my personal prayer language ability came forth—many Gifts of the Spirit were in operation in my life for the *first time!* These gifts had never before been a part of me—or to my knowledge—the ability to use them! *I finally* brought forth Tongues, by fervently asking for them—once I understood—*slightly*—what they were according to God's Word. And I realized—not yet how they were to be applied or used—but rather that, according to what I read—I should—or could have them! Remember, I am a Baptist, and before I was going to proceed into something as strange as speaking in Tongues, I had to 'check it out' in the Bible!

But I repeat—*before these Tongues were brought forth*—I found myself capable of operating in Gifts of the Spirit that I had *never had access to before,* or at least was totally unaware of. The first was the Gift of Faith with which I prayed, not with an attitude of a 'wish for' or a 'oh I better not say this aloud in case it doesn't take place'—which was my attitude of unbelief before this Baptism! My comment in fact had been: "I don't have the faith to believe for Miracles, and one can't 'con' God—He knows I don't have this faith!"

But this Gift of Faith—and the Word of Knowledge from the Holy Spirit gave me such an assurance, that with *no* doubt whatever, I prayed first, for a friend with a 'whip-lash' injury of 16 years. God spoke in my heart—the Word of Knowledge: "pray for Marie!" I had no idea that she even needed prayer. Immediately the ability to lift her hands completely was restored. Then I voiced this same 'assured prayer' for healing of a cancer, and immediately the cancer was dismissed from the body being prayed for. This was the Gift of Healing being accessed also!

And then the Gift of Discernment was given me and the Lord told me to lay my hand on another and to rebuke a demon that was troubling her. The Holy Spirit did not tell me the name of the demon, He just said: "Lay your hand on her stomach and rebuke the demon!" It must have been the spirit of unbelief or fear, because she said later that she wanted the Baptism, but didn't want to speak in Tongues, but the moment I laid my hand on her in obedience to the Lord, she burst forth in the most fluent expression of Tongues that I have ever heard. And this was on the very day that she asked for the Baptism, (telling the Lord within that she wanted the Baptism, but not 'those Tongues')! She had just been prayed for to receive the Baptism and had been slain in the Spirit. And remember, I had not had the Tongues come forth yet myself!

Right here, lets just tackle the opposition—can a Christian have a demon— "in my flesh dwells no good thing"—are we still in the flesh—though spiritually blessed? Of course! Case closed! If that sounds too 'cut and dried'—remember—I know this one I just wrote about was already a wonderful Christian—but the Lord spoke in my heart to lay my hand on her and rebuke a demon. Let me assure you that—since that time—I have been called upon to cast out demons from lovely Christians too many times to deny the reality! And the difference in the life and the expressions of joy and peace after such deliverances are such a blessing to behold. I pray the Body of Christ has so matured in this area that further deliverances will be performed!

We who have been baptized in His Holy Spirit should have this 'Fire of the Christ Within' pouring out of *our* mouths! This is a good way to 'pray without ceasing'—we can still drive autos, run sweepers, do our daily work with just Prayer in the Spirit streaming out of our lips and under our breath. We are building up our own faith as Jude 1:20 tells us to do! Wouldn't you like to be a 'Holy Ghost Fire Fighter'? Tongues streaming forth from our lips are as a 'Fire Powered extremely hot water fire hose'—of 'steam'—really—spiritually—that enables us to wash away all of the ugly mud caused by the floods of the evil one! Tongues are not *too holy* to be used commonly even as we use the Written Word! And more, when used with positive results following, Tongues are the *sign* for believers and unbelievers that here is *Power!*

Again—the misconception is that these Tongues because they may cause fear or misunderstanding for the unbelieving should not be used? Paul's life shows that the Gospel itself *must be preached* in spite of persecution, misunderstanding or whatever else from unbelievers—or believers!

Tongues are the Living Water of Christ Jesus Words issuing forth out of our bellies! We must let them out! This Living Water is just what Jesus said it would be—the Holy Spirit issuing forth from our bellies bringing with Him—healing and Illumination and wisdom of spiritual realities, which we need to bring forth for self as well as for others!

My plea in this book is that Rebecca, Isaac's wife, a type of the Bride of Christ, bring forth so much Worship using Song of the Spirit, that it rises as that 'Old Faithful' pillar of cloud that I saw in my vision—and that God takes it and condensates it and pours it back on a thirsty, hungry world! For those who have these Waters of Christ within, but haven't received the *dynamite type hydraulics, the drawing power* issued in the Baptism of the Holy Spirit, enabling them to bring these Living Waters—out of their 'belly-wells' in the form of Tongues—they just have not understood that they might—and should—do this! If they will only—lay aside their own 'lack of understanding' and trusting in Jesus alone—ask Him for the Baptism of the Holy Spirit, they too may bring forth these Miraculous Waters, and use—or employ them *as well as* the written Word of God, the Bible which *they are presently drawing from and using!*

They will be able to weld the *two*-edged Sword. I believe the Bible is calling the speech out of our mouths—speaking the written Word of God in our native language—one side of the Sword—and the Tongues—spoken—are the other side! Hebrews 4:12, "For the Word of God is living and powerful, and sharper than *any two-edged sword,* piercing even to the division of soul and spirit and of the joints and marrow, and is a *discerner* of the thoughts and intents of the heart." I believe that this Scripture is not only declaring the excellent superiority of the razor or laser-light sharpness of the 'Sword of the Spirit' but that also, it is telling us that the Word of God is a 'two-edged' Instrument!

I believe also that this scripture is a proof text concerning Tongues. To *discern is an act of the will.* It is a function of a brain. This word discern as it is written on the page and read has not the power to discern. But in the use of Tongues, we are utilizing the one side of this spiritual sword that engages the Holy Spirit in Speech—and *He most certainly is doing the discerning, and enlightening it to our understanding!*

I believe that the Holy Spirit wants the Body of Christ to have the opportunity to read about, examine, and begin to truly understand and *use* Tongues. I believe that God is about to bring forth, in fullness, prophecies that He has given many, through the years. I am praying that this book will be a success—really a great success and tool, with many receiving a new understanding and desire to receive and use their Tongues from the Holy Spirit and that thereby the poison will be drained out of the Body of Christ, the Church!

Oh may the Bride of Christ go forth as men and women, having our gowns 'steam-cleaned'—not only in the fires of persecution that are spoken of in the Word of God—but also with a 'steamy cloud' issuing forth from our lips as we join together singing a 'love song' in the Spirit, of Worship to our Marvelous God! This is really how we contribute to our Lord's standing and singing in the midst of the Congregation as written of in Hebrews 2:12, saying: "I will declare Your name to My brethren; In the midst of the assembly I will sing praise to You."

And as we sing in the Spirit, it is as the deep within our wells, calling to the deep things of Heaven, and an anointing is brought down upon us, which can be experienced—felt by us and those around us joining in this Song in the Spirit!

An example of this experience is as follows: I remember going to the altar of 'Sheepfold Ministries' daily at 6:00 a.m., not really wanting to be up at that hour, but it was my obligation to be involved in the morning 'prayer watch'. As I stepped into the Church and heard the Song in the Spirit coming forth from the mouth of my black brother Jeremiah, as he was already kneeling at the altar Worshipping the Lord in clear high tones, my heart and spirit were filled with the desire to join him. All thoughts of sleep and selfish distraction were eliminated and I rejoiced to drop to my knees and join in the Heavenly Song. This happened over and over again. It was during this time that I thought of the scripture concerning 'deep calling unto deep' at the noise—the sound of His Waterspouts—and felt that this experience revealed a portion of illumination regarding this Scripture!

Chapter Six

Beyond the Wilderness and into the Promised Land!

C ome with me now to this place, this kingdom, this spiritual 'Cloud of Glory' that I have been baptized into. We must learn to walk and move and talk and pray and have our whole being in this new land of Invisible Light! This whole new world, though invisible, is as real as the visible world, more so probably. I had been given spiritual eyes to see into this Spiritual World! As the scales of darkness fell away, I, though thinking beforehand that I was so rich in spiritual wisdom and needing nothing more than 'more of the same', had my eyes anointed with eye-salve, and now I stood looking into a whole new Realm.

"In the Spirit" is no longer an expression of words that mean the same thing as, earnestly, or sincerely, or fervently, which are words describing an attitude toward our daily walk in the Lord. "In the Spirit" now means the same as; in, or of this new realm! This is a place of living and moving and being that is not of the flesh, nor of the carnal realm, but rather involves us in a life and behavior and attitudes and new understanding of the things which please and follow after the Holy Spirit of our Holy God! Thus, to "pray in the Spirit" means to use the Language of this new place, the unknown Tongue, the Language spoken only by the residents of this Realm. To "walk in the Spirit" means to walk not by sight, but by faith. To "live in the Spirit" means to endeavor to have our entire being following after the Spirit, rather than listening to the carnal call of the flesh, which listens to self rather than to the Spirit.

I was to learn that inside of this 'Cloud of Light' the inhabitants are given supernatural weapons with which to battle, for outside of this cloud, on the side facing Egypt, there is darkness. The children of the Lord who are dwelling in this land of natural sight and natural light are being blinded by the rulers of the darkness of this world.

This darkness is so great that for the most part, the children of the Lord are not even aware that these rulers of darkness - these powers and principalities

- even exist, though their Bible is full of examples of such! They even scoff at the mention of the reality of demons, although their Lord has been reported to have had to deal with the same. But because they cannot *see* them nor discern their presence, they think they do not exist. The darkness makes the virgins sleep. The bride must go forth crying, "Behold the Bridegroom cometh!"

The Inhabitants of the 'Land of Light' must now learn how to rout the powers of the evil one that they *are now aware of.* They must learn to use their new supernatural weapons with which they have been issued. These are not carnal weapons, but spiritual, and are mighty to the pulling down of strongholds, which speak of entrenched enemy bastions, not imaginary foes!

We will explore this area of weaponry in depth, for the Lord of Hosts has given us an ultimate weapon, which He wants *all* of the Inhabitants of this Realm in the Spirit to know of and to use. Oh, how He longs for all of His children to come into this place.

There is only one entrance to this Realm. The Dove is hovering over us, even as Paul spoke of all our fathers being under the Cloud, the Pillar of Cloud that went before the Israelites, the Cloud that was representative of the *Shekinah Glory* of God, which entered and so filled the temple in answer to Solomon's prayer that the priests could not stand under it to minister. Solomon was a type of our wonderful Prince of Peace.

This Cloud, the Dove, this Power, this Glory of God that is the Holy Spirit of God, must come down upon us. We must be encompassed about, surrounded by, baptized by Jesus into this Cloud of Glory! Those of us who have Christ in us, who walk in His footsteps, must be anointed with the Invisible Holy Oil, even as was He! To anoint is to pour upon the head. To anoint is to pour blessings *upon.* Again, in the Old Testament only kings and priests could be invested with this authority and power by the prophets chosen by God. But in these last days, God is pouring out through His Appointed Prophet and Great High Priest Jesus Christ of Nazareth, our Lord and Savior—His Holy Anointing Oil. Could we picture that this Holy Oil is made up of the love and the power; the energy, and sweet essence of Christ. And all are topped off with a flame of fire, tongues, with which to ignite the one receiving! It is for *all flesh* who will desire it.

Remember that Jesus, who was sinless, came to John to be baptized. He was baptized of water and the Spirit that day. Are you sinless through Christ's Righteousness today and already water baptized? Come as did He to fulfill *all* righteousness and ask to be baptized in the Spirit. Just now, He is waiting. No one is watching but Him. No one can read your mind or is reading over your shoulder! I rebuke every spirit of doubt and unbelief and fear and pride in you who are reading, in the Name of Jesus. Ask your Precious Savior to baptize you with His own Holy Spirit. Or just tell Him you *want more of Him*, as I did as a little child, in my ignorance of this experience. He will do the same for you as He did for me! Praise God. Thank You, Jesus!

Song in the Spirit is one of the most joyous discoveries in this new Land. This song is a rejoicing deep within, like the beginning of a new fountain that wants to bubble up into a spring, even as Israel sang this song. "Spring up oh well; sing you unto it." You know not how, but from within you there wants to come forth a shout, a song, a flow, as the beginning of a new river of Living Waters. This is a new song! It comes from the depths of your being. It may at first be expressed only through a flow of tears of rejoicing and gratitude as you begin to grasp how deeply He really loves *you!*

Or you may be blessed with a song in the Spirit, and words will come forth that you never spoke before, accompanied by a melody not composed by man, but by His Sweet Holy Spirit. It will be a song of deliverance and joy and wonder at His Goodness. And if you knew to wait for it and to pray for an interpretation, it would be given. (He has given me most songs in this manner.) But no matter, your Savior knows the interpretation, and it is music to His Ears. Don't be concerned about what your voice sounds like to your ears. In the Song of Solomon, He, Jesus the *King,* says: "Let me hear your voice; for your voice is sweet." Chapter 2:14 (b)

As this new stream begins to flow, this river of worship will come forth and water the things around you, and that dry land, that wilderness area, will begin to blossom like a rose and everything around you will begin to bloom. Even as Moses was told to *speak* to the rock in the wilderness for release of the gushing of the waters, so these Living Waters will come out of the *Rock, Jesus,* who is hidden in the depths of you - in your belly, as you *speak* and *sing* in Tongues! Our dear Savior cried out on that last Day of the Feast of Tabernacles and invited all who would to come to Him for Living Waters! (John 7:37) With the Words of His Speech—Tongues—the water will come out of the *Rock!* A wonderful mystery is this!

Even so do the priests of Israel to this day cry on the last day of the Feast of Tabernacles for water, the latter rain waters for the yearly harvest! And to think, that we, who are baptized in the Holy Spirit, have this ability to bring forth Living Waters for this End-Time Harvest of the souls of men! Oh God, forgive us of the error of leaving these Holy Waters, these Living Waters in our bellies, while we use our tongues to speak our native language rather than Your Heavenly *Tongues!*

Weaponry!

Is it not time for the Body of Christ to begin to look into this matter of Tongues with completely open hearts and minds, seeking unity of the Spirit concerning His Language? This ability was given unto men with the great sign of visible Tongues of Fire resting on the heads of the first disciples. This sign was accompanied by a Rushing Mighty Wind that shook their habitation. All of this took place on a great Feast Day called Pentecost and ushered in a new power and ability to witness to the death and resurrection of our Lord Jesus Christ. Should we not put aside all of our preconceived ideas and understanding of this manifestation that *He is responsible for,* that we might come into a new Unity of the Spirit?

Oh that we, the Body of Christ, might come into a new Oneness in Him! Oh, that as members of the Army of the Lord we might be united in One Fighting Unit against the foe using *every weapon* of the Spirit that we may possess? Surely it is time, seeing that our Lord prayed for this unity in the Garden on the night of His agony. For too long Satan has divided us on this issue.

Lord God, if indeed Tongues are one of the most powerful weapons that you have given us in our battle against evil, help us to have a clear understanding of this weapon and how to use it. You are the Commander in Chief. What Commander would not make His soldiers aware of the battle weapons, and then not teach them how to use them? We know that your answers and instructions are in Your Word; give us spiritual eyes to see them. Ephesians 6:10–12 gives us a command as soldiers of the Lord. "Finally, my brethren, be strong in the Lord, and in the power of His might." We are then told to put on the whole armor of God that we might be able to stand against the wiles of the devil.

We are told that we wrestle not—against flesh and blood, but against principalities, against powers, against the rulers of the darkness of this world, and against spiritual wickedness in high places. We are instructed to take unto ourselves the whole armor of God that we may be able to withstand in the evil day, and having done all, to stand! A list of the battle armor is given:

Wrap your loins, (the bowels and the parts affected by emotions and sexual desires) with a Girdle of Truth.

Put on a Breastplate of Righteousness. This covers the heart and keeps us thinking right. We have a better understanding than did Aaron. His was set with natural Jewels. We have in our Breast Plate of Righteousness, the *Jew-El-* Jesus Christ the Righteous One!

Be shod with the Gospel of Peace, and be ministers of reconciliation, especially with one another.

Take the Shield of Faith that is capable of quenching all of the fiery darts of the wicked.

Now we come to the most important part of the body - the head. With this member we think, see, hear, nourish and command the rest of the body. This most important part needs to be covered with the helmet of salvation. And to this head is given the ultimate weapon, the Sword of the Lord! We need to learn about this *Sword!*

Speaking forth the Written Word is the part of this Sword that is available to every Christian, while only those baptized of the Spirit can use the other side of the two-edged sword, the Tongues! A wonderful clarifying Scripture that helps us to understand the reality of the Word being a Sword that comes out of our mouth is found in the *original Hebrew*, in Psalm 149:6.

While living in Israel and studying Hebrew, I came upon a small book of Psalms printed in Hebrew and English. Rather than the King James Version which reads: "Let the high praises of God be in their mouth, and a two-edged sword in their hand," the Hebrew version reads: "Let the *exalted high praises* of God be in their *throat, a sword of mouths*, in their hand!" To me, the scripture read in this manner brought revelation!

The throat is located in our neck. This is the place of our voice box. The Song of Solomon Chapter 4:4 says, "Your neck is like the tower of David built for an armory, on which hang a thousand bucklers, all shields of mighty men."

After much searching of the Word of God, and asking the Holy Spirit the meaning of this strange verse, Pastor Wallace Heflin Sr. received the Lord's reply: "The voice box is in the neck!" This answer helps us to see the importance of *speech*, and its ability to overcome mighty men, defeating satanic giants with *speech!* And to, as it were, hang the trophy of these around the neck, even as warriors put 'notches in their gun belts'! Having heard this revelation I saw more than just praises given in our native language, I saw *'exalted high praise'* as being the *Language of the Spirit—Tongues!*

In Judges 7:17 Gideon told his 300 warriors to watch and to do what he did and in verse 18, "When I blow the trumpet, I and all who are with me, then you also blow the trumpets on every side of the whole camp, and say, 'The sword of the Lord and of Gideon'!" I believe that exalted praises are the 'Perfect praise sword' supplied by the Holy Spirit. Then: A sword of mouths is as the Sword of the Lord...and of Gideon. Or, we could say: "A sword of the Lord and of Grace." or "A sword of the Lord and of Mark...Harry...Betsy!" I believe that we can see in this scripture the type of a Christian, who needs not many to go with him, but only those who truly believe by faith that God is able, no matter what! Then He gives us His Sword with which to go into battle!

Ephesians 6:18, states that we are to pray always with all prayer and supplication in the Spirit! That phrase "in the Spirit" is explained by Paul when he says in, I Corinthians 6: 17, "But he who is joined to the Lord is one spirit with Him." and then: I Corinthians 14:14, "For if I pray in a tongue, my spirit prays, but my understanding is unfruitful." Is this not truly identifying Tongues. He said: "If I pray in a tongue—my spirit—joined to the Holy Spirit—prays—or is speaking, unknown words" his understanding was unfruitful! His mind 'didn't get it'! But he was praying in tongues and he said that this was 'praying in the spirit'!

It is the Holy Spirit, not our spirit, giving the Words that we speak in this way, so they are His Words! The Bible tells us that they are not our words, our minds do not understand them, they could not possibly be our words—and thus, being His Words—they are, and may be called: the audible spoken Words of God!

This prayer begins as speech and usually 'high-gears' into song in the Spirit unless it becomes travail, which usually ends in song when the travail is over. Travail is something that I knew nothing about until after being baptized in the Spirit and having travail just come upon me one day when intense prayer was needed in a situation.

When the Church, the Body of Christ is singing in the Spirit and refuses to stop before there is the awareness of the anointing of God—the blessing out of Heavenly Zion—and then stays in the Holy 'Hush' that follows; visions and revelations are often given in this atmosphere! Let us learn to let the Holy Spirit 'take the baton' and lead us into His Green Pastures where we can find our souls refreshed! Is this not the refreshing that He is speaking of when He tells us in His Word to labor to enter into His Rest? I believe this is a large part of the mystery of silence and rest as He gives to His Beloved in rest! In quietness and confidence, shall be our peace, our strength, our rest!

Because this Sword of Mouths is the audible Word of God it is filled with creative power! As mysteries are spoken, they will never return empty or void. God watches over His Word to perform it. This is as a laser beam of light and a guided missile that knows how to dispel the powers of darkness. The Spirit does all of this through the Word as we allow Jesus Christ in us to speak forth! He takes up serpents and cleanses the air waves as we speak these Precious Swords. This Word, as the Tongue of Jesus—the Living Word—is living and powerful and divides asunder between joints and marrow, soul and spirit and *is* the discerner of the thoughts and intents of the heart.

One thing more concerning Paul's admonition concerning *speaking* in Tongues as we are all gathered together. Certainly we are not all to begin to *speak* in Tongues at once, any more than we would *all* begin speaking in our native language at the same time. However, *speaking* and *singing* are *two dif-*

ferent things! We all do sing together. Even so, we should *all* sing in the Spirit together!

God's Strengthening Process—led of the Spirit, into the wilderness!

Although our Lord Jesus was driven into the wilderness to be tempted by the devil, immediately after His Baptism in the Holy Spirit, as written of in Matthew 4:1, more often than not it seems as though the Lord allows us a 'Honeymoon Experience' of a few months at least before we are led into these areas of the 'New Growth'! And the joy that fills us because of our new position in our Lord does fully sustain us as His Joy *is* our strength! However 'Hinds Feet' are not given automatically, but rather are acquired as we learn to walk, *and run,* in the Spirit.

At the beginning of this walk, if we experience tension and discord, we must check ourselves to make sure that we have not begun to walk in the flesh. Remember though, that following after Christ does not assure us a constant life of peace outwardly, but rather inwardly. On the contrary, God is bringing many sons into perfection and this process can cause much suffering and humiliation and hurt to the son involved, for *He chastens and scourges every son whom He receives!*

Hebrew 12:4–6, "After all, you have not yet given your lives in your struggle against sin. And have you entirely forgotten the encouraging words God spoke to you, his children? He said, "My child, don't ignore it when the Lord disciplines you, and don't be discouraged when he corrects you. For the Lord disciplines those he loves, and he punishes those he accepts as his children." (NLT)

This is a pruning process by the Great 'Husbandry-Man'. We can rebel because we still have our free will; but to yield our will to Him will always bring ultimate blessing and fruit for self and others; so why fight it? He always wins. It just takes longer if we resist, and we are the losers if His Perfect Will cannot be carried out in our lives.

Christ Jesus was perfected through suffering. He who was already perfect had that perfection brought to fruition and shown to Himself and others through His example of perfect yielding. Then He was gloriously resurrected. So we should live this new life knowing that this *'Way of Life'* is a way of suffering and of death, but each time that we submit to this severe pruning, there will be more glorious growth! There will be a moving up to higher ground, which has its own valleys, but we get to know him better in these valleys—as our Lily of the Valley—than we do on the mountain tops. And we need never go back to the lower ground from which we have ascended, unless we backslide.

After we have gotten to know this level to which He has brought us, we may then go on to still higher ground. As soon as one crop of fruit is harvested, we must be pruned so that we may bring forth more fruit. (How does this happen? More often than not, just as we have obtained some victory in Christ; perhaps a wonderful 'move of the Spirit' takes place in a meeting. Then before very little time has passed, a discomforting problem of major portions appears!)

But remember, through the testimony of the victory of the battle that is fought and won, the Vine becomes thicker and we acquire a more full knowledge of Christ and His ways. When we consider the unseemly growth with but little fruit that we observe in un-pruned vines, it makes us more thankful for the patience and care given us by our most Patient Gardener. We could wish that this process were less painful, that there were some other way, but this is *His Way*. Knowing this beforehand helps us to desire to endure, and once we have shown this desire—His Strength is always adequate for any test.

Steadfast praise is our battle cry of *Victory!* When we truly begin to submit to this way, we do indeed find that we begin to know Him in a sweeter way than was possible through any other experience. And this knowing does settle and establish us as the Spirit promised us through Peter's letter. This is the precious result of the fiery trials.

I Peter 5:8–11, "Be of sober spirit, be on the alert. Your adversary, the devil, prowls about like a roaring lion, seeking someone to devour. But resist him, firm in your faith, knowing that the same experiences of suffering are being accomplished by your brethren who are in the world. And after you have suffered, for a little while, the God of all grace, who called you to His eternal glory in Christ, will Himself perfect, confirm, strengthen and establish you. To Him be dominion forever and ever. Amen!" When we agree with the Word that we are trees of righteousness, the planting of the Lord that He may be glorified, we see that a similar process is necessary. Evergreens go through pruning, severe wintry blasts, freezing rains, wet blankets of white snow to cover and limit. But at the same time, this protects them from overexposure and prepares them for future growth. We are being nurtured as perennials, not hot-house plants and annuals. So let us rest in Him that whether we are in a period of growth or blossom or fruitage or pruning, we go through it all, trusting in Him who *never* fails us! Hebrews 10:35, "Cast not away therefore your confidence, which has great recompense of *reward!*"

We must remember, too, that we are but earthen vessels, clay pots! Clay, until it is fired, can be very easily broken. He does not desire this for us, but rather designs that we be strengthened through the application of fire! Each time a vessel is fired, it becomes stronger. As the heat is intensified, the vessel becomes capable of holding that for which it was created. We were created to hold and show forth His Glory! Job was not tested because He was unrighteous, but rather, Satan desired to sift him because of his righteousness! It is necessary to understand all of this, for so many of us do not know the difference between discipline, which is necessary for growth, and chastening, which is for correction. Scourging (of whatever sort) is also necessary for growth and applied in a similar manner, but given for different reasons and results such as acceptance by our Lord as Sons!

Remember also the beginning of Chapter 12 of Hebrews verses 1–3 and our 'Pattern Son' Jesus, "Therefore, since we have so great a cloud of witnesses surrounding us—those of faith listed in Chapter 11—let us also lay aside every encumbrance, and the sin which so easily entangles us, and let us run with endurance the race that is set before us, fixing our eyes on Jesus, the author and perfecter of faith, who for the joy set before Him endured the cross, despising the shame, and has sat down at the right hand of the throne of God. For consider Him who has endured such hostility by sinners against Himself, so that you may not grow weary and lose heart."

When trials and testing are allowed to come our way for the strengthening process, seeing that we have yielded to our 'Heavenly Potter's Plan', the accuser of the brethren, Satan, uses our ignorance of God's plan to make us feel that we are being punished rather than strengthened. This gives us the inclination to get out from under the Mighty Hand of God, rather than humbling ourselves under it. Hebrews 12:11 says it all so well. "Now no chastening for the present seems to be joyous, but grievous, nevertheless, afterward it yields the peaceable fruit of righteousness unto those who are exercised by it."

Many times we do not understand being 'under the Mighty Hand of God.' We have even allowed ourselves to think of Him as having no hands but ours. True, in many instances, He has limited Himself to the use of our hands, or rather, has given us the privilege to be used as His Hands extended, but it is His Hands that hold it all together.

Psalm 98:1, "It is His Right Hand and His Holy Arm that have gotten Him the victory." It is His Hand, as well as His Word that kills, that makes alive, that wounds, that heals, as we see in Deuteronomy 32:39, "See now that I, even I, am he, and there is no god with me: I kill, and I make alive; I wound, and I heal: neither is there any that can deliver out of my hand." Psalm 16:11, "Thou wilt show me the path of life: in thy presence is fullness of joy; at thy right hand there are pleasures for evermore." Psalm 17:7, "Wondrously show thy lovingkindness, O Savior of those who take refuge at thy right hand from those who rise up against them." Jesus Christ is at His Right Hand. Mark 16:19, "So then when the Lord Jesus had spoken to them, He was received up into heaven, and sat down at the right hand of God". It is His Right Hand that supports and makes us great, Psalm 18:35, "Thou hast also given me the shield of Thy salva-

tion: And thy right hand upholds me; And they gentleness makes me great."
And by His Right Hand are mighty victories given to His anointed. Psalm
20:6, "Now I know that the Lord saves his anointed; He will answer from His
holy heaven with the saving strength of His right hand." (All Scriptures in
these paragraphs are from the New American Standard Bible.)

Chapter Seven

A Psychoanalyst Receives Deliverance!

H aving spoken of the wonderful realms of deliverance possible through the speaking in Tongues, I want to share this story of deliverance with you. I met Robert, the chief psychoanalyst, in a drug rehabilitation program for a consultation concerning one of his patients. Suddenly, he startled me with a question completely off of the subject. "Can you please explain to me concerning these 'Unknown Tongues'?" Evidently, he had heard a little on the subject and wanted to know all about those 'Tongues'!

I was planning to go to a prayer meeting in that neighborhood that was about to begin, so as quickly as possible I discussed speaking in 'Tongues.' He wouldn't let me end our conversation, but rather continued to question me. In my desire to 'run-off' to the meeting, my spiritual antenna was 'tuned out.' I was missing the sound of the spiritual hunger that he was broadcasting.

When it dawned on me that this man was searching for truth, I gave him my full attention. I more completely explained the prayer in the Spirit to him, and then spoke to him of his need to believe in and ask Christ into his life and then to be baptized in the Holy Spirit.

He opened up and told me of all of the ways that he had been searching. He had studied Transcendental Meditation, Yoga and Hare Krishna. He had used Tarot cards and sought information from an Ouija Board! He had read books exalting false prophets—had stretched out his palm to have it read, and had gone to a tea leaf reader. In short, he was searching everywhere, and if there was anything offered, he accepted it!

After I shared the Gospel with him and he understood that he could ask Christ into his heart, he said that he would do it that night before he went to bed. I suggested that I lead him first, in a prayer of confession and renunciation that would close the door to Satan concerning the false help that he had sought.

He agreed. I took his hands in mine and led him in a prayer of deliverance.

"Lord God, I confess that I have delved into those things that are abomination in your sight. Forgive and cleanse me."

I felt a thrill of joy go up my arm as we held hands and prayed. When he opened his eyes and looked into mine I said, "Bob, you want to ask Jesus into your heart right now, don't you?"

"Yes," he said. As we prayed together, he asked Jesus to come into his heart and to baptize him with the Holy Spirit.

"I'm going to sing in the Spirit and while I do, if you hear any words within, speak them out." I then bound up the spirits of doubt and fear and unbelief and pride. Experience had taught me that this is helpful in bringing forth prayer in the Spirit, for when the spirits are bound, the human spirit is free to respond to the Holy Spirit. But as I spoke this command, I heard myself rebuke all other spirits operating in him and commanded them, "*Out* in the *Name* of *Jesus!*"

As soon as I did that, I thought, "*Why did I do that? I don't want to put him through deliverance!*" I had just wanted *to bind the spirits that would hinder the Tongues from coming forth.*

He began to stutter and speak a word or two in Tongues. As he did this, his whole body began to shake under the anointing of the Holy Spirit. I stood aside, shocked, and then said, "The Lord is cleansing you!'"

"Yes," he said, "I know, I know!" Then suddenly, he lurched from his chair, fell to the floor face down, and retched! Then he turned, looked up at me with an expression of shocked surprise and gladness on his face and shouted, "He's real, Jesus is real! That was a demon that came out of me!"

I *had not mentioned the word "demon"* to him that night. I had said that he had opened himself to evil spirits and to Satan, but the word "demon" had not been used. I said within, "Lord, I know what's happening. The books on deliverance say a woman should not minister to a man alone, but you are putting him through deliverance, and I don't think you want me to leave him in this condition."

Then suddenly, I can't explain exactly how I knew that a spirit of murder began to manifest itself in him, except to say that *I saw a vapor-like form settle down over him* as he lay there on the floor. (I say vapor, but if you think of an icicle, it has form, but one can see through it—this is how I saw this spirit.) This man, who had been so pleasant, began to snarl at me and behave as though he wanted to reach out and strangle me. A chill of fear went down my back, but immediately I said within, "No, I will not fear! Either every Word in the Bible is true—and I am going to stand on it—or I shouldn't even be in ministry, but I *know* the Word of God is true!"

With this declaration, I dropped to my knees—which put me just a few feet closer—right in front of him! I lifted my hands and began to sing a prayer.

"I thank You, Lord God, that every Word in the Bible is true and that You are my Defender and High Tower, my Rock and my Deliverer. I thank You Jesus that by the shedding of Your Precious Blood on the cross, Satan was defeated."

Then, while he lay on the floor not three feet away from me, straining to get to me—though he could not move from that spot as though invisible hands were holding him—he continued snarling at me with a deadly look of murder and hate distorting his features! I spoke this command to that spirit. *"I bind you with the cords of the Blood of Jesus Christ. I rebuke you and command you to come out in the Name of Jesus Christ!"*

I continued to kneel. I refused to budge one inch, and with hands lifted to God, I began to sing in the Spirit. *As the Song went up, the Anointing came down. I could feel it streaming out of my hands as they shook with the Presence of the Power of God. All of this took only minutes.*

Suddenly, that spirit released him. It was the quickest deliverance with this strong of a demon that I had experienced up until that time. I was overjoyed!

Bob stood, to his feet, shocked and apologetic, with an expression of worry and concern on his now relaxed features.

He spoke, "I—I wouldn't hurt you for anything but that thing was try-ing—was trying to—hurt you!"

"It was trying to murder me!" I stated. He looked shocked that I knew what he could not bring himself to express verbally. I said, "Don't worry, the Holy Spirit is here and you saw how quickly He delivered you. You're being cleansed tonight."

He suddenly beat upon his chest and cried, "Satan, you come out of me!"

"Bob, you belong to Jesus now, and you don't have to holler at the evil one." (Now that I think of it, I am glad that he did so!)

"You need only speak the command in Jesus' Name. In fact, you just relax. And as thoughts come into your mind of the things that you have to confess to—specifically—you speak them out, and I will speak the command and the Holy Spirit will do the rest!"

He said, "Abortion, a spirit of abortion."

Startled, I asked, "How can a man have a spirit of abortion?"

Weeping, he cried, "It's true, I made my girlfriend have an abortion."

I said, "Well, that is how you opened yourself up to a spirit of murder!"

"Necromancy—you have a spirit of necromancy." I spoke as the Lord gave me that Word of Knowledge.

"What is that?" Bob questioned. He didn't have a clue as to what the word meant!

"Have you ever tried to contact the dead?"

"Oh! My roommate in college—he killed himself—I was only trying to help him!"

"Well, that is how you opened yourself to a spirit of necromancy."

"Out—in the Name of Jesus!" I commanded that spirit of necromancy to leave him!

Next Bob said: "Pride—about my genitals—that's why I wear these tight pants."

(I was getting an education.) The spirits of adultery, and lust, and fornication, and homosexuality as well had taken up abode in him. They all needed to be exorcised. It was strange to see some of them leave his body in the way that was suggestive of the act that their name implied.

"Profanity, the spirit of profanity needs to come out," said Bob.

I commanded the spirit to "Come Out!" Bob pursed up his lips and blew as if to whistle and then laughed in amazement as he exhaled and said,

"Grace, I couldn't even swear at you, I tried to, or rather, that thing that was in me tried to, but couldn't. Jesus is neat!"

Next the Gestalt spirit, which is a false system whereby one goes into a closet to scream out their frustrations, came out of him with a scream. I explained to Bob that this system was an imitation of what Jesus told us to do. We were to go into our closets and pray to Him in secret and He would answer us openly!

At this point he was half lying and half sitting on the floor with his head propped back against his analyst's couch He was totally exhausted. I looked at him and began to smile. He said, "What, what are you smiling about?"

"Well, forgive me, but this is just so unusual, you have your head on your couch seeking answers, and here I am advising!" I was still on my knees, intermittently singing in the Spirit in worship as all of this deliverance was taking place.

I spoke this humorously but Bob interrupted me by rising to his feet and saying so seriously, "No, don't apologize, that is the way that it should be." He pointed to his books and said, "A lot of that is pure baloney! Jesus has been telling me that. I saw Him, He was standing right here. Jesus Christ is the Way, the Truth and the Light!"

He was preaching to me and it was music to my ears! I said: "Bob—you are preaching!"

He replied: "I have to tell my girl! Jesus told me that when I saw Him, I have to tell her!"

With that statement, he reached for the phone. "But wait," he hesitated, "she is not going to understand any of this. Can I tell her later when I'm with her and can explain, is that wisdom?"

I assured him that it was!

Then, he got a little panicky as he thought about his patients, and said, "I know they're all filled with demons."

I assured him that Jesus would guide and protect him if he just prayed. He told me that I must speak to his fellow psychoanalysts about Jesus. I told him that his testimony would be adequate; that we overcome the beast by the word of our testimony and the Blood of the Lamb. When I said this, his face went white with astonishment and fear!

"The *beast!*" he cried; "that was my 'nickname' in college because of my beard!"

"Don't worry; you belong to the Lord now."

He replied shyly, "That's really why I wear this beard! I really think it makes me look a little bit like Jesus, or at least, maybe one of the apostles."

How strange, Bob was giving me a 'peek' into his heart and I was seeing there not only a hunger for Truth, but also the pride he had because he didn't smoke or drink or do drugs. Who could have imagined that he had been a host to *Legions!*

Bob said: "You have to come back and pray with my friend, another doctor in this program, He is a Psychologist and I know he needs deliverance too!" I said: "Bob, you have the power to put him through deliverance now." (I think I was commissioning him a little too quickly, but I wanted him to know of the authority that the Lord gives us in the Baptism!)

As I was leaving, he said, "I can't even thank you can I, because the Holy Spirit did it all!" That statement made me really rejoice. In this entire deliverance ministry with Bob, God had been glorified! "Well thank you for coming," Bob said, "I think God had this all planned."

"Yes," I agreed. The picture of the Great Shepherd reaching down over the steep cliff to rescue the little lost sheep comes into my mind just now. I thank God for the new lessons He taught me through His rescue operation. Within weeks of this, two others on the staff received as he had, but without the exorcism!

I started out one day to go north to visit a friend in the hospital. The Lord impressed upon me to go south—to the Center where Bob had received his deliverance! I argued a bit.

"Lord, I don't even know if the Center is open in the day-time". I really wanted to visit my friend and was not in the 'mood' to witness. This is a terrible confession, but it happens to me every now and then!

Finally, I dropped by the center to say "Hello" to Bob, and as I entered the foyer I found the friend that he had wanted me to speak with sitting at a desk upon which sat a Bible. This was my confirmation that I was indeed to be here. I asked the Lord's forgiveness for my hesitancy.

Jim, the friend that Bob had asked me to minister with, was engaged in a phone conversation, and when he recognized me, he behaved as though he were going to stay on that phone *all day in an effort to avoid talking with me.*

After about 15 minutes of waiting, I finally remembered to *bind up* every spirit of pride and fear and unbelief operating in this one, and as I did so, he immediately ended his conversation. Binding up spirits, always makes a difference. He cordially spoke with me and I asked him if we could go to his office to talk. Surprisingly, he instructed his secretary that we were not to be disturbed.

As we sat down in his office, I said, "Jim, I know that as a professional you have a procedure, well I have one also, could we pray before we begin?" He agreed. I took his hands in mine and just as the prayer ended he opened his eyes and said, "You see, Grace, I am beginning to doubt *that there is a God.*"

I said, "Oh, that is no problem," and began to pray once more. "In the Name of Jesus, I command you out, spirit of *Doubt!*" Amazingly, that freed his human spirit to be able to listen, and within a very short time, he was bowing his head and asking Jesus to come into his heart and to baptize him in the Holy Spirit! As we stepped out of his office, Bob was standing right there! I said, "Bob, meet your new brother in the Christ!" Such rejoicing took place!

As we entered a third office, each of us still spilling over with words of praise, I noticed a black man standing at a filing cabinet looking for a file, but obviously listening to us. He behaved as though he was disinterested, keeping his arms resting on the filing cabinet, while he continued to file some papers. I spoke to him.

"Well, how about you? I know you have a mother or grandmother praying for you somewhere and I know that you know what this is all about. Come now, come join us while I show these two how to have a prayer meeting." With a slight smile of resignation, he closed the file and allowed me to take his hand as we four joined together in prayer. I could feel the tightening of his hand, which always reveals the emotion within. As the prayer ended, I opened my eyes and saw tears running down his cheeks. While wiping his eyes, he explained.

"You were right! When I was a young man, I went to church with my Mama and asked Christ into my heart, but I have been backslidden for years." Oh, did we have a time of rejoicing then! We held our first prayer meeting there in Bob's office, openly sang praises to God with hands joined, then uplifted to Him, and the anointing came down. "Amazing Grace, how sweet the sound" is what we sang and I, of course, repeated Song in the Spirit to the well-loved tune!

I shared with them some instant prayers that I have found to be so effective: *"Lord, give me Your Peace,"* when the heart is pounding and the stomach is churning because of anxiety, fear, or turmoil. *"Lord, be my strength,"* when we are weak and faltering with temptation or can't minister because of fear. He *will* strengthen us with His Strength. And then the *prayer and song in the Spirit,* which is a testimony of love and a singing swinging sword!

I shared with them, that the *application* of the Blood of the Lamb gives us protection, and the Written Word of God is sufficient to equip and enable us for any battle! I also made them aware of how effective it is to *bind up* the *unseen spirits of darkness,* that the human spirit may have liberty to respond to the Word of God!

Each of them had a personal experience of such deliverance and was better equipped to minister to others in that drug program from that day onward!

Robert and Jim, their friend and I were greatly blessed, with the strength that comes from the 'Joy of the Lord' that was flowing from the ministry happenings of that day!

Chapter Eight

Deception and Death, Dished Out by the Evil One.

I n these last days, so many are involved with witchcraft, directly or indirectly, for this is the spirit that is manifested in rebellion. I Samuel 15:23 says, "For rebellion is as the sin of witchcraft, and stubbornness is as iniquity and idolatry." (KJV) The 'I will,' is being manifested, rather than the submissive attitude of "Thy will be done in my earthen vessel." There is need for deliverance after Light has been cast upon the results of this rebellion. Oppression and even possession by the evil one are the physical and spiritual results when one disobeys God by following after those things which are an abomination unto Him. A list of such abominations may be found in Deuteronomy 18:10-13.

A further act of rebellion, which results in unhappy consequences, is to refuse to hearken unto the words of God that would be spoken in His Name through the mouth of the Prophet that He promised to raise up from among the people like unto Moses. In Deuteronomy 18:15, Moses said, "Unto Him ye shall hearken!" John 1:45, "Philip found Nathanial, and said to him, "We have found him, of whom Moses in the law, and also the prophets, wrote—Jesus of Nazareth, the son of Joseph."(NKJV) That Prophet is Jesus Christ Himself, the Son of the Living God. John 3:36, "He who believes in the Son, has everlasting life: and he who does not believe the Son shall not see life, but the wrath of God abides on him." (NKJV)

That Son, that Savior, that Redeemer of all of mankind has said that He alone is the Way, the Truth, and the Life. He alone can give peace. Peace of mind and soul and body is the Perfect Peace that Jesus gives to those whose minds are stayed upon Him. Peace through any other person or through any method other than coming unto Him is to go in the path of error! Seeking a false peace is an imitation and a trap that will close upon the unsuspecting when Satan is finished 'toying' with them. He enjoys their gullibility and stupidity, and then torment and ultimate destruction, is their destination, unless they repent and turn to the Savior for deliverance.

We have a supernatural hunger to delve into the supernatural; a longing to explore the mysterious areas of the unknown. We have this for we were created to inhabit the supernatural realms of eternity, worshipping and fellowshipping and enjoying the supernatural God who created us. We were created to enjoy eternally this wonderful God and His universe, in an atmosphere of peace and love and joy and serenity. And we are being drawn and convicted of sin and righteousness and judgment by His Holy Spirit that we might turn from the darkness of this world unto this marvelous Realm of Light.

But we are also being drawn by the supernatural evil spirit of Satan. We can be tricked and lied to and deceived by this master of deception. He, through pride, vaunted himself against the Most High God, and fell into the darkness and is doing everything in his power to drag man down along with him into his domain.

Lucifer, that fallen angel of imitation light, uses the spot-light, the strobe light, the black light even—many times—in an effort to titillate and draw men away from the True Light of the World. He has convinced many that it is not sophisticated to even believe that he and his demons exist. When we read the dictionary definition of the word "sophistication" we begin to understand how cleverly Satan has deceived us already. Most of us who use that word think that it means dignified or having to do with proper behavior. Let's read the definition.

Sophistication: *to make worldly-wise, to mislead or pervert; deceptive; misleading; reasoning adroitly, cunningly; and speciously; seeming to be genuine, correct or beautiful, but not really so, being artificial, rather than sound!* (American College Dictionary)

He has also crept as a snake into our conversation without us being a bit aware. We say, "*Good Luck*" or "*Lucky,*" which is a 'nickname' for *Lucifer,* when we really mean, "*God Bless you*" or "*You're blessed.*" We use the word *fortunate* when we really mean *happy* or *blessed.* We say—*'fortunately'* when we really mean *'happily'.* The Word of God tells us not to be involved with *fortune or luck!*

This evil one, whose wiles—a trick; a stratagem; an artful or beguiling procedure; deceitful cunning; trickery; to beguile, entice, or lure—American College Dictionary—we are to stand against! He knows that he cannot interest a free people in following after abominable religions or systems by emphasizing their more 'gory' practices and final results. Mutilation and enslavement of self and others, are Satan's final goals, so he uses more 'Sophisticated' methods of bringing out the more 'Sophisticated' aspects of these sophisticated *false* systems!

One such method is found in Transcendental Meditation, a mental exercise of a false religion. The Gestalt Therapy, mentioned earlier, is another - the act of going into a closet to *scream away frustrations.* This is the imitation of going into a closet to pray as taught by our Savior. Jesus teaches us to closet ourselves alone and apart to converse with Him. And we find in the Word from Isaiah 30:15, "In quietness and confidence, He shall be our strength", rather than through the self-effort of screaming.

The euphoria, the feeling of alertness that one may experience initially when following after these practices—sounds like drug addiction—same sponsor, different station—is afforded because of the release from tension that Satan directs. He is the main cause of tension—he can affect a release when you are being lured.

His *lures*—he too is a fisher of men, he is always imitating success—are very similar to those found to be so effective on Eve - *doubt;* which is a *certain lie,* covered with *uncertainty.* "Hath God said?" Genesis 3:1. He very well *knows the answer,* but hopes you don't and he blinds you to the answer, with a question raised and a promise of wisdom. Genesis 3:5, *"For God doth know that in the day ye eat thereof, then your eyes shall be opened, and ye shall be as gods, knowing good and evil."* What his hearers don't know is that this joker is being honest for a change. A god is a stone cold object with no power even to feed itself. It is dead with no power whatever, other than that given it by its followers.

The implication: "Ye shall be wise expanding your mind to *know mysteries."* Being a liar, he gives the opposite, making men fools.

This liar tells men they will not die. *"'Pot' can't hurt;* you can handle drugs." And then he rewards his followers with sickness and weakness and shame and death. His main method throughout the ages has been to make men *doubt.* If he can make you doubt God's Word, you are responsible for the consequences.

Doubt leads to unbelief - unbelief in the Word of God. Unbelief in the Word of God leads to not believing on the Son of God. Not believing on the Son of God leads to condemnation. John 3:16–20 says, *"For God so loved the world that he gave His only begotten Son, that whosoever believes in Him should not perish, but have everlasting life. For God did not send His Son into the world to condemn the world but that the world' through Him, might be saved. He who believes on Him is not condemned; but he who does not believe is condemned already, because he has not believed in the Name of the only begotten Son of God. And this is the condemnation: that the light has come into the world, and men loved darkness rather than light, because their deeds were evil. For everyone practicing evil hates the light and does not come to the light, lest his deeds be exposed."* (NKJV)

We do not throw light on the evil one to cause men to fear Satan, but rather to expose the way in which this thief is trying to rob, kill and destroy! Our prayer is that you deny satan, and his desires and designs for your life, and receive the Lord and His Will for your life.

Know this: the depth of evil is to *deny God*, the Lord who made you, and to turn from the *Light* revealed in His Word because your deeds are evil and you can't bear to give them up. If you receive *not* the love of *truth, Jesus Christ,* that you might be *saved,* for this cause, *God Himself* shall send strong delusion that you should believe a lie and be damned, eternally. Romans 1:18-through to the end of the Chapter *"For the wrath of God is revealed from heaven against all ungodliness and unrighteousness of men, who hold the truth in unrighteousness;" "Wherefore God also gave them up to uncleanness through the lusts of their own hearts, to dishonor their own bodies between themselves:* For this cause God gave them up into vile affections; for even their women did change the natural use into that which is against nature:" (KJV) Then comes a string of 'woes' on unto the end of the Chapter! Oh, that man would deny satan and fear God, rather than fearing satan, and denying God!

The fear of the Lord - *healthy respect and awe of Him and His Word* - is the beginning of wisdom. It is clean, enduring forever. It is the beginning of knowledge. It will prolong your days. It is a fountain of life to depart from the snares of death. If you will only listen, and understand, and renounce Satan and your own sin, and turn to the Light of the World, you will be saved. Call upon Him while He is near, just now!

A Word Concerning the Binding of Evil Spirits!

Over and over through the years, I have seen dramatic results in the reactions of others when I remember to bind up satanic spirits. I have just told you of the change it made with the one who was on the phone obviously not wanting to speak with me, and then later when he displayed a spirit of doubt concerning belief in God.

God has given us the spiritual weapon of the ability to bind up evil spirits. Psalm 149:6–9, *"Let the high praises of God be in their mouth, and a two-edged sword in their hand; To execute vengeance upon the heathen, and punishments upon the people; To bind their kings with chains, and their nobles with fetters of iron; To execute upon them the judgment written; this honor have all his saints. Praise ye the Lord."* (KJV) When I am about to witness to another concerning Jesus, I find many times that a spirit of fear of man will begin to attack *me*, whispering: "This one will be offended if you speak to them. They will reject and embarrass you."

As soon as I realize that I am being intimidated by an evil spirit, I say within, "In the Name of Jesus I bind you *spirit of fear of man!*" I rebuke every spirit that would keep me from doing the will of God. *Immediately* the fear of man is gone! Next I say within, "In the Name of Jesus, I bind up every spirit of doubt and fear and pride and unbelief operating in this one." (The one I am about to speak to). Then I pray, "Lord, what would you have me say?"

Often He says, "Tell them how much I love them!"

I remember sitting next to an airline hostess on a plane in New York City. She was off duty and busy painting her finger-nails. I began to speak with her about the Lord. She looked at me with disdain in her eye and her expression said, "Get lost, I'm not interested—why are you bothering me?"

I cringed and thought, "Oh, Lord, I forgot to bind the spirits of doubt, fear, pride and unbelief." I took a minute and bound the spirits. I apologized to the Lord and asked Him what I should say next.

I sensed the Lord saying. "Tell her I love her!"

I turned to her once more and said, "Jesus loves you *so* much." You would have thought that I was speaking to a different person. She responded with warmth and paid attention to everything I shared with her, and before the plane had landed in Pittsburgh, she had prayed with me and asked Jesus to forgive her sins and to come into her heart and to baptize her with His Holy Spirit!

Here is one more example. Years ago I had a friend who could not seem to speak more than a few words in the Spirit. She prayed and we prayed and nothing seemed to help. She used to say, "I pray every day with my prayer list. If only I could say more than just those three words in the Spirit." This went on for over a year.

We used to say, "When Mary begins to pray in the Spirit with fluency, we will really learn some new lessons."

One day, a minister came to her home to pray for her husband, who was very ill. Mary spoke to him knowing that he would understand her request. "Oh, if only I could have more Words to pray in the Spirit!"

The minister said, "I am going to command that *if a spirit is hindering your prayer language, that it name itself* and when I speak this, you say whatever comes to your mind."

As he spoke the word of command, Mary replied, *"Pride."* The minister commanded the spirit of pride to come out of her and *immediately* the Tongues began to flow!

When I heard the story of her longed-for deliverance, I said, "Mary…you, I would never have guessed that you had a spirit of pride!"

She replied, "Oh, it's true, I would never leave my house if I thought even a hair on my head was out of place!" From that day on, we, who by this time had begun to understand and were binding up the spirits of darkness, included this chief one that was the calling card of Satan—the spirit of *pride!*

Rebuke the Fear of Man—Bind up the spirits— and let the anointing teach you!

When it comes to bringing forth a message in Tongues or Prophecy during a church service, we must do the same thing. There is so little understanding in the Body of Christ concerning this manifestation of the Holy Spirit, and Satan hates the vocal gifts of the Spirit so much, that he causes as much confusion and trouble as he is allowed to.

When I am aware that the Holy Spirit has come upon me with the anointing and that He desires to use me to speak forth, either the prophetic word in English or a message in Tongues, I must *first rebuke the fear of man,* which can tie up the tongue from speaking and the hands from clapping and the feet from dancing. I then *bind up any hindering spirits* such as jealousy or contention and even my own flesh from getting in the way of the Spirit. I then yield my spirit afresh and anew to the Holy Spirit, ask Him to strengthen me to speak all that He desires me to speak and then wait as His perfect timing leads me in knowing when to speak.

I John 2:27, *"But the anointing which you have received from Him, abides in you and you do not need that anyone teach you; but as the same anointing teaches you concerning all things, and is true, and is not a lie, and just as it has taught you, you will abide in Him."* (NKJV) (My Bible just opened to this exact Scripture, so I felt it was the Holy Spirit guiding me to use this translation.)

Years ago when first I read this scripture, it puzzled me. "Lord, I asked, surely you are not refuting the teaching ministry?" (This is the Gift I felt that He had given me.) "What does this scripture mean?" I pondered this question for a long time, until one day, while standing waiting for a trolley; it suddenly dawned upon me that this Scripture was speaking of the way that the *anointing teaches one about the anointing!* Here is what I mean.

Before the Baptism of the Holy Spirit, I had *not a clue* as to what the anointing was all about. Except for the wonderful warmth upon the heart that was the Holy Spirit's conformation of a truth, such as when I wanted to know if I were really 'born again', or when I would lead a soul to the Lord and feel that warmth again as though it were a confirmation of a 'Well done', I knew nothing of the anointing until I was baptized in the Holy Spirit! *Then,* immediately, the very day of this baptism, I began to *experience the movement* in my very being, along with the Joy of the Lord, which fills one to overflowing!

As the Holy Spirit, over and over, comes upon us, with His Presence and Power (I began to realize), this is undoubtedly, the anointing! Therefore, the anointing itself, which is the manifestation of the Holy Spirit teaches us about this manifestation! This manifestation is called, the anointing!

Most times, before I receive a Word of Prophesy to share with the congregation, I become lost in the Lord, through Worship in the Spirit, through Song in the Spirit (quietly, for few are singing in the Spirit) and His Spirit, then *falls upon me* helping me to understand that He wants to use me in the vocal gifts—either to bring forth a Song in the Spirit with—usually a singing interpretation, or a Word of Prophecy, with or without Tongues. I believe that this is what Luke was expressing when he said in Acts 10:44, "While Peter was still speaking these words, the Holy Spirit fell upon all those who heard the word." And again in Acts 11:15, "And as I began to speak, the Holy Spirit fell upon them, as upon us at the beginning." (KJV)

I know that these scriptures are expressing the powerful occasion of the initial Baptism of the Holy Spirit that took place upon those being ministered to. But I would say that this is also the reality of what is available and what takes place, with those of us, who have experienced this Baptism. This marvelous experience of 'the falling upon us of the Holy Spirit' in or through the presence of the anointing is beyond anything that is available in the natural earthly realm. This is exactly what is needed for those in the world today. We were created to give Him pleasure and when we do so, according to His Word, we are fulfilled, in part—by the anointing that teaches one concerning the anointing!

I have seen great moves of the Spirit being dissipated by well-meaning men—and women trying to keep things in order by the action of having prophecy be tested *before* it is publicly spoken forth—rather than by the Biblical injunction to test prophecy as it is given. The anointing which can break every yoke is even *upon the voice of the one anointed, as prophecy is given,* just as the anointing is upon the words that are spoken—or should be!

Scripture speaks to those who are given the *terrible obligation* of bringing forth a message from the Lord. Jeremiah 1:17–19, *"Thou therefore gird up thy loins, and **arise, and speak unto them all that I command thee**,* be not dismayed at their faces, lest I confound thee before them. For, behold, I have made thee this day a defended city, and an iron pillar, and brazen walls against the whole land, against the kings of Judah, against the princes thereof, against the priests thereof, and against the people of the land. And **they shall fight against thee**; but they shall not prevail against thee: for I AM with thee, says the Lord, to deliver thee." (KJV)

I was given this very Word as a personal prophecy even before I ever was called upon by the Lord to give a Message in Tongues or Prophecy! (This certainly puzzled me for a long time, and actually is not completely clear to me now! How can one, a woman, be a city, an iron pillar, and bronze walls? I assume that this Word is speaking of our Lord's strengthening process!)

It is a wonderful thing that God strengthens us to continue on serving

Him in spite of the tendency of the flesh to get out from under His Mighty Hand. Especially so, when one feels they are being put to the test of being a living sacrifice, (as called for in Romans 12:1) *"I beech you therefore, brethren, by the mercies of God, that ye present your bodies a living sacrifice, holy, acceptable unto God, which is your reasonable service."* This being a 'living sacrifice', often takes place by the impaling of the 'cross of misunderstanding' inflicted, sometimes, by a Christian brother or sister! Hurts inflicted upon us by our loved ones who know Christ create deeper wounds than those hurled at us by those who are still under Satan's control.

This helps one to understand a situation such as the agony of the Vietnam or more recently, an Iraq Veteran. To serve one's country (or church) by wielding and using weapons effectively against the enemy out of duty or love or obligation or a combination of these principles and then to be ostracized or have others behave as though one's motives were wrong or impure is such an unkind cut that hurts deeply.

No sooner had I written the preceding paragraph than the Lord reminded me that it is from among that same Body, His Body that the 'Balm of Gilead' is applied. As I remember the expression of love on the faces, and the kindness of the words of those whom He has used as the 'Medics' in His Army, I am reminded once more that even the barbs have not come without our Father's permission. It makes me realize anew that our Lord allows sorrow and misunderstandings to come, for it is a strengthening process, as we stand through it, though it little seems to be that at that moment of its application. Hebrews 12:11 warns us, *"Now, no chastening seems to be joyful for the present, but painful; nevertheless, afterwards it yields the peaceable fruit of righteousness to those who have been trained by it!"*

I also realize that this is the difference between one who belongs to the Lord and one who does not. We ever have the Great Shepherd to comfort us. "Oh Lord, how do they bear wounding, who have not Your Precious Care? Help us, Lord of the Harvest, to lead the lost to your bosom." Amen.

'9–1–1'—A Wake-up Call? Nay—this is an Emergency!

Not just a routine morning reminder—that the time of slumber is spent—that the daily business of life is once more about to commence; Nay—but rather an alarm of great portent—a warning from Heaven is sent! "Come back to Me, My People! Come back to Me and repent! My Blessings upon you have been poured out—from the time of your birth 'til this day. Only spiritually blind could deny it! Only obtuse could say: "Where is HIS blessing upon us?" "Where is that for which we didn't pay?"

"Oh, Oh, Whoa, Woe! You've forgotten the God of your fathers. You've gone your own way without Me! You've said in your heart, "Who needs Him? We will go our own way, we are free! We will do my own thing; He's not looking, He doesn't know, nor does He see."

"Oh My people of America think now, let's reason together this way. From the time of your birth 'til today—the blessings of beauty and abundance have all been yours—without pay! The only price was by your Fore-Fathers paid—as they bowed in humility and—to Me prayed. They dedicated this land to Me! They asked My Blessing each day. I honored their faith and obedience. This is why you are free to say: "We are the land of the brave and the free."

"But you have used that freedom to become 'gay'. Your sons and your daughters worship creatures. "Their Creator is deaf, dumb and blind—says they."

"For days on end you've forgotten. You have dismissed Me and left My Commands, You have chosen instead paths of ignorance. You have chosen to make your own plans. The Fear of the Lord that brings wisdom—which is clean and healthy, giving life—has been replaced by apathy, by division, quarreling and strife. Self-will has replaced Thy Will. What is left but to maim and to kill!"

"Let's abort the babies," your courts demand! "Who needs these 'gifts from heaven' that we haven't planned? We will not be led by one we cannot see. Who is He to tell us, that we can't be free? Free from inconvenience these births would entail, Let those who oppose us—our foes—go to jail we want to be free—free to die and go to hell. In hell where our friends are, we will have a ball. We'll laugh and fornicate; free drugs for all! The Father of Lies has told us it is so—a continual ball, a 'Hell-o-wean Brawl', where men can enjoy doing whatever they like, and women likewise can enjoy being dikes!"

"In hell, without opposition, from 'stuffy preachers', who blast us and tell us, that we are vile creatures. Who 'nag' us and warn us that a Savior is grieved, when we reject His Free Gift, His Salvation Reprieve! Who wants to go to Heaven and worship Almighty God? We don't want to be under—His Shepherd's Rod—we would rather worship self—we have made ourselves god. Our feelings and flesh just won't be denied, Forget full-term babies and their unheard cries—as the scissors and suction to their brains are applied. We will do our own thing—have our orgies and flings! You can't make us behave as moral beings; it's just so much fun doing abominable things! An affair is too exciting, to think of the one, whose heart we are smiting!"

"Your courts have ruled to bar My Name. They forbid in school the telling of My Fame. Your children learn not to laugh and play; rather they mourn and fear each day. The slaughter of innocents—the spilling of blood—cries out from your flag of a chilling flood. A flood of blood from your aborted babes pollutes the land, the land of *the free—free to behave—merci—less—lee!*"

"It is time to awake, study the good old Book. It's time to read—take a second look. I said in My Word so very long ago: "I sent blasting and mildew, famine and grief! I was trying to get your attention. When blessed you forget Me—therefore I must blast—less taking for granted your blessings—your end comes at last—and forgetting your God, you must into hell be cast. Where the worm never dies—the fire is not quenched. No 'party' there—only hearts that are wrenched. Bodies broken and bruised for eternity—for they believed the lies of the enemy! He hates you don't you see—for you were created—for and—by ME!"

Do you see it my friend, we're so near to the end. And our Father, who loves us, is allowing Satan to do his worst, in hopes that thereby, we are chased unto Him. It's in our nature it seems; this human tendency to sin is odd. It can rarely be stopped and turned around, 'til calamity chases us to God. Therefore the hurricanes, the fires and the floods—those elements that cause us such grief—must be allowed by a loving God, to call a people to Himself. If we won't come in times of blessing, Father must change the scene; Must allow distress as the only means, to draw a people unto Himself, whatever the way—to prevent lives of complacency from leading us—into paths of destruction and decay!

Jesus said: "I AM the Truth, the Light, and the WAY!" None other on earth or in heaven has this right to say. Our Heavenly Father can only be known, through His Son, Jesus Christ. Come to Him now, be a 'Born-Again One'! And those who are born again, knowing the Son, Are the remnants, crying out to Him, else all—would be undone! Every Nation and peoples, who have forgotten their God, will be turned into Hell—so says the Word. Pray not for the Blessings that have already been given. Rather thank God that America— bountifully blessed—will turn to Him and repent of her slothfulness.

Our complacency has allowed what we have become. Will we cry out to Him, that we be not undone? Will we call sin a sin, rather than disease? Will we battle Satan by falling to our knees? True love won't tickle the ears of the hearers, rather in love we must catch listening ears. Speak the Truth of God's Word, before it's too late; speak the Words of the Spirit; before the closing of Heaven's Gate.

Every founder of a religion that leads down into hell lies moldering in a grave. Only the Son, that Day-Star Divine, with His Heart so truly Brave, Sacrificed His Life, then rose up from the grave. Christ is now awaiting that Last Trumpet Blast! Soon all of this earth will be a memory past. He'll come back for His Own, bought with His Blood. Will you be in that Glorious Fold—

to be caught up by the Shepherd, the Redeemer of old? 9-1-1 means emergency, a life or death-call. Do you hear the Sound? He is calling to all! "Get ready! I AM on My way!" The Day is far spent; the hour is late. He is waiting for you at Heavens Gate! The Night will soon be here, the Holy Spirit warns—it is so near! Jesus is knocking today, beloved don't turn Him away. Open to Jesus, He'll come and He'll stay, Jesus is calling today! Open your heart's door just now, Open and gaze on His smile, He will fulfill you—make living worthwhile. Oh Jesus is calling today—beloved don't turn Him away— go out to meet Him prepare ye the way. Be wise and pray:

"Lord Jesus, forgive me—and come into my heart today!"

Speaking in Tongues can be Stolen, Beware!

When I was in the Baptist church in Russia, in 1972, I discovered that this congregation could have the State's permission to gather together only if they would sign an agreement not to Preach or Minister in the realm of Healing or Speaking in Tongues. Doesn't that give you some idea of how much Satan hates Tongues and fights against them?

Satan hates Tongues. He does everything in his power to hinder, bind and prevent their coming forth. He tries to confuse the issue once they do come forth. He does everything from lying to outright stealing, to keep them from being repeated!

He knows that when we speak in the Heavenly Language, perfect praises and prayers are coming forth from our lips! These will not return void or empty.

Remember, Satan is a liar, a thief, and a murderer. He will lie, cheat, steal and kill, whether it be a tangible thing such as the destruction of a body, or intangible as he attempts to kill faith in any of God's provisions or promises. Let me give you an example of one of his most obvious tactics - theft!

My friend Marilyn had asked for the Baptism of the Holy Spirit, but she had fear concerning speaking in Tongues. This happened years ago, when I knew very little about deliverance. I heard of a meeting being held by one Don Basham, who, at that time, had a Deliverance Ministry. Another friend and I decided to go and have this spirit of fear cast out of our mutual friend.

On the way to the meeting, I shared the Scripture that I understood concerning the subject of this Language, hoping to encourage Marilyn to desire this wonderful blessing which could build up her faith and edify her in the Spirit.

At the end of the evening, we took our timid friend to the minister and asked him to cast out the spirit of fear so that she might speak in Tongues. The minister obliged, came against the spirit of fear, and then nudged me to listen, for I had my head bowed and eyes closed in prayer.

I looked at my friend and praised God, for the Tongues were flowing out of her. She then stopped, turned to the minister and said, *"Oh, that was wonderful, I enjoyed that."*

The minister replied, "Yes, we all do, we all enjoy it."

We thanked the minister and turned to walk down the hall leading out of the church. We had not walked ten steps when Marilyn turned to me and asked, "Why did he say that?"

I looked at her blankly, not understanding her question, and in puzzlement asked, "Why did he say, what?"

"Why did he say, "Yes, we all do, we all enjoy it?"

I answered, "Well, Marilyn, you had just spoken in Tongues and…"

"I did not!" she exploded adamantly.

I called to our friend, who had walked ahead and had not heard what Marilyn was saying to me, but had been present and heard all that took place during the deliverance. "Joyce, come here and listen to *this!* Marilyn can't remember speaking in Tongues or talking to the minister in English." We were what could honestly be called dumbfounded—struck dumb with astonishment!

We tried to recall her memory with repetition. "Marilyn, you spoke in Tongues and then said "Oh, that was enjoyable, I enjoyed that." And that is why the minister said "Yes, we all do, we all enjoy speaking in Tongues!" Now it was her turn to be amazed. She could not remember even the words she had spoken in English! I think that if Joyce and I had not been friends of hers for years, she would not have believed us.

This situation is not now unusual to us. It happens all the time. So many times we hear people tell us within days and even moments that they have *no* recollection of having spoken in Tongues, when we and others have heard them and *know* that this is exactly what they have done. Usually these same ones are apt to become irritated with any who try to help them to see that they have already spoken in the Spirit. How is this possible? Remember Matthew 13:19, which says, "When anyone hears the Word of the Kingdom, and understands it not, then comes the wicked one, and catches away that which was sown in his heart." It is possible. These examples point to the fact that Tongues are a portion of the Word of the Kingdom, and they can be stolen.

By the way, Marilyn did speak in Tongues. Weeks later—while on her knees in prayer for my oldest daughter Amy who was in the hospital at the time! Marilyn burst forth into prayer in the Spirit. This time, the *language* was not stolen and her testimony is like that of most others. It changed her prayer life! She found a new joy and desire and ease in prayer.

Before I leave this illustration, I want to say that while Marilyn expressed enjoyment in the prayer in the Spirit, many do not 'feel' anything. Tongues are speech in a Language. As with any speaking, it is not the Language, but rather the content, and the subject matter of the words, that bring about in others or causes within the emotional responses. As we are caught up in the Spirit of Worship and receive His Heavenly Anointing, that always accompanies true worship and obedience, we enter into His rest. We experience the Fruit of the Spirit which is Peace!

The most important reason for using Tongues and not letting the evil one steal the experience or the time that should be given over to this speaking is found in Ephesians 6:18. We are *told* to pray always with all prayer and supplication *in the Spirit*. This speaks of an area of obedience to the Lord. We are told to pray in the Spirit not *if* or *when* we please, but *always!*

Jude 1:20 also tells us to 'build up our faith' praying in the Holy Spirit! Is your faith weak, because you are not doing the proper building? Think about it!

Does this help you to see what the evil one is up to in his theft? He was and *is* the great disobedient one. He wants to try to make us walk in his path of disobedience, that we become weakened and ineffective. He certainly doesn't want us flashing and slashing with our *'Sword of Mouths'!* Especially he is jealous of the ministry of worship taken away from him and given to us. *He wants to steal our fire!* Let's use our 'Pentecostal Fire' to burn his bridges and wreak havoc in his kingdom of darkness. Let's join together and submit unto God, resist the devil and watch this *thief flee!*

'Hell!' By Joyce Petrichek

—and there will be wailing, and gnashing of teeth!

The end is the Beginning. Ever losing—never winning. Hope—there is none—nor is there fun. No pleasure now in sinning! No chance to pray—not ever. *Your choice*—God's bonds did sever! No Pure White Light—for all in *night!* And peace—you'll know it *never!* Old friends—you'll never find them. You'll gnash your teeth and grind them! And weep for eyes that did not see—the god you chose did blind them. There'll be no joy bells ringing—no happy children singing—no glad refrain from souls in pain—no angel glad news bringing.

Hellfire—forever burning—too late to be discerning—you chose to wait—now it's too late.

And there can be no turning. No one to hear a lost soul's cries—a soul that lives—but ever dies.

Each soul alone—with god of stone—for each believed his lies. Each soul entombed in sorrow—no happiness to borrow. No hope—no prayer, No joy is there—there only is tomorrow. A soul in Hell is only free—to weep for all eternity! For each does know—and hence, his woe—He *chose* his Destiny!

Chapter Nine

'Missionary Stories'

The Dance, World-Wide T.V., Sister Stamps!

Many have taken the position that dancing is only worldly and sinful and should not be engaged in by Christians. Some dancing may be such, but this should not keep us from the dance that is unto the Lord. The Word says: in Psalm 149:3, " Let them praise his name in the dance: let them sing praises unto him with the timbrel and harp". And again in Psalm 150:4, "Praise him with the timbrel and dance: praise him with stringed instruments and organs." and note, it doesn't say, "Dance in the Spirit," but rather just, "Praise him with the timbrel and dance!"

We start off in the flesh—this is the only place we can begin. But many times as we get lost in the Lord, the Spirit takes over and we feel almost as a puppet on His string, but most times this doesn't happen. Still we are to praise His Name in the dance, even as David did in II Samuel 6:14, "And David danced before the Lord with all his might; and David was girded with a linen ephod!"

On my first trip to Russia in 1972 I met Rev. Ruth Heflin. She had just joined our group coming to Russia from Lapland, where she had just ministered revival among the Lapps! She told me at this time, that ten years before, she had a vision of Jesus while at the Garden Tomb in Jerusalem. He appeared to her and told her first, that just before His second coming, He had an important work for her to do in Israel, and then He said this; "David was the only king who fed his people a triple portion and he did it because he danced unto Me. He danced 11 miles uphill accompanying the Ark!"

Jesus said to her, "If you would feed the people of a triple portion, dance unto Me!"

She said that this was harder for her to do than it had been to go into the mission field of India. In her eyes, only the older lady Pentecostals did such things as dancing. However, endeavoring to be obedient she went to the

'Calvary Pentecostal Camp Meeting' for six weeks as she did every summer to 'charge up her batteries' and every day while there, she spent some time dancing unto the Lord.

At the end of this time, she was given a word that because of her obedience, she was being sent to Kings and Potentates and those in high places throughout the earth. Ruth then shared that she had since been to more than one hundred countries and had been before many rulers ministering! I learned later that she would even go into the bathroom on airplanes to dance before the Lord!

I began to dance unto the Lord. I remember one incident especially where the Lord showed me the power of the dance to deliver. Years ago while in Canada at a Christian convention, I felt that the Lord wanted me to dance. Although seated at the back of the dimly lit auditorium, I resisted because there were many in my group who did not understand the dancing and would criticize. I finally arose to dance when I felt an anointing go from my knees down to my feet and heard the Lord say: "Will you?" The Lord was graciously asking or directing me a second time to dance!

I arose stepped into the aisle and quickly became lost in the beauty of the song being sung, closed my eyes and was waltzing to the beautiful melody when I was startled by a hand being placed on my shoulder and I heard a man say, "Sit down, miss, we don't do that here."

I smiled politely at him and said, "Oh no sir, I'll just finish out here," and danced into the nearby foyer which I knew was empty when we had entered the auditorium.

When the song was completed, I turned to go back into the meeting and was once more shocked as a woman rushed up to me, threw her arms around me and exclaimed, "Oh that was wonderful!" She continued, "I was so fearful because I have been asked to lead the music service tomorrow and I was just plain scared! All the fear is gone now! As I watched you dance the fear left! Now I am looking forward to tomorrow's meeting!"

I was amazed and thought, "Lord, you used the dance to release this one from fear." I went and sat quietly in a chair that was just outside the meeting hall. I was just sitting there thinking on the wonder of the things of God in the result of that dance, when the one who had been singing stepped up to me, took my hand in his and said, "My dear, I don't agree with what was done in there," pointing to the auditorium, "but I appreciate how you handled it!" It was Roger Mac Duff, the one who had sung so beautifully that I couldn't resist dancing unto the Lord. Once more I was shocked and surprised and so happy that, as usual, the Lord was saying through the mouth of two witnesses, "Right on!"

Betty's Testimony of Healing, through her Dance!

Years later, a marvelous experience of healing took place through the dance. Betty Peace had stripped the cartilage in both of her ankles. Her doctor told her that she would be on crutches for at least ten weeks. She had to wear high top shoes and stay off of her feet as much as possible. A few days after the accident—and the doctor's orders—she came to a meeting being held at Burning Bush. This is a Retreat Center in Saltsburg, Pennsylvania, where I was ministering for the Body of Christ by restoring the entire facility! Betty joined me and another, in worshipping through song in the Spirit, as I was playing the autoharp. Suddenly, I felt led of the Lord to ask Betty to stand and dance. She thought at first I was joking until the other friend present assured her that she too felt the Lord was speaking to her to try to dance.

Slowly and with pain, Betty stood and began to move back and forth in time with the music. When she had taken only a few moments of dance steps, the pain left. She laid her crutches aside and was completely healed before the dance was over! The next week she drove her van over a thousand miles on a trip to Florida, where five wonderful friends from the Ohio 'Guardian of the Joy' joined us for—eventually—ten wonderful weeks at the Gerald Derstine Ministry in Bradenton Florida. Her ankles were not only strengthened, but from that time she seldom had a problem with them! Her feet and ankles have walked many miles for our Lord and were never again hindered by accidents! Dance unto the Lord! Betty is now in heaven dancing with the saints! The testimony of her *total healing* from cancer can be read in Chapter Eighteen. Travail with prayer in the Spirit was the instigator 24 years ago when first we met!

The First Radio Broadcast—that led to 'World-Wide' Television

An amusing but wonderful event took place in 1973 when Velma and I decided, that the Lord was speaking to us to begin broadcasting a 15 minute weekly program on radio. We went together to be interviewed at WPIT, our Christian Station here in Pittsburgh, PA.

After a short conversation, we quickly became aware that the attitude of Michael Kamacheck, the then Vice President in charge of programming, was speaking to us as two ladies who were going to be politely dismissed as he felt that we just didn't understand all of the obligations, financial and otherwise that would be involved in such a commitment. It was at this point that I began speaking of our previous trip to Russia, at which time we had successfully smuggled Bibles into that land.

Shocked and surprised at the disclosure that we were able to do this, his attitude and tone changed immediately. "How did we ever complete such a task?"

He himself was of Russian descent—Ukrainian—and he had found it impossible to get Bibles into Russia! After I excitedly shared some of the adventures of that assignment, he questioned us concerning our finances. Velma didn't tell him that we had just $65.00 in our account at this time, she rather mentioned the brand new Ford Van that we had just purchased the week before, quickly receiving all we needed for the purchase, after one elderly woman who was attending our meetings began a Fund Drive with just a roll of nickels! Before we left that day, with a contract signed, Velma had also been asked to record an opening prayer for each Broadcast day!

By the third broadcast I was wanting to sing in the Spirit over the radio, as I know that the Words of this song and sound going forth brings blessings; cleans up the airwaves; and frustrates the 'prince of the power of the air'. Velma said: "Bring your harp and sing!" I was so happy, it was my birthday and I considered this a marvelous birthday present.

Just before taping the broadcast, with Michael once more doing the engineering (he was filling in for the summer for the regular broadcaster), he came into the studio and said: "Oh by the way ladies, there is to be no speaking in Tongues on the radio!" My heart sank. I asked dejectedly: "Why not!" He said: "Oh, I don't know, it has something to do with Brother Dan and Sister Ann!" They had a program on at this station.

Velma spoke up answering cheerfully: "Oh we're not going to speak in tongues; we are going to sing in the Spirit!" He said: "Alright!" (He hadn't a 'clue' concerning this subject) I laughed within and immediately my joy was restored.

I began the broadcast playing my autoharp, singing a verse from 'Amazing Grace' and then went right into tongues using the same melody, and then back once more to the words in English! When the broadcast was over, Michael burst into the recording studio and exclaimed: "Oh Velma, we are going to have to edit some of your talk because we can't cut out any of that beautiful music!" Oh happy day! Was this not a great birthday present! And since we spoke of missionary trips I think many thought we were singing in known languages. If there was any 'flack' from Sister Ann or Brother Dan we never heard any of it!

A few years later 'Living Waters, the Fountain of Israel' became a daily radio broadcast under the direction of sister Carly, her husband Max and me,. This is when we were operating our combination 'Christian Book Store' and 'Straight Gate Hair Styling Shop'. We dedicated Saturdays, the Shabbat to Jewish Ministry! Max was our announcer. He has a marvelous radio voice! Song in the Spirit was a regular occurrence! I have shared all of this because I think it was the underlying reason for the great blessing that *later* happened *in Israel!*

The Worldwide TV Door—opened in Israel!

In 1998 the Lord directed me to give up my job with Passavant Memorial Homes and move to Israel. I resigned, moved to Israel in June, and shared a three-bedroom house in Bethany—El Azariah, the Arabic name—with 2 other ladies. We each paid $150 a month. This was a lovely affordable arrangement. On an afternoon in September, while singing and rejoicing with the ladies while playing my autoharp, Brother David—the one who had rented the house for us—stopped in for a little visit. He came into the living room and joined us in Worship. The Spirit of the Lord came upon him; he laid his hand on my shoulder and began to prophesy: "Your song and your voice will go into the Nations!" Startled, I said within: "Lord, I just got here; I don't want to travel yet!"

The very next day was a Wednesday; the time we had established for our weekly evening 'Prayer meeting'. Brother David stopped in and told us that Reuters News Agency would be coming in that evening to tape our meeting. He said that they would only be here for maybe five minutes, and that we were not to respond in any way to their presence, but just to continue on with our meeting. They wanted a 'candid' taping. I had been part of a Television Ministry in the States producing and providing a children's segment, so I had no apprehension concerning the Reuters crew when they arrived with their cameras.

Our meeting had just begun so I opened after prayer, with my usual practice of leading our group in worshipping the Lord with Song in the Spirit. We then went on with more song and testimony. Brother David gave about a fifteen minute talk as usual, that was always anointed. We closed our meeting by holding hands and repeating the 'Lord's Prayer'. We then added a prayer for the television crew who had stayed, not for 5 minutes, but for the whole hour or so of the meeting! This surprised and pleased us, but we didn't mention it to them. They were very courteous and nice with us.

The Reuters crew packed up all of their equipment and went to their cars when some one of them discovered the flat roof of the department store next to our house. They came back in and asked if we could do just about 5 minutes more of that singing that had been done at the beginning of the meeting, as with infra-red cameras (of some sort or other) they could tape us from that roof—right through our window. We agreed and they taped.

Within the next 9 months Reuters came back twice more, CNN came and did two '15 minute segments'. NBC, CBS, FOX News, Norway Television, German Christian T.V., BBC from England did a Christmas and Easter Special. Peoples Magazine interviewed us. Zola Levitt sent a reporter in to televise. Every week from that night on our 'Prayer Meetings' were filled with camera crews setting up beforehand and camera men quietly scurrying around squatting to keep from getting into one another's viewfinder, as more than one interviewer came at the same time. Over and over I would open my eyes—my habit was and is to close them when I am worshipping the Lord—to find a huge 4 x 6 inch camera in my face! We closed the meetings by standing and asking the reporters to join hands with us as we prayed the Lord's Prayer and always asked God's blessing upon them. It was surprising that when the meetings were over, rather than scurrying away, many reporters and T.V. men and women remained for tea and conservation which mostly centered on questions about our Lord! Thank You Holy Spirit for the opportunity to witness to many who might never have entered a Church!

Shortly after the weekly filming began, Brother David asked me if I would move into an apartment just a few doors away so that we could have more space for what was happening and also our neighbors were becoming distressed at all of the lights and sound coming out of our house. When he showed me the lovely apartment, high up in an apartment building that was completely furnished beautifully with a huge living room; a dining room with wood inlaid table and stuffed chairs of French Provincial lines—my favorite—a huge kitchen with full appliances and a bedroom with a balcony—a 'many-times' conformation of the Lord's doing all through my years of travel—overlooking the mountains of Moab I was really interested. And when Brother David further suggested that: "If *someone* would just move in here and have the apartment ready for the Wednesday night meetings—why they would only have to pay the $150 a month that they are currently paying for one bedroom in the smaller house!" My reply was: "Let's get busy and clean it up!" It had sat empty for months. Brother David signed a rental contract, and we were 'on our way' with our new TV 'Home' Studio!

Many times I later sat on that balcony with tears of thanksgiving streaming down my face, as I realized anew that this was the way of the prophecy—that Brother David had spoken—of being fulfilled. My voice and Song in the Spirit went into many, many, many lands via television. As example, Sister Gwen Shaw while holding her 'First End-Time Handmaiden and Servants 'Holy Spirit' Conference, in Israel, January of 1999 asked me to stand during one of the meetings. She then said: "Sister Grace, we were in Spain last year and we turned on the television to view CNN and we saw our little handmaiden playing her harp, and singing in the Spirit. What a surprise!" She then had Brother David and the rest of those living in Israel stand and commended us for our love and devotion to Israel.

One day I was reading the 'Great Commission' from Matthew 28: 18–20 from the Amplified Bible, "Jesus approached and breaking the silence said to them, All authority—all power of rule—in heaven and on earth has been given to Me. Go then and make disciples of all the nations, baptizing them into the name of the Father and of the Son and of the Holy Spirit: Teaching them to observe everything that I have commanded you, and lo, I am with you all the days—perpetually, uniformly and on every occasion—to the [very] close *and consummation of the age. Amen—so let it be.*" I thought to myself: "Lord, You have Your Evangelists and Christian Television sending the gospel throughout the earth that souls be saved before You return to Earth and that is so wonderful! Lord, you have let me and our little 'band of Christians' go *to the secular world*, that they may hear and share in the sound of your Marvelous Words and Tongues—coming forth through Song in the Spirit! "Thank You Lord for this wonderful 'Miracle of Communication' throughout the Earth by Satellite Television—that was certainly motivated, mandated and maneuvered by You alone!"

The Amazing Sister, Reverend Mertis Stamps and Sister 'Winnie'!

Having just shared concerning some things that took place in 1973 I want to include here a short story concerning the beginning of the Mexican Ministry of my dear friend Sister Stamps. Hers were the first Churches on Foreign soil that I was invited to minister in. I honed my preaching skills concerning Tongues and learned to speak with an interpreter, and to sing songs in Spanish, all through the gracious kindness and encouragement of this marvelous woman!

I met Sister Stamps in 1974 on my third trip to Israel. I can see her now, a lovely black woman sitting across from me at the shared dinner table of our restaurant. She was quietly looking around with her eyes of wisdom that displayed such a subdued combination of discipline and reserve. Her smile of acceptance welcomed me to begin conversation. We enjoyed the sharing of our mutual love of the Lord Jesus and His Israel. Later as we talked she told to me of the beginning of her ministry in Mexico. It is a precious story, one that glorifies our Father God and I want to re-tell it to you.

Mertis was the co-pastor at 'God's Extended Hand' a ministry that was being led by the able direction of Reverend Winifred Smith—Sister 'Winnie' to all who loved her. My sister Carly and, friend at the time Max Cheney, were then working and ministering in her 'store-front' 'Rescue Mission' to the home-less and down-trodden on the streets of San Diego—one of five Bars that Winnie had restored from 'local dive' to 'Local Church! Her story should be told. She is with the Lord now after serving until her 88th year in the restoration of body and soul of 'needy' men and women! She herself was completely restored of lungs 'riddled' with tuberculosis brought about in part by 'chain-smoking' during her days as an alcoholic! As a young woman she came dying, into 'God's Extended Hand' 'store-front' Rescue Ministry; was saved, delivered, and became the proprietor of this Ministry and served it faithfully for over 50 years!

Mertis was working diligently at her post, when the Lord began to speak to her over and over, what was to her, a strange sounding expression: "Frijoles and Arose". She questioned the Lord in this manner: "Lord, I know that You arose from the dead, and I know that you are the 'Rose of Sharon', but what is 'Frijoles'?" The expression went around and around in her head, with her repeating her replies to the Holy Spirit. After a few days while talking with her neighbor she mentioned this expression and told him of her responses. He threw back his head and laughed heartily! He was Mexican. He said: "Frijoles and Arose, this is Spanish for beans and rice!"

Shortly afterward, Mertis was given a $50 bill and was told by the donor, that the Lord would tell her what to do with it. And indeed He did. The Holy Spirit put it into her heart to 'break' the $50 bill down into 50- $1.00 packets; get on the trolley to Tijuana and when she got off to just wait and He would send women to her. She was to give each a packet and tell them that she would be back the next week, and that they were to tell others that she would return.

When Mertis shared this with her friend, Sister Wanda Peters, another of the ministers at the Rescue Mission, Wanda said: "This I've got to see!" And she accompanied her to Tijuana. (Neither Mertis nor Wanda drove 'autos' at the time. Mertis still does not, and obviously she did not speak Spanish…she does now!)

The two 'adventurers for Jesus'—one white, one black—boarded the trolley to Tijuana. When they arrived, they stood in a field nearby and one by one and two by two, women…young women, old women, women with children and women without children, (mostly brown women…I added the colors for I think that God enjoyed the love expressed in and to, His 'human rainbows'). They arrived, and received the 'packets' from the mysterious ladies. The further 'wonder' of it all is that as soon as the 'packets' were distributed and they had no more to offer, the 'parade of women' abruptly came to an end!

From this sweet humble beginning, the last time I spoke to Mertis she has been instrumental in establishing 29 Churches, which are all eventually turned over to the Native Pastors that she, with the help and direction of the Holy Spirit have raised up into these positions of Service to our Lord! Mertis has just 'waged' a battle with Cancer. "Lord we rebuke that horrible scourge. We speak deliverance to Mertis!"…unless Lord, You want to take your diligent, faithful servant Home at last, to be with You!" A wonderful ending to this story is that after four months in a rehabilitation center, Mertis is cancer free and back in action with her Churches. Thank You Jesus!

Chapter Ten

"We, Can 'Pick'—the Spirit's Holy Fruit?"

A Vessel for His Use!

W e are created in His Image and are being conformed to that Image, but it is just an image. We are no more Him than would be our images if they should come to life as we gazed on them in our morning mirrors. He must teach us this lesson that we see that we are the vessel, the house, the ark. We are lovely vessels if reflecting Him, but nevertheless, we are only a vessel which houses His Glory. We are not Him, we are not the glory, but certainly, we are His vessels. Or we may think of ourselves as water pipes through which His Living Waters flow. Or vases—just clay pots originally, but when strengthened—we become 'fired ceramics'—that is—we can at least hold water and give a drink to the weary! Sometimes we are even given a platinum trim—a very high temperature of 'firing' is necessary. All of this change comes, through the process of continuing on in Him—from Glory to Glory! No matter, the trials of testing necessary, which strengthen us as we stand in Him.

Or we may think of ourselves as timbrel or trumpet or organs—or 'songbirds' through which lovely music is made unto Him! But always we should consider ourselves as just the instruments in His precious Hands! When we have learned this truly, He is pleased to begin to use His Instruments, knowing that they will not try to 'touch and receive His Glory' unto themselves. This reminds me of a lovely song written years ago by Margaret Hemsher called:

'A Tool in His Hand'

"All I want is to be used—by my Lord. Be a tool in His Hand—for my Lord.
All I want is to be nearer—never apart.
Keep my close Jesus—close to Your Heart!"

If a beautiful sound is brought forth from a trumpet, the trumpet player is praised, or the trumpet *maker,* but not the trumpet, as though it had anything of itself to do with the sound produced. And if this instrument is not used for public display but rather brings the owner personal enjoyment—privately—should it not be content. We are His Instruments! We should be content to minister unto Him, whether in congregation or at home, just so we minister unto Him!

Further—a cup which brings a drink of refreshing water is not praised. The water is appreciated. The one supplying the water is praised. The cup is incidental, except to its owner. If it happens to have any beauty, the one who made the cup is praised. No one ever says, "Oh you beautiful cup, you gave me a drink."

Love is the final word and ultimate weapon. That glorious thirteenth chapter of I Corinthians sandwiched between chapter 12 and 14 speaks of love, without which no instrument, or weapon, however beautiful or fearsome, can be properly wielded. Even Song in the Spirit will produce a clanging sound if the words are just mouthed and not brought up out of a heart filled with a desire to express a love song to our Creator. I am so glad that we are not admonished to *choose* between the gifts of the Spirit and the fruit of the Spirit. But rather are encouraged to exercise and live in the realm where we are to follow after love, desiring spiritual gifts, that we may be fully equipped to minister and feed others *His Fruit* of love, joy, peace and all of the other Perfect Fruits in His Basket—the Fruit of the Holy Spirit!

A Most Wonderful Life-changing Discovery: The Fruit of the Spirit is 'His Fruit'!

I have discovered that I no longer need strive *to be* 'more loving.' No longer need I *try to be* 'more patient' or *to be* 'more kind.' I have learned a *secret* of bringing forth the *Fruit of the Spirit!* I have discovered that it is not *my* fruit that I am to try to increase, but rather I am to go to the Holy Spirit and *'pick'* His Fruit!

Jesus is the Vine; *I am not a fruit,* but rather a *branch* abiding in Him. If I am to *bring forth* Fruit, it is from the Vine, through the branch, and then the Life-Giving Invisible Spirit is the one to whom the Fruit belongs, and from whom it is given! He is the One who distributes it, through us His branches!

The Word tells us that even the heathen love those who love them. This is the natural, carnal capacity for love that all have in measure, because we are created in God's Image. This natural fruit can be compared to raisins in contrast with large 'Canaan Land' grapes! We are not to try to increase this, *our* fruit, for the feeding of others, because it won't work. If we take that route we wind up being exhausted, even self-condemning when we see ourselves incapable of bringing forth all of the different kinds of fruit that we *mistakenly* think we are to '*be*'!

Examples: "If I just try harder I can '*be*' more loving! If I just try harder I can '*be*' more patient!" Stop it! We can never '*be*' a fruit! Remember, we are *branches in the Vine.* The Fruit is the Fruit of the Spirit, not the fruit of Mary or the fruit of Joe! I stumbled upon this awareness, which has been just about the *most valuable lesson of my life,* a few years ago. I was in a trial that was so numbing that I cried out, "*Lord, I can't give anything to anybody just now. If I'm to minister in any way, You will have to put it there, I'm empty.*"

To my amazement, I discovered that though I was going through the hardest trial of my life, I was filled with more love than I had ever had before. I prayed, "Lord, this is great, *in a pinch!*"

The Lord answered, "*In a pinch?*" And suddenly it dawned on me. I was to go to Him in this same way, always! Before this I had learned how to get rid of the *blight on the branch that I am*—that is—the sins of the *flesh*—by not striving to 'be better' or 'do better'—but rather by confessing my sins to Him—specifically—and then praying—"Jesus, YOU be my strength in this my weakness." He became the 'better' in me as I experienced His strength pouring into me, and the temptations were overwhelmed and weakened and dissolved and forgotten, by that strength!

I had not known that I was to apply the same lesson to 'fruit bearing,' and so was caught up in striving to increase my natural capacity for love, patience, kindness, gentleness, long suffering, etc. The Word in II Timothy 2:24 says, "And the servant of the Lord must not strive; but be gentle unto all men, apt to teach, patient." KJV There is no need to strive—in fact—we are not to do so! We have only to *ask!* Listen now while I explain—*this is so very important!*

John 15:16 tells us, "He has chosen us and ordained us that we might go and bring forth much fruit, and that our fruit should remain." We know that many have considered this foremost as referring to the souls of men (which is true) - but let us see it now in this light. It is only called *our* fruit because we are the ones who go and pick it. That is, we ask the Holy Spirit to deposit it—to put His Fruit—in us. It is *His fruit!* Love, joy, peace, and all of the other Fruits of the Spirit are emotions and attitudes. They are not bananas, apples and peaches! These natural fruits can be taken into us though our eating processes. His Fruit can be taken into us by the same process—by us asking Him to put them into us—His vessels—His baskets—and then receiving them by faith. This is the same process by which all of the attributes of God are received! Follow me now while I explain what took place as the Holy Spirit taught me further concerning this truth!

A few days after this truth dawned on me—that I didn't have to strive to *become* this fruit—*nor could I receive such by striving,* but rather, I had only to ask the Holy Spirit to put His Fruit in me. I was to 'pick it' and I would immediately receive it, for the immediate occasion! I learned that His Fruit may be picked to be dispensed at the time of the asking. This fruit is so delightful for we are the first partakers as it goes through us and then can be expressed to another! This may be somewhat different from the fruits that eventually will become ours to be known by, as in: 'By their fruits you shall know them!' I don't have this all figured out except that I know by experience that what I am about to share with you is of the Holy Spirit—and it works wonderfully! Perhaps after 'picking' fruit from Him over the years, as I have done, we become known in this light. I have never yet learned a better way to bring forth; enjoy and distribute the Perfect Fruit of His Spirit, to others!

My first experience after this discovery: I was in an auto stopped at a red light. My children were scuffling, the traffic was heavy, the temperature uncomfortably hot, and I began to get 'up-tight'! I was ready to *'blow-up'* at the children. Suddenly, I remembered what the Holy Spirit had been showing me and I said, "Lord, give me *Your Patience."* Immediately, I became so calm and peaceful that even though the children got louder and the traffic heavier, I could care less! I said, "But Lord, they need to be reprimanded, but I don't even want to scold them." He replied, *"You asked for MY patience; and it is Infinite!"* (This actually—truthfully happened!)

A few days later I began the day in a dismal mood. I couldn't shake it. I knew what was causing the distress—my natural flesh in which dwells no good thing—and more than likely a spirit of depression trying to influence me. I wasn't aware of the specific reason—whether I had dreamed a bad dream—or what?

Then, I heard a knock on my front door and as I went through my living room to answer the door, I prayed, "Lord, whoever is here, you will have to give me whatever fruit I need." When I arrived at the door, there was no one there. As I walked back to my kitchen puzzled, I said, "Lord, if there had been someone at the door, you would have given me the Fruit of the Spirit to feed them with. Lord, I am at the door. Whatever fruit I need to get me out of this bad mood, feed me!"

Immediately, I began laughing and filling up with joy! I said, "Lord, that is exactly what I needed, Your Joy; Your Fruit (I picked it), shall remain (I get to eat it, too)!" John 15:16, "Ye have not chosen Me, but I have chosen you and ordained you that ye should go and bring forth fruit, and that your fruit should remain, that whatsoever you ask of the Father in My name, He may give it you." KJV I had just asked for this Fruit—and He gave it! Oh Joy! And that is exactly what happens when you pick it for others. *It goes through you, the branch, and because you get to experience the emotion in order to give it to others, you are the first partaker and are thereby blessed in wanting to bless others. Try it…you'll see!*

Later, when I considered the troubled actions of my husband—he came up the drive—got out of his car and slammed the door muttering angrily! I thought: "Lord—if he knew to apply what I am learning—He could ask of You to give him patience in the traffic and he wouldn't come home in a bad mood! But Lord, what fruit do I *need* just now?"

"Gentleness and kindness," were the answer. I said, "Lord, feed me that fruit." To my joy and surprise, I began thinking kind, gentle, loving thoughts about Larry! I forgot all about his anger! In fact, I became so absorbed, then, in the wonder of this reality in the Spirit that I was discovering—that I forgot all about Larry, and was surprised when he came to me and apologized for being so 'grumpy'! It was the *first time he had ever done such a thing!* I decided that my face and 'body language' must have been registering *God's emotions of kindness and gentleness.*

I have shared this many times and challenged the hearers to try it. One funny incident was told to me. After hearing my message in church one morning, a woman went home to discover that the upstairs bathroom tub was running over, water was everywhere, and her husband was sitting watching television, doing nothing to alleviate the situation. Just as she was getting ready to explode, with her teenage daughter looking on apprehensively, she remembered the morning lesson. *"Lord, whatever fruit I need right now, that Sister Grace spoke about,* please put it in me!"

She said her daughter, her husband and herself were so surprised at what happened next. In a calm voice, she spoke to her daughter and together, the two of them quietly wiped up all of the water. Then she entered the living room and spoke kindly to her husband. They all had a nice afternoon and she had to return to church that afternoon to report the miracle. "Honey, do you know what I would have said and done if I hadn't heard that message! *I just can't get over it. This* 'Fruit-Picking' really works!"

I'm thinking now of the *substance of fruit.* Most are soft, like bananas and pears and plums and peaches. If not, they need to be chewed or softened by cooking before the body can assimilate them. And then I remember a message by Randy Shankle concerning a message on the 'Ankle'! He spoke of the marrow of the bone. This is a soft, gelatinous-like substance that runs through the bone, feeding it and making for growth. If the marrow is damaged or in some way hindered, the bone will not grow, but rather becomes dry and brittle.

Is this not what we see in our own lives when even the carnal fruit is missing? And this can certainly be applied when considering the Body of Christ.

Being bone of His bone, we need to pick, eat, and share plenty of the Fruit of the Spirit that good growth may take place!

"Taste and see that the Lord is good," Psalm 34:8 says, "Blessed is the man that trusts in Him." Whenever I realize myself being 'in the flesh'—that is being impatient—unloving—or displaying any of the other—'fruits of the flesh'—I run to the Holy Spirit and 'pick'—His 'Holy Fruit' of His Holy Spirit!

Chapter Eleven

'The Nun's Story' Sister Mary Andrew—More Holy Fruit!

N o segment of the Christian Body can be left out from the need to receive the baptism of the Holy Spirit. I met a Catholic nun at a prayer meeting in a Baptist church that had a totally black congregation (except for the two of us)! She was a 'fiery' little redhead named Sister Ellen. She was filled with the joy of the Lord and I immediately 'took' to her.

She said to me, "Grace, I have been a nun for forty years. Three months ago at the Charismatic Conference at Duquesne University, (the very place where the Holy Spirit fell in 1967, bringing with Him, the Charismatic Renewal in the Catholic Church)! I found myself praying with a Charismatic priest. He led me in a prayer to be born again and baptized in the Holy Spirit. I asked the Lord Jesus to come into my heart and then asked Jesus to baptize me with the Holy Spirit. I want to tell you, I feel alive now in a way that I have never felt before! Oh, if only all of the nuns in our convent could have this experience. I'm humble enough to tell you that I don't understand my Bible enough to explain scripturally what has happened to me. Could you come to the convent and share with the other nuns what this is all about so that they too could receive this wonderful experience?"

"Could I, I would be delighted to do so!" I arrived at the convent and was pleased to find that a lovely nun named Sister Mary Andrew had come to the morning meeting. I shared the following illustration with those gathered.

"There is a Trinity involved in the reality of knowing Christ Jesus. Christ With you, Christ In you, and Christ Upon you! You have Christ with you when you believe all that I know that you believe as a Catholic - that Jesus Christ is God in flesh, was born of a virgin, gave His life willingly to die in our place, was crucified, died and was buried. He arose from the dead, ascended into heaven, and is going to 'come again'!"

"Step One: Believing all of this, that Jesus Christ is the Savior of the world, one will have a measure of life, Christ with them, as opposed to those who do not believe and are spiritually dead. But having Christ with one is like being or having a baby in a womb. There is life there, you know it, and God knows it, but one can't go and tell and speak and share Christ with others."

"Step Two: Takes place when you hear that one can have, not only the Body and Blood of Christ in the Eucharist, but one can have His whole self within! He is standing at the door of your heart knocking, wanting in. When you ask Jesus to come into your heart, He comes in! And the baby comes 'skittering' out of the womb as it were. You are born again of the Spirit! Now you can go and tell and do and serve others by sharing the 'Good News' as 'Birth Announcements'! You can tell them: "Look, this is how you get 'born again'." Then they can get 'born again' the same way!

"Step Three: Takes places when the Reborn One, the Born Again, the one with the Holy Spirit of Christ in their heart hears that they may now have the power of the Holy Spirit poured out upon them. As they believe this and ask Jesus to baptize them with this Holy, Heavenly Oil it is as though the Dove, the Loving One, the Holy Spirit comes down upon them and takes them into His Heart! And oh, such a deluge of love is poured upon one! Now we can minister not only to one another, but unto God Himself with His Heavenly Words in a Song of Love!"

When I had shared this little illustration of Christ with you, Christ in you and then Christ upon you, Sister Mary Andrew exclaimed: "Oh that is beautiful, I teach the children religion. I am the religious coordinator of the first and second graders and I am going to share this with them!"

I said, "Sister Mary Andrew, may I lead you in a short little prayer, maybe only ten words? I know that you pray the prayer book prayers, but if I lead you in the prayer to ask Jesus into your heart and then to baptize you in His Spirit, you will know experientially what Sister Ellen is all excited about, what I am talking about and you will really be able to share with the children!"

"Yes, I would like that," she said!

Oh, I was so thrilled with her response. I took her hands in mine and led her in the prayer. "Lord Jesus, forgive my sins (for all have sinned and come short of the Glory of God - even nuns) and come into my heart and baptize me with your Holy Spirit."

I then KNEW that she was being baptized. Her face lit up like an angel's. She lifted her hands in the air and with eyes closed gave Jesus the most beautiful smile. I turned aside to allow her to be alone with her Lord; for I knew He was giving her the same marvelous experience that Sister Ellen and I had already received.

Sister Mary Andrew's Testimony!

She and I became very best friends and I wanted so much to know what her experience had been that I might share it with others of the Catholic faith. About a month later, I asked her, "Sister Mary Andrew, is there a difference in your life since we prayed together and you asked Jesus to come into your heart and to baptize you in His Holy Spirit?"

She pondered the question awhile and then said, "Well Grace, I've always loved God, that's why I became a nun. I have been a nun for twenty-five years. Before this experience, I had to pray and pray and pray to have a sense of the Presence of God, and many times I did feel His Presence, but it was just hard work! But now," she exclaimed as she wrapped her arms around herself in a hug, "He is in me. He's upon me," and poking me in recognition that I knew just what she meant, said, "You know, you know!" I knew! We both laughed in joy.

Months later, during the 'afterglow' that we had following the weekly praise meetings that we began in the convent of 'Our Lady of Grace'—Sister Andrew said to me, "Gracie, I think that I must have been born again already when we prayed because I had asked Jesus to come into my heart every time I took the Eucharist. I suppose I just didn't realize that according to His Word, He did come in—so I was not resting on the fact that He was there, so didn't have the joy that comes with the knowing! I just kept asking Him again and again to come in. But I don't know how I missed the Baptism of the Holy Spirit. I took first Holy Communion and then later was confirmed. I guess it is just so important an experience that the Lord wants one to ask, really realizing what we are seeking—or asking for!"

The Story of how those 'Praise-Prayer Meetings in the Convent began!

A month after the experience shared above, I received a letter from Sister Andrew. She had gone to College for the summer to complete her Masters degree. In this letter she said: "Gracie when I return to 'Our Lady of Grace' I must speak to you before I see the Monsignor!" I thought: "A Nun wants to speak to me before she sees the Monsignor…hmmm?" When she returned we went to lunch and she told me this story:

"After receiving the Baptism of the Holy Spirit, the Holy Spirit kept prompting me to ask the Monsignor if we could have meetings here in our 'Lady of Grace' Church so that others could receive this marvelous experience. I am a very shy person. I kept resisting speaking to Monsignor until the last day I was here before leaving to complete my Degree. That morning I was at Mass, and once again the Holy Spirit urged me to speak to the Monsignor."

I finally prayed: "Lord, if this is You urging me to speak to Monsignor, You bring him to me!" I thought: That settles it for that will never happen!

No sooner had I said that prayer, than the Monsignor finished the Mass, removed his surplice, walked up the aisle, entered my pew, sat down beside me, took my hand in his and said: "Sister Mary Andrew, how have you been?" I quickly began: "Oh Monsignor, I have received the wonderful Baptism of the Holy Spirit, just as it is being received by so many at Notre Dame. You know this latest experience in our Catholic Church began right here at Duquesne University in 1967! Oh Monsignor, could we have meetings here in our Church that others might receive this experience also?"

He replied: "Yes, Sister Mary Andrew, when you return in the fall, you may begin these meetings!" She exclaimed to me: "Gracie...I don't know anything about such meetings, how can I lead one?" I smiled at her sweet humility. "Sister dear, have no fear, the Holy Spirit will direct and lead them and they will be wonderful!"

She was hesitant concerning Tongues, the Heavenly Language. The idea of speaking in words that she did not understand seemed so strange. She had to 'check it out' with the Lord. When she was convinced in her heart that according to the Word, Tongues were for her benefit and something that the Lord desired her to have, she brought forth the Living Water. That is probably a key, for bringing forth—the desire to do so. After this, she would invite me to speak to the youngsters before they had their confirmation service. I was so especially blessed, when I saw tears in the eyes of one young priest who attended one of these meetings.

Sister Mary Andrew is with the Lord now, but over and over through the years I have shared her testimony with others, especially Catholics, and it has led them to reach out and receive the same wonderful relationship experienced by this precious Nun, and Sister Ellen also! This is the same experience that we who have been born again and baptized in the Spirit have as reality in our lives. The reasoning seems to be, "If it were alright for a nun, it is right for me!"

Over and over since that time, when I hear someone say, "I have God with me," I reply, "Wonderful, now do you know that you may have Him in you, and upon you?" And over and over again I have the joy of leading them on into the experience of being Born Again and Baptized in the Holy Spirit.

The Lord used those dear nuns to open the door to the whole church, and for two years at the weekly praise prayer meetings, I had the joy of seeing those gathered—dancing unto the Lord. This first took place at the first meeting, when at one point I said:

"The Bible tells us that we are to dance unto the Lord."

Immediately Sister Andrew said: "Well then we shall!" And she 'leaped' up and began to dance as we sang and clapped our hands to *'There Is Power, Power, Wonder-Working Power in the Blood of the Lamb,'* and other solid Scripture songs!

We experienced joy unspeakable and full of glory! This willingness and obedience to do whatever the Bible tells us to do as soon as it is made known to them was one of the most delightful characteristics I discovered in my Catholic friends! Through Bible studies and testimonies, we had the joy of seeing ourselves and others grow in grace in our Lord. What a wonderful blessing, to be involved in helping others to draw from the 'Well of Life' that we become when we have Jesus Christ the hope of glory in and upon us!

Those in the neighborhood began to ask: "Why are the convent lights on Fridays unto 2:00 a.m.?" The answer: nobody wanted to go home—we were having such a good time in the Lord!

How 'right on' that Mary took the name of Andrew, with her vows—the one who led his brother Peter to the Lord—for I have used Mary Andrew's testimony over and over through the years to lead others into the knowledge of how to be 'born again' and 'baptized' in the Wonderful Holy Spirit.

Chapter Twelve

'Fasting'—for a 'Change'!

If the Members of the Body of Christ truly understood the marvelous rewards that the Lord God gives on behalf of those who will enter the obedience of fasting, there would be many more people involved in using this wonderful Spiritual Weapon! The Weapon of fasting is Mighty to the pulling down of powerful strongholds. Not only are there resulting blessings in the lives of those who will fast, but also, the lives and situations of those who are being lifted up in prayer and fasting have been changed dramatically!

The Bible is filled with stories of life changing results when the Heroes of old were obedient to the call of the Lord to fast. Moses stands out as the one who began this process, although the Bible speaks of others who fasted in their acts of mourning: Abraham for Sarah at her death (Genesis 23:2), and Jacob when lied to, concerning the supposed death of Joseph (Genesis 37:34).

When the Lord God told Moses to come up alone into the Mountain of Horeb in the Sinai wilderness, he was not told that this encounter would be accompanied by a 40-day and night fast! God set the pattern then of requiring an obedience that could result in extreme measures. The Wonderful result was that the world received the Ten Commandments! However, being the first to break all Ten Commandments (when he threw them down in anger- smile) Moses had to enter another 40 day fast, straight upon the commencement of that first 40 days!

Our Father in Heaven, is it not time for America to fast? Is this a Wonderful Solution to the Terrorism that is threatening our land? Fasting is one of the fastest ways of growing in the Spirit!

Matt. 6:16, "Moreover, when you fast, Be not, as the hypocrites, of a sad countenance, for they disfigure their faces, that they may be seen of men to fast Verily I say unto you, they have received their reward. But you, when you fast, anoint your head, and wash your face; that you be not seen of men to fast, but of your Father who is in secret; and your Father, who sees in secret, shall recompense you." "Hey there! Is this not a great incentive? Yes it is!"

Our Heavenly Father sees in secret, what we do in secret—in obedience to His Word—and rewards us openly! That is the Word of God from the lips of our Beloved Jesus! And I and many others, who fast, have found it to be so! Christians, who fast, know that God answers prayer and honors the fear of the Lord expressed in serious fasting! Just as the Lord rewards the tithing of our first fruits, which in this day speaks of our financial fruit to begin with, even so is fasting, a giving of our selves, our time and attention and a bit of a sacrifice of our daily bread! And our Lord doesn't say: "If you fast, but rather—when you fast…"

I Kings 19:4–8 tells us that, Elijah fasted for forty days and nights and came to Horeb the mount of God, in the strength of the food given by an Angel. This reminds me of when I was given food and drink, in the Spirit, during the first time I was led of the Holy Spirit to neither eat nor drink during a 7-day total fast in 1970.

I am going to share with you a very strange, mysterious, happening that took place during this first time that I was in a period of extreme fasting. This fast was accomplished, through 'feeding' and standing in His Strength alone!

The 'rewards' mentioned in the Word were ones which I thought were to be given only in Heaven, but I was made to understand that when the Lord spoke of 'rewarding one openly', this meant also while we are down here on Earth! Knowing that we are to be careful not to speak of our fasting, I only share this experience, and many others, because for a number of years, the Holy Spirit has been prompting me to write my personal testimonies concerning the wonderful results of fasting! (When Brother Bill Bright encouraged us to share concerning fasting that others be encouraged to do so, I first felt free to share concerning my times of fasting, but did not do so. I will do so now!)

I was taught to fast at a young age. I have already spoken of going to the Kathryn Kuhlman 'Miracle Services' here in Pittsburgh. I learned that Kathryn encouraged everyone attending the meeting to fast; that is to do without food from the midnight before the meetings until the midnight of the Miracle Service. We were to just drink water. This comprised a 24 hour fast. I entered these fasts, and while I was happy to at least be subjecting my flesh to the obedi-ence of the Holy Spirit, I was not aware of any certain, personal results of fast-ing, other than attending really great meetings which, of course, was the reason for those fasts! *(So I was seeing results, but was not realizing the connection!)*

In August of 1970, while attending the Miracle Service in the Presbyterian Church, I received the Baptism of the Holy Spirit—the marvelous experience I have already shared! That very day began a whole new revelation to me of the power derived from fasting. I went home from that meeting overwhelmed with a new awareness in my life, of a love for Jesus Christ that I had not had before, though I had thought previously that I loved Him with all of my heart! Comparing me with me, not anyone else, I had a new love for everyone around me. And while I thought that my love for God had been full, I immediately entered a New Realm of Worship and Praise that had not been in my life until that very day. It was the Realm of 'in the Spirit'!

This meeting took place on a Friday afternoon. The following Monday evening, at my home church, as we gathered for refreshments, I went to put a cookie in my mouth and could not swallow! I was taken aback and suddenly realized that I had not had any food since that Friday afternoon service, nor had I even thought about food! At the same time I began to realize that I was having a tremendous sense of Power flowing through my forearms, from the elbows to the fingertips! As I thought about this, I attributed this to the fasting, but of course, also to the Baptism of the Holy Spirit that had just preceded it. This was the beginning of a marvelous time in my life. I have shared all of this because I wanted to give the background of the incident of extreme fasting that took place just 4 months later in December of 1970.

Every week—from the time of that following Wednesday when our entire Bible Study received the Baptism of the Holy Spirit—without fail, we gathered together in great excitement as the Holy Spirit taught us concerning this Baptism. It was now December and the Joy of the Christmas season was in the air. We were excited about the Word we had received earlier in the month concerning the celebration of His Birth: 'Born to die for you and I'. We were encouraged to display the Christmas Star as a Star of David, and the Cross along with that statement! This is the true message of Christmas! We were challenged to see who would be brave enough to share this Word. I remember how bold of an action this seemed to be at that time! Many responded wonderfully. Carolyn had her husband cut these symbols and message in plywood. They then placed them on their front lawn. Others placed this message on their windows! God blessed each of us in a special way that Christmas!

Then Came—The Long Fast!

Later, our little group of Holy Spirit Baptized believers was worshipping the Lord while standing in a circle holding uplifted hands in adoration. I thought that everyone heard the Word of the Lord that came to me. This is the reason I discussed it. He called us to enter a 7 day total fast! We were to have neither food nor water for 7 days. I spoke of this to the others and they said I must be mistaken. They told me that it was impossible to enter such a fast, that it would harm our kidneys.

I replied, "But if the Lord desired and directed it, there would be no problems." My group of loving friends said that they had no intention of entering such a fast and warned me that I should not do so either.

I determined to obey the Lord. Late into the third day of this proposed fast, being so very thirsty, I decided that my friends might have been correct. I broke the fast. During the following days I immediately began seeing the Scripture from the Old Testament: *Micah 5:4*, "And he shall stand and shall feed in the strength of the Lord…in the majesty of the name of the Lord his God." As I read this just now in the King James Version, I see that this is not speaking directly to us. Perhaps this read differently in my Moffat Translation. I have given it away and cannot find another. Anyway, I was given the idea that I was to stand and feed in the strength of the Lord. One of the guiding scriptures of my life has been Philippians 4:13, "*I can do all things through Christ who strengthens me.*" So this was the same thought, to my understanding.

And then from the New Testament I heard in my spirit: "Their god is their belly!" Philippians 3:19, "Whose end is perdition (destruction), whose god is their belly, and whose glory is in their shame, which mind earthly things."

I prayed, "Lord, you really do want me to go into a 7 day total fast. Alright Lord, I will do it, *in Your Strength!*" I immediately began again. This was just a few days after I had broken my fast of 3 days.

By the 5th day my mouth was so dry that I had to put coffee in my mouth and swish it around and then spit it out. Why coffee rather than water? I can't remember, but *I was careful not to swallow even a drop.*

On that same day, I was in my automobile driving up a hill. I can see this so clearly in my memory bank even today.

Suddenly, the Holy Spirit spoke in my spirit: *"Would you like a glass of water?"*

I was shocked! "Lord, I said within, in a tone of voice that said: "Why would you even suggest such a thing?"

"See it!" said He. "Picture a glass of ice water in your mind's eye."

"Oh!" I saw I suppose in my imagination, or in the mind of my spirit, a tall glass of water filled with ice cubes and with sweat beads running down the sides.

He said: "Drink it!" I put the glass to my lips and swallowed. After just the one swallow, the glass disappeared. I had within me the feeling one gets when one drinks too much water. I call it a 'logy' feeling. Sort of waterlogged and not wanting anymore water. I was refreshed, not thirsty and totally stunned and surprised! I had never heard of such a thing! Nor have I since!

Later, while still in the car driving, the Lord spoke again, "Would you like a cup of tea?"

I said, "Lord," as though to question, "what is this all about, what are You up to?"

He replied, "See it!" I saw a steaming cup of tea. "Have some," said He.

I took just a mouthful and once again, it disappeared and I was comforted, as one is by a nice soothing cup of tea.

Now, rather a bit later, on the same trip, I was driving down the highway.

The Holy Spirit said to me, "What would you like to eat?" By this time I knew He was speaking of spiritual food and named something simple.

"No," He said, "you can have anything you want, think of something you would really like!" Well, I imagined a plate upon which sat a filet mignon steak, and a lobster with a thought of dipping it in drawn butter. (I used to like lobster before I realized that, supposedly, it is really just a giant cockroach of the Sea—a scavenger!)

The Lord said, "Take and eat." I took my fork and took one bite and immediately it was gone. I had no hunger anyway, because by the 3rd day and certainly by the 5th when fasting, hunger is no problem. But I had a feeling of contentment as though the Lord had just taken me out to a lovely dinner!

This incident never happened again during that fast, but something similar happened a few years later when I was going through a 21-day water fast while at Calvary Pentecostal Camp in Virginia. Mother Heflin taught at the 11 a.m. Bible Study every day.

At one point the Holy Spirit spoke to me and said, "Would you like some peanuts?"

This made me remember the December 1970 'happening' and I smiled and said, "Okay!" Many days after this, at the same time, in the eleven o'clock Bible Study, the can of Planters Peanuts showed up in my spirit.

Now I am not known as one who likes peanuts especially. My husband came to camp to take my children and self home at the end of the summer and this 21 day fast. He presented me with a can of Planters Peanuts! He knew nothing of this experience of my 'Eating in the spirit'!

I said within, "Lord, You are surely confirming this experience of eating 'Food we have not known of'!"

Now having said that—quoting our Precious Savior, I must explain. The first time I shared this strange experience with a Pastor I was strongly rebuked. He became angry at my recollection and said that this was not a scriptural way of fasting!

I thought to myself, *I didn't ask for this experience or even imagine that such could take place, it was the Holy Spirit who initiated it.* I had told that Pastor, who had himself been on many 40 day water fasts, thinking that surely he must have had such experiences. I never have shared again until recently, when I felt the

Lord wanted me to speak of the experience, and thought maybe this might be a way that He will sustain us during the 'End-Times'—if necessary!

Since then, I remember the Lord's Words to the disciples in John 4:32, "But He said unto them; I have meat to eat that ye know not of." And then again in John 4:34, "Jesus said unto them, "My meat is to do the Will of Him that sent me and to finish the work."

I had thought that this meant His Food was obedience, which of course it was. But lately, in considering His Words and what took place in my life, I began to wonder. Lord that which happened to me took place when I was obediently doing Your Will. That 7 day total fast took place only days after the 3 day fast. Is this part of what the Lord Jesus Christ was saying? Did similar instances take place in the lives of Moses and Elijah and our Lord when total fasts were entered? Hmmm?

Some of the Blessings of Fasting!

The Lord had me enter this fast every 10 years, in 1980, again in 1990, and then in the year 2000. I speak of this to say that such fasts are possible with no bad after effects and only marvelous results, as I will share further. *In fact, the fasts became easier* and the last one in December of 2000 was one of the easiest fasts I have ever gone through. I was up on the top rung of a ladder hanging Christmas Ornaments in the Jerusalem House of Prayer Revival Center in Sheikh Jarrah on the 3rd day and only had to swish my mouth with mango juice in the last 2 days. I love mango juice, but I didn't swallow any! I am now older; so age isn't a barrier to doing His Will, although I thought it might be and waited clear into the end of the year in December of 2000 before I began my decade fast—at the age of 67 years. I believe this act of obedience has added years to my life and surely I will do the same in 2010 and possibly 2020 if our Lord tarries! Actually, I enjoyed Thanksgiving at the home of my son Glenn and his wife Becky in Orlando Florida in 2004 and stayed a week longer. The Lord surprised me and once more led me into a 7 day total fast. At the age of 71, this was the easiest fast of them all!

Especially since the Baptism of the Holy Spirit, I have been led by the Spirit to enter many different kinds of fasting, such as 21-day water fasts, three-day fasts, and a 40 day Daniel fast in which I only ate fruits and veggies. It was a most delightful fast as it was summertime, and I could have all of the watermelon and cantaloupes and raisins and dates that I desired. Occasionally I would have liked a hot meal or some coffee, but I had none, and my reward was to begin my travels into other nations in 1972! A Word of the Lord to that effect came to a group of us attending a 'Jesus Festival' in Washington D.C.

In one period of my life I was led to fast—again secretly—one day a week for a ministry just getting started. That ministry blossomed and bloomed and I know that fasting had a part in the growth of it.

Always the Lord has blessed in many different ways. Perhaps I will share particulars as they have had dramatic results. These fasts have often been on behalf of my children, neighbors, others, and even sometimes on behalf of self, and so testimonies of the wonderful results can many times be borne out by facts.

Hoping to encourage others to fast, I will share the startling, and remarkable results, which I have experienced, especially, of the '7 Day–Total Fasts' entered into in 1970, 1980, 1990. I see that I have already spoken of the year 2000 though not the results.

A dance before the Lord in the middle of the night—then a Word is given!

Two weeks after the fast of 1970, as I awakened in the night hours to begin my normal nightly hour of Bible reading and study, I heard within: "Come dance with Me!"

I immediately said, "Yes Lord, I will love to do that!" I danced into my living room, and while dancing I worshipped Him by singing to Him in Tongues. All the while, I was lifting my hands unto the Lord, moving these in a swirling circular motion. As I did so, I began to hear precious Words and I said: "O Lord, these Words are so lovely, may I write them down?"

His reply was, "Yes, you are supposed to!"

As I sat down to write, the Words were so beautiful that I stopped writing and began once more to Worship, and as I did so, my recent habit pattern of lifting my hands to the Lord and moving them in sweeping circles began once more. As my hands swept across my throat and chest in this circular movement, I realized that *tremendous heat was issuing forth from my hands and I could feel it—pouring onto my neck!* The Lord said, "This is my confirmation to you that I am using your hands to bless My People."

"Be always ready at a moment when I may use your hands to bless My people." It seemed to me that He was saying that this blessing would take place, as I lifted hands to Him in Worship—in this 'swirling manner' while singing in the Spirit—Tongues!

Just then a little spider appeared, crawling out from behind my refrigerator! Without thinking, I immediately lifted my hand with palm forward; thrust my arm toward the spider and just held it there in mid-air. As I did so, and realized what I was doing I prayed.

"Oh Lord, what if I use my hands to hinder or to bind?"

He answered: "This too is a blessing is it not?"

I answered. "Oh, yes Lord!"

The Lord said also: "When one is constantly immersed in warm oil—one loses the initial sensation!" I understood but vaguely what the Lord was speaking of concerning blessing! I realized that a stream of anointing was pouring out of my hands as I worshipped in this manner.

My English Language was Gone!

The day after the wonderful 'night-time' occurrence of this charge, by our Lord, I was *unable* to speak any words in English! Every time I went to speak, Tongues of the Holy Spirit came forth instead! That evening as I boarded the Trolley to go to Pittsburgh to attend a meeting, during the entire trip, the surrounding road-way, which is usually deserted except by a few, was filled with workers and others! It was as though a parade was passing by. I held up my hands to the window at the beginning of the trip but soon felt foolish. I said: "Lord, I feel 'funny' holding my hands up this way!"

He replied: "You are not holding up your hands, you are holding up mine!"

Now, please listen—I know that sounds strange and I am hesitant to repeat what the Holy Spirit said, but really, with Christ in us—He *is* coming forth, *from our hands and eyes and speech*—is He not? And this is the manner in which I have considered, or understood all of the 'ways' in which He uses us for the blessing of others!

That evening at the meeting—at last able to speak in English, though I didn't share what had happened—I was told prophetically, that Jeremiah 1:17–19 was a Word—especially for me! As I read it: verse 17, "Therefore prepare yourself and *arise, And speak to them all that I command you.* Do not be dismayed before their faces, lest I dismay you before them. For behold, I have made you this day a *fortified city* and an *iron pillar.* And *bronze walls* against the whole land, against the kings of *Judah,* against its *princes,* against its *priests,* and against the people of the land. They will fight against you. But they shall not prevail against you. For I am with you, "says the LORD", to deliver you." (NKJV)

This Word is the reason that I have stood and spoken a message in Tongues and the Interpretation when the Lord directs, even though often through the years, especially during my earlier years of ministry, when ministers, mistakenly I believe, insisted that a message must be written down and judged before being spoken audibly! I was also rebuked concerning what others considered the 'wrong-timing'!

Also, I remember that the night before, during the disclosure to me by the Lord…

He said: "You know what the evil one thinks of this anointing and his probable response, what will you do?"

I responded bravely: "Lord, I will lift my hands and bless the Lord from whom all blessings flow!"

I then asked: "But Lord, how will I know it is you speaking?"

He said: "If you are ever lead to lift your hands in worship unto Me, it will only be of Me, the evil one would not desire it, for *I will never let your hands fail a blessing!*"

Saturday, the day after, I met a friend from church, and wondering and marveling at the memory of not being able to speak anything but 'Tongues' for an entire day, I shared the experience with her. She insisted that I must share this experience in church the following day. I protested that it was a personal experience and not for general expression.

She replied, "Oh no, sister, you must share your testimony to bless the people with what God is doing!" She persisted, and so the next day in church I shared the experience, and I am so happy that I did. There were a number of ministers at the service that day, who confirmed what I shared and added Words of Prophecy, one of which was: "Speak more slowly, for there is more that I would give you to speak."

I thought, "Lord, am I to speak in Church again?" The whole experience astounded me.

His Power Shakes His Tabernacles!

Later, as I lifted the hands of others to bless them as the Lord had instructed, I found that a tremendous anointing of power flowed and it created a shaking in my hands and in the hands of those who were open to receive what the Holy Spirit was doing. This shaking brought so much persecution that I found myself protesting to the Lord. He reminded me that in the message I had received that night, when the Lord said, "You have some understanding of what the evil one might do in response to what I have given you, what will you do?"

I had replied, "Lord, I will just lift my hands and Praise God from whom all blessings flow!" *This was spoken in belief and love and not in full awareness of just how often and, how much the evil one would harass me through others!*

One day as I was ministering to a group of women, I passed from one to the other, not really praying for them nor praying in the Spirit, but rather I was saying within, "Lord, You know what You are doing, and I know, but does it have to be so obvious?" (When I lift the hands of another in prayer, the Power of God comes into them and shakes and is obviously seen.)

As I reached for the hands of a fourth woman, she burst forth in a strong Tongue in the Spirit. Startled, I stopped and listened. She then interpreted her Tongues: "Minister unto Me, question Me not, question Me not, just minister!" This admonition ended *my* protests.

Through the years I find others, even ministers, who do not understand the shaking of the Holy Spirit as He comes upon one in power and anointing. They comment and even mock, or criticize such movement, of the shaking. May they realize that it is recorded in the book of Acts, that the very house was shaken by a tremendous move of the Holy Spirit, a Mighty Wind, as others received the Baptism of the Holy Spirit! The Lord of the Church is still shaking His *temples, His tabernacles,* as He *fills and uses them.* Question Him not! This is very sound advice. Let us hear what the Spirit says to the Churches!

Results of the 1980 'Extreme Fast'!

A Trip to Europe, England, America and then the Gift of Music—the Spirit's Gifts!

In 1980, this 7-day Total Fast took place during Holy Week in Jerusalem. I was living there at the time and this is the one week that Virginian Hams and goodies abound. It was a testing of love for Him over food! Just weeks after the fast ended, I was given finances to go from Haifa to Greece on a ship, travel money to make my way across Europe to England, and then in England, was given an airline ticket to America. (Just now as I write this, I realize that those finances, and that wonderful trip, were a part of the blessing of the Fast!)

Before this trip to America—temptations came!

Lay your Head on My Breast

Mother Heflin came to Jerusalem just before I returned to America in 1980 and gave me a prophecy that was also a part of the music coming forth! The Prophecy from Mother Heflin: "Be not involved in much busyness, but come, lay your head upon My Breast and you will learn things there that can be learned in no other way!" I did not receive that Word graciously and with the joy that I should have, but later I did!

While living in Israel, I had been involved in a little 'club' for children in the development town of Ofakim. It was an effort by the Israeli Welfare Department to guard the dignity of the Moroccan Jews who had emigrated from that country. The children needed to learn skills with art and games, etc., while their mothers could learn habits of cleanliness using the automatic washers and dryers. It was a pilot program for the Department, and they were recording the gatherings with Television recording equipment. I had been asked to learn how to run and be in charge of the recordings. I had been involved with the children's portion of a program on television in the 70's in Pittsburgh. I had a seven minute spot that I wrote, produced and performed in for the children. I told a story while paintings of 'Hook's marvelous Art Work' were displayed, and then played my Autoharp, sang, and led the children into a little prayer! This was on 'Keys of the Kingdom,' shown on Channel 53 in Pittsburgh, underwritten by Sheepfold Ministries! I loved being in that ministry, and here was my opportunity of getting into Television work in Israel.

Instead, the Word had come: "Be not involved in much busyness!" I rebelled! I started off for the 'Club' on the day scheduled for the learning session. Each step I took I could hear within, in cadence with my walk: "Go- back- home! Go—back—home!" I stopped halfway there; turned and looked up into the sky and said, "Lord, does everything that you want us to do have to be a sacrifice? Well, I know that I have sacrificed before and I know You know all about it, but I haven't really told You so, but now I am telling You! If I have to give this up it will make me unhappy!" And then I stopped; paused in the midst of my complaining and took stock! "Oh Lord, what does it matter except to please your Dear Heart!"

As I turned to go back to my apartment, suddenly I realized what the prophecy had said: "Come, lay your head on My Breast..."

I cried, "Oh Lord, Your Heart is in Your Breast! Oh forgive me! Who could have such a Wonderful invitation?" I went back to my apartment; opened my Bible to Psalm 119:165 and read, "Great Peace have they who Love Thy Law, and nothing shall offend them!" A wonderful 'great' peace filled my little kitchen there in Ofakim as I read and I was ready to spend the whole summer just reading His Word and practicing how to lay my head on His Breast. Within two weeks I was miraculously back in America! He wanted me to go *all the way back home* and then the blessing of the 45 Songs began!

The Songs Begin!

Shortly after, when I came home to America, every time I took my autoharp in hand to sing and Worship the Lord in the Spirit, I was given a new melody. No sooner had I written down the melody than words came for the tune. I was given 45 Songs! I have since put them into composition in a book of music called '*Living Waters, Doxology of Praise*'. I have never written a song on my own, I am not a song-writer, but rather a song-secretary! I just record what the Lord gives to me as I sing His Song of the Holy Spirit to Him in Worship!

Twice I have received a melody to words that were not given to me. Once when I was reading a poem by a Mrs. C.L.Shacklace from a piece of 7th Day Adventist literature titled: "Oh Galilee", a beautiful melody came to me and would not leave until I had written down the score. I have tried to find this woman, but cannot and maybe this is why I find myself writing about this song and poem now. The other melody was given to be sung of Isaiah Chapter 53. See this in Chapter Fourteen: Spotlight on the Royal House of the Lion of Judah!

Checker Playing!

The Lord had directed me to put the music into composition with 'explainettes'—my word denoting an explanation of what the song meant, or the circumstance of how it came into being, and/or the Scripture that it glorified! Mother Heflin had taught me that 'Moving with the Lord' is like playing checkers! When it is your move He doesn't move, but after you move, then it is His move! The Lord had told me that when I had put the music into composition, He would bring an artist into my life to do the artwork for the 'eye-gate' and then He would have me do a tape for the 'ear-gate.'

I spent a year at my drafting table—this was before I learned of computers and music software. I drew all of the little notes and struggled with the timing. I remember at one point when I had just put a song into composition, my good friend Ken Barker said, "Shalom—his nick-name for me concerning my trips to Israel—I think that this song should be written in ¾ meter, rather than 4/4 time."

Well, that really discouraged me and I said, "Lord, I never went to Julliard—I wanted to—I have only studied composition from my year of piano playing in 6th Grade and my books from the library! I just am not capable of completing this work!"

Previn & Perlman!

The very next day, or was it that same afternoon, I turned on the Television to the Public Broadcasting Network and I heard Andrea Previn, the former conductor of the Pittsburgh Symphony and my favorite violinist, Yitzhak Perlman discussing a work of one of the 'Old Masters'. Their conservation:

Andréa said, "But Yitzhak, I think that the music goes: ba-bum, ba-bum, ba-bum!"

And Yitzhak replied, "I think it goes this way." And he gave another sound of a beat.

I was stunned! I said, "Lord, do even accomplished musicians find confusion in determining the beat and rhythm of a song! Well then, I certainly can continue without feeling inadequate - lead me Lord!" And He did and I finished my compositions!

The Artist Appears!

The Lord graciously moved on the 'checker-board' when I had completed the compositions, and brought into my life Alice Twitchell. She was an accomplished artist who had works displayed, and was part of an Art Museum in Ashland, Ohio. She has since gone on to be with the Lord. She agreed to draw the illustration of my songs, and just the other day, I was looking at the original book of art, which she presented to me as a gift. I believe she sketched 55 different pieces of art. I have had them copyrighted and have scattered them throughout my books. A tape of some of the music—19 songs—has also been recorded.

A Thousand Dollars—with a 'snap' of the fingers—just like that!

Just now I am thinking of how the printing of the Music Books was paid for. This, too, was a miracle and may have been involved with that 1980 Fast! In 1983 I met my friend Betty Peace. She had a friend who had a small printing press and it was given to me. I enjoyed learning how to print on this machine, and had planned on printing my Music Books. The process left my hands smudged with ink and the office in Betty's home smelling of chemicals!

Betty would say, "You did the compositions, the explainettes, and the layouts. You don't have to do everything! You are a musician; your hands should be playing your harp. If you would just put that press away, *I know that the Lord could give you a thousand dollars, just like that!*" And she would snap her fingers for emphasis as she said it! "You could have your music printed at a Commercial Publishing House." (At the time—through looking back on it—I remember that her husband 'Mack' had a problem with his lungs, and Betty was probably, in her kind way, wanting to eliminate the chemicals without discouraging me as she knew how much I was enjoying the printing machine. "I'm sorry Lord for being so unthinking!" Thankfully, my sister Carly came to Pennsylvania for a visit, and before she left, Mack was completely healed of his lung problem! See the testimony in the Chapter on Healing, Deliverance and Direction that have been accomplished.)

Betty repeated this admonition daily, and finally one day in exasperation, for I was having difficulty with the printing press as a small but important piece had broken off; I cleaned the machine, put all the apparatus away and declared, "Well Betty, my printing days are over. The press is cleaned. Be happy!"

She replied: "Good, now the Lord will supply that $1000 and you can have your books printed commercially and be on their way!"

That very night we went to visit with a dear friend, Clara Byers. We had enjoyable evenings praying and fellowshipping with her at different times. We had not seen her for quite a while. At this time, Betty and I were presenting a weekly radio broadcast locally on w.a.v.l. Apollo, and Clara had enjoyed listening. We chatted, enjoyed one another's company, and prayed together, and that evening just before we left, Betty began telling our friend about my experimenting with the printing press. She also mentioned her statement concerning the thousand dollars. Clara looked at the two of us and began laughing. She lovingly said, "Now I know why the Holy Spirit led me to put a thousand dollars into my personal checking account this morning!" She went to her desk and wrote a check!

Betty and I were stunned, startled and surprised. Betty said: "I didn't know why that statement kept coming out of my mouth–'God could supply you a thousand dollars, just like that, if you would put the printer away!' Now I truly realize that it was the Holy Spirit's leading!" Amazing story is it not—but it is true!

By the way, Brother Lantz—he was known as the 'Candy Man' for he always carried a bag of 'Black Cow' Carmel Suckers for the children—insisted that he pay the $20 every week for the broadcast! His lovely wife, Sister Lantz, agreed with this, and many times, when they would see me while shopping, Sister Lantz would roll down the window and wave the $20 bill for me to receive it! Brother Lantz has been with the Lord for some time now, and I had the privilege of giving the eulogy at his funeral. Often, I am asked, "How did you pay for this or that?"

My answer is always as Ruth taught me, "The Lord will provide!" And He does, if we will only just trust Him to do so!

The Music Book is Marred—The wrong tempo!

I was later distressed to discover that I had made some mistakes in timing, but I made the discovery while at the first i.s.o.m., the International School of Ministry held by Sister Gwen Shaw. The year was 1988 and the school is located in Jasper, Arkansas. The very first end-time handmaiden, Dorothy Buss, played a piece from my newly printed book complete with artwork, on the piano.

As I listened, I was crushed! I said, "Oh Dorothy is that how I have written that song?" I knew it wasn't how I had heard it in my spirit. I sat down by Sister Gwen and hesitantly poured out my woe concerning my already printed Music Books. Sister Gwen patted my hand and said, "See Dorothy, she will correct it for you." I protested that it was too difficult with too many songs to correct. That dear sweet Dorothy, my dear friend and such a marvelous musician, corrected every song. Sad to say, I have still not redone the music. Perhaps the Lord will let me hear the Angels play it in heaven, since they are probably the ones who gave the music to me through the Holy Spirit as I worshipped in Spirit and in Truth!

A Multitude of Blessings—the results of the 1990 Fast!

In 1990, again during Holy Week, my 7 Day Total Fast was done on behalf of my oldest daughter, whom I had not heard from in two years. I knew she was troubled and having great difficulty. On Easter, the day of the ending of the Fast, I rejoiced, lifted up my hands and praised God, knowing that God had heard and was in the process of defeating Satan's plans against Amy.

Two weeks later while at St. Isabel, California, the place where I had accomplished the fast—always in the strength of the Lord, my daughter Jenny called and rejoiced that Amy had gotten in touch with her! I was able to send Amy an airline ticket to visit me, and, 15 years later, Amy had gotten an associate degree from College, with a 3.9 average, was nominated and accepted into the Phi Theta Kappa Honor Society.

Today she is completely free of the bondages of the past and is living a good, healthy life! She has so much fun and enjoyment taking her dog 'Sprite' on trails and watching him jump into the lakes for swimming. Sprite is also her companion as she is the driver of an eighteen wheel truck! Life is just good; thanks for this are given to our Wonderful Savior, and the part that Deliverance was accomplished, through the value of fasting! A sad note here is to relate that 'Sprite' was killed just a few months ago, and the new Labrador puppy given to her to help ease her pain of loss, was stolen at a Truck Stop. Still Amy brightens when speaking with me and says: "Mom, I am blessed and highly favored in the Lord!" My heart sings when I hear her say that and tears of thanksgiving fill my eyes at the remembrance of God's goodness.

I have learned that fasting is one of the fastest ways of growing in the things of the Lord. The Lord always honors what He initiates. Fasting and faithfulness in His strength are two wonderful spiritual weapons in our arsenals, while the Bridegroom is presently away at the right hand of the Father, making preparations for our Wedding Feast!

Results of my 'decade fast' in the year 2000

Upon arriving back in America, I was worshipping the Lord at a morning prayer meeting in the 'Ark', the wonderful End-Time Handmaidens Worship Center in Jasper, Arkansas, when I heard the Lord speak in my heart, "I am taking you back 20 years in life for I have a work for you to do!" As I read this just now—it reminds me of a Word of the Lord given me by Ruth Heflin while at Pentecostal Camp in Ashland Virginia during the 70ties. Ruth walked over to me—placed her hand on my head and said; "Even as I put Adam into a deep sleep that I might bring forth a birth—even so I will put you into a deep sleep that a spiritual birth come forth. It shall be a great birth. You don't understand it now. Nor will you understand when it takes place. But afterward—you shall hear the telling thereof." My hope is that this birth has to do with others beginning to understand the importance of seeking and using the Tongues of the Spirit—through the printing of this book! As strange and shocking as those words sound, I believe them! Thank You, Lord! Nothing is too hard for You to do! Help me, Lord, to use my time in glorifying You!

I must add now, what has just happened in my life! September 22, 2006, the Day of Rosh Ha-Shanah, the Jewish New Year, Benny Hinn and others around the globe blew the shofar signifying a Glorious New Year. I blew my little shofar also. Immediately the pain in my hip was gone! I began on my music once more and realized I was preparing 'Awake O Israel' for our Church presentation! I just spent a wonderful week in Israel for the Feast of Tabernacles and received wonderful words of prophesy from Sister Gwen Shaw in confirmation concerning what the Lord had just told me of my work in Bethany and I came home to complete editing this, my book which contains almost all of my booklets. *I have awakened*—and am overjoyed at the prospect of the future! Thank you dear reader that I can share this happiness with you!

"Lord, don't Let 'Razz' close his eyes in death—
until he knows You as Savior!"

I usually fast on Sunday mornings before going to Church. I feel it prepares me more adequately to be ready to come forth in a Message in Tongues, with Interpretation if the Holy Spirit leads me to do that, and I am in a Church where prophetic song and Words are not rejected. I also feel more ready to speak in class during Sunday school. I usually fast while I am writing booklets or poems or letters. Fasting seems to keep my mind 'zeroed in' on what the Lord would have me do, write or say! Many times the Lord leads me to fast, simply as I feel in my Spirit that it is time to do so.

One Saturday morning I awakened and felt that the Lord was impressing upon me to fast. I said, "But Lord, it is Saturday! You usually don't have me fasting when the family is home and there is shopping, etc., to do!" Nevertheless, I had no hunger at all and so began to fast. About the middle of the afternoon, I 'snapped'–spoke crankily—at my husband about something and I said within, "Lord, if this fasting is making me cranky, maybe I had better stop."

I heard one word: "Satan." I knew then that it was the evil one and my own flesh making me cranky! I said, "Oh, Lord, You really want me to fast! All right, I will continue to do so!"

About 15 minutes later, the phone rang. It was my next door neighbor Agnes. "Please come quick! Razz is on the floor and looks like he is dying!" Razz was her husband. I ran to my neighbor's house. There lay Razz on the kitchen floor. His mouth was wide open and he had the pallor of death upon his face. His wife was leaning on the kitchen sink immobile!" I had already learned from experience that when one seems to be unconscious, never-the-less, many times, they are still capable of hearing and understanding.

I dropped to my knees and took his head in my hand, and said in his ear, "Razz, ask Jesus into your heart!" There was no response! He just lay there with his mouth hanging open. Again I cried into his ear, "Razz, ask Jesus into your heart!" Then I spoke loudly in Tongues into his ear and a third time cried, "Razz, ask Jesus into your heart!"

Suddenly a huge smile spread across Razz's lips. I cried to his wife, "Ag, look, Razz asked Jesus into his heart! He asked Jesus into his heart!" Just then Razz, with his head cradled in my hand breathed his last and was gone. Thank God, I know he is in heaven.

I had witnessed to Razz just a year before for the last time. He had listened to me and said, "Aw, kid, 'you can't teach an 'old dog' a new trick! I'm sorry." He refused to pray a sinner's prayer and just before leaving I said to the Lord, *"God, please don't let Razz close his eyes in death until he knows You as Savior!"*

A Fifty-two Hour Drive from California to Pennsylvania!

As I shared this story, it made me think of many not so dramatic, but powerful stories concerning fasting. When my son Glenn was living with my mother and dad in San Diego, California, just after graduating from high school, I really wasn't happy that he was there. I felt he should be home and I wanted to tell him about the Baptism of the Holy Spirit!

I had just read Merlin Caruthers's book on *Praising the Lord* in all things. I prayed in obedience, "Lord, I thank you that Glenn is in California, and does not yet have the Baptism of the Holy Spirit!" I smiled at the seeming 'lunacy' of the prayer—being the very opposite of what I desired!

Shortly afterward, I felt led to enter into a 21-day liquid fast. I had no idea why. The Lord confirmed to me that this was of Him, so I was obedient!

On the 19th day of this fast, my son Glenn burst into my living room and cried: "Mom, what am I doing here?" I was overjoyed to see him and didn't respond to the question I didn't really understand.

He repeated, "Mom, what am I doing home? My buddy and I planned to stop at the Grand Canyon and become guides, or maybe go to Vegas and become dealers!" (Oh God, thank you, I had no idea he had such a thing in mind!) "We got into that car and drove 52 hours straight! We never stopped! What am I doing here?" I suddenly realized that this happening was the result of the fast!

Well, for the next few weeks, Glenn kept coming home after spending just a few hours with his friends. He wanted to bake cookies and spend time with his mother! Finally, the Lord spoke to me. "Just behave as though Glenn is any of the other teenagers that you have ministered with and lead him into the Baptism of the Holy Spirit!" Oh, I finally 'got it!'

I said, "Glennie, you are never sorry that you asked Jesus into your heart when you were a little boy, are you?"

"Gee no, Mom," was his reply.

"Well, the Lord has another gift for you and it is just as easy to receive as it was to be born again. The Lord wants to baptize you in the Holy Spirit."

I explained that this was an experience of the Holy Spirit coming down upon him and taking him into His Heart! I asked him if he wanted to receive this gift now. He said, "Yes."

I prayed with Glenn, lifted his hands unto the Lord—and began telling him about the 'Tongues.' He said, "Mom, we have done a lot tonight. Could you tell me about this later?" I went to bed and left him staring at his hands.

A week later, as I was taking the laundry to the basement, I passed him in the game room. He said to me, "Mom, you could never freeze to death could you?"

I went on to the washing machine with the clothes. Passing him on the way back upstairs, I said, "Glenn, what do you mean, I could never freeze to death?"

He replied, "Well Mom, suppose you were in Alaska and you were freezing, all you would have to do is put your hands up and pray and that heat would come into your hands and you couldn't freeze!"

I said, "Well, I guess you are right. Wait a minute, how do you know heat comes into my hands?"

He said, "Well Mom, ever since you prayed for me, something strange is happening to me. Every time a friend gets a headache or is in pain or something like that, heat comes into my hands about the size of a quarter right in the center of my palms, and I feel like praying for them."

I said, "Glennie, the Lord has given you the gift of healing. Come over here and lay those big hands on me." I had tension in my neck and was in pain. He laid those big warm hands on my shoulders and I felt the Heat of the Spirit, like warm oil radiate down through my neck and over my back! All of the pain and tension left! *I thank the Lord and attribute all of these things in large part to the act of Fasting unto the Lord!*

Chapter Thirteen

Visions—Remembered and Shared!

'Bon-Fires'

T he year was 2002. The month was August. I was attending the Annual International Missionary Ministers Forum in Dayton, Ohio, under the leadership of Rev. Doris Shwartz. Each was given an American flag and while a woman with a magnificent voice was leading in a song of patriotism and spiritual warfare we were waving them. During all of this, a vision began.

I saw a huge 'tepee' shaped bonfire composed of brown planks, or boards rather than logs. I believe that the Lord was showing that logs leave spaces between them, but these planks were standing firmly, tightly joined together in unity! Fiery flames were shooting out at the top! While singing together we were being filled with the Fire of the Spirit. Next, I saw behind us a huge map of the United States. We were in the middle of the map. I saw scattered in different areas smaller replicas of this larger one. I had the understanding that this represented other, smaller groups who would go forth *being 'Bonfires';* starting 'Revival Fires' in many areas of America!

Next I saw a huge Garrison Flag of the United States. Its pole was planted in the Eastern part of the map, and the wind was blowing the flag toward the West. My eyes filled up with tears as I sensed in my spirit that the tip of the flag had been dipped in the Blood of the Lamb! The joy that this caused came from the realization that this American flag being dipped in the Blood of Jesus' spoke either of forgiveness for the sin of the spilling of the innocent blood of aborted babies, or it meant that the *cessation of this crime would take place!*

This thought brought much joy to me. It reminded me of what had happened several years before. As I was attending a Christian Convention, I looked up at the American flag on the platform. I was startled to have the thought that the red stripes were as a river of 'innocent-baby-blood' flowing out across the land and *the flag seemed to be hanging in remorse and sadness and shame because of this condition!* Therefore, the joy came now, seeing our flag being cleansed!

Next in this vision I saw a huge Eagle, with its wings spread out across America from East to West. It was as though The Mighty Eagle God, who had led the Israelites out of bondage so long ago on Eagle's Wings, was declaring through this vision that He would do the same for America!

Then I was told to write this vision—as well as others! Before this—when I heard or read the Scripture I had thought, not of putting down the contents of a vision—a picture or thought, given in our spirits—but rather I thought of a vision as a concept or plan of ministry given to one to share and act upon for the benefit of others as in: Habakkuk 2:2–3, "Then the LORD answered me and said: "Write the vision and make it plain on tablets, that he may run who reads it. For the vision is yet for an appointed time; But at the end it will speak, and it will not lie. Though it tarries, wait for it; because it will surely come, it will not tarry." NKJV As I re-read this Scripture just now, it thrilled me to remember that all through the years of waiting, I have been encouraged by the truth that God will fulfill what He has promised, if we will but wait and trust and believe for the vision to be fulfilled. I am still waiting and believing Lord, for the bringing forth of this book—into all the world

'My first Vision: I Saw Him!'

This took place when I was 12 years old! I had been invited to go to Salvation Army meetings to be involved with the crafts program as a 'Sunbeam.' Always enjoying crafts and not wanting to be rude in refusing the invitation, I went. The family who invited me, having nine children had just moved into our neighborhood and I overheard my schoolmates laughing and teasing, calling them the 'poor kids'. I thought this was mean-spirited and ugly, so when one of the children invited me to go with them to their Church, I just couldn't refuse. I am eternally grateful that the Holy Spirit 'set me up', resulting in His turning evil into good! After a few meetings, we were told that *this* evening we were going to have a party, but first we were to go up to the Chapel and hear stories about Jesus.

Growing up in a Methodist Church, always sitting next to my Grand pap Jacob, I knew I enjoyed hearing about Jesus, so I gladly went to the Chapel. I had attended Church regularly since about the age of six, but I had never been told that I could or should be 'Born Again!' This fact never before, to my knowledge, had entered the sermons, nor delightful children's stories that I had heard! But this night, I heard for the first time in my short life that Jesus Christ was standing at my heart's door knocking, and if I would believe in my heart that Jesus Christ was Lord, and would open my heart and ask Him to forgive me my sins, and come into my life, He would come in, and I would be 'Born Again!'

I remember that just as soon as I heard and understood this, I couldn't wait to *run to the altar* and ask Jesus into my heart! I kept thinking, "Oh, I wish the Chaplin would hurry up and finish so that I can invite Jesus into my heart!" Finally, the sermon was over and we were invited to come to the altar and pray. I remember that *I ran to the altar*, dropped to my knees, bowed my head, shut my eyes, and asked Jesus to come into my heart!

Suddenly, I saw Jesus! He was standing above me, on the platform just above the altar! He had on a beautiful white robe and He was standing with His Arms outstretched toward me! He had the most beautiful smile on His face! He was so handsome! Those who speak of His lack of beauty—no form or comeliness—found in the 2nd verse of the 53rd Chapter of Isaiah are seeing his appearance while hanging beaten and battered on the cross. My heart filled up with joy! But then my mind began to question. "How can I see Him, I have my eyes shut, and my head is bowed down?" I knew nothing about visions!

While bathing in the 'light' of this vision, my joy was interrupted as some-one knelt down beside me, put her hand on my shoulder and said, "Now honey, people are going to spit on you and call you dirty names and throw stones at you, but you must bear all, for you are now a Christian!" This woman scared the 'be-jabbers' out of me with her verbal 'word-picture'! I could see in my minds eye people rejecting me and throwing stones and spitting at me! I ran from that place, never to return! But thank God, I always carried in my heart and memory that wonderful vision of Jesus! Every time I heard His name or mention of Him, I had the warm glow return to my heart. I didn't know that this was the confirmation of the Holy Spirit, bearing witness with the truth that Jesus was in my heart!

I also heard Kathryn say many times during these formative years, "If you are 'Born Again,' you will *know it!*" Because of this statement that she often repeated I believe that she must have been one of those who received the Baptism of the Holy Spirit, at the same time that she was born again. I thought that this meant that your life would change so dramatically that you wouldn't fail to know of it! My life seemed to be the same. *I somehow thought that because I didn't 'know it,' that this meant that I was not born again.* Of course, I was a baby Christian needing growth, spiritual food and water before such changes could be seen. And so, I who had been given a glorious vision of Jesus the very day I asked Him into my heart, was in confusion! I asked Him in over and over and still didn't *'know it'!*

It is very sad that someone did not tell me, as I later learned by reading Billy Graham's book 'Peace with God' that if I had asked Jesus into my heart, I should rely on His Word alone that He had in fact come into my heart, according to Revelation 3:20, "Behold, I stand at the door and knock; and if anyone hears My voice and opens the door, I *will* come in to him and will dine with him, and he with Me." (NAS) That means right now.

Rather, I was taught to rely on the fruit in my own life as being assurance of whether I was born again or not! Jesus didn't add any requirements, He said, *"IF you invite me in, I will come in." Not maybe, or might, or sometime later if you go to Church regularly or when you get yourself all cleaned up!* We can't get 'all cleaned up' without having Christ in us first! Oh, if only I had had that assurance, according to the Word of God taught to me, the very day I asked Him in. I could have avoided years of confusion that led to wrong choices!

'My second vision—before the Baptism—was the opposite of the first!'

Because I didn't have a clear understanding of what it meant to be born again. I thought it meant that something would happen to make me instantly sinless, without anymore temptations. I didn't realize that Jesus was tempted and that the temptation isn't sin! Rather, the *yielding to temptation* is the sin. *I didn't know this and expected that if I were really born again, I would no longer be subject to temptation.* After asking Jesus into my heart and still finding my self subject to temptation and yielding to it, I finally hit upon a plan! I had just asked Jesus into my heart for the 'hundredth' time while watching an Evangelist on television. Almost immediately I went to the kitchen to open a beer. With my hand on the bottle cap, I 'looked at my action' and said to self: "Look at you; just because Jesus didn't come into your heart, you are going to open this beer and probably get 'loaded'!" I thought: "I know what I'll do to get born again! I will do everything I can, to get as good as I can, and then Jesus will save me!"

So for the next *three years,* I went to Church every Sunday. I stopped smoking and drinking and I tithed of all of my finances. After three years of this regimen of self 'won't power', I still *wanted to* drink and smoke and do other things that I was tempted to do! I decided that Jesus just didn't want to save me, and I didn't blame Him. I just thought that I was a hopeless case. And then I reasoned that since I knew Jesus tells us in the Bible that if we think a thing in our hearts, we are guilty of them, I might just as well do what I was tempted to do! Such bad 'self-advice', but that's what my hopelessness led me into thinking—and doing!

I immediately began drinking—which I am told 'numbs' the frontal lobes of our brain—the place of our moral restraint. I got inebriated, and began to do what I had been tempted to do which I am not going to reveal. Just place here any of the things that you know are wrong, or have been your own areas of temptation and you probably won't be far off the mark. Sin in any area—is sin!

For the next ten months, I yielded to all that I had been tempted to do. I became numb. As alcohol numbs the frontal lobes, sin numbs them also so that I began to have no 'qualms', no misgivings concerning the sins that I had, not fallen, but walked into! This surprised me, but released me from any convictions concerning my sins. I was completely 'clueless' that my 'step by step' 'ignoring' of the Holy Spirit's convicting voice, had stilled that 'Precious Policeman' of my soul. I had 'seared' my conscience as with a hot iron! I can never stop thanking God for what came next for, thankfully, came the vision!

I had just made plans on the telephone that would have changed my entire destiny. After the phone call, I went home, lay on the couch, placed my hands behind my head and began to rejoice about how happy I was going to be with my new preparations. Suddenly, on the wall before me, I saw just the head, with a face of the ugliest, most horrifying features I had ever seen, or one could ever imagine! The features were bloated, as one would look who spent their time in debauchery and depravity! This evil apparition had upon the side of his forehead a deep scar that looked as though he had fallen into a fire. I thought at the time that this must be Satan and that he had somehow been burned in his own fire. I learned later that this was a spirit of 'seared conscience'!

As I stared at this ghoul, I heard him say with a sneer in his expression and wicked glee in his voice: "Now I've got you!" This literally scared the hell out of me! My phone-call plans were completely 'scrapped' and I ran back to God as fast as I could go! Within weeks I was restored in the following manner.

My son, who is now 53, but was then 7 years old, had just seen the story of David and Bathsheba on television. He came into my room and asked me to read him the story from the Bible. After the story, he placed the Bible on my lap, kissed me goodnight and went to bed.

The Bible was opened to I Corinthians 6:9–11, "Don't you know that those who do wrong will have no share in the kingdom of God? Don't fool yourselves. Those who indulge in sexual sin, who are idol worshipers, adulterers, male prostitutes, homosexuals, thieves, greedy people, drunkards, abusers, and swindlers—none of these will have a share in the Kingdom of God. There was a time when some of you were just like that, but now your sins have been washed away, and you have been set apart for God. You have been made right with God because of what the Lord Jesus Christ and the Spirit of our God have done for you." (NLT)

God came to my rescue as I dropped to knees beside my bed and prayed. I said: "Oh Lord, I am not cleansed, I am in that list! And for the first time in my life I am going to give you the *most cowardly prayer ever,* but I have to pray it!" (While I was growing up my mother had always said: "Never say you can't girl, always say you'll try, you'll win the battle, surely by and by." Therefore I was always under the impression that I had to do the best I could before I gave the rest to God. Such was the sorry understanding of God I had.) I prayed my 'cowardly prayer': "God, I *can't* change myself. If You don't change me, I am never going to be changed!"

From the left corner of the room, I didn't see the Lord, but I heard Him give a *great sigh of relief,* as I heard Him say: *"Do you finally see it!"* "See what" was my response! I didn't know what the Lord was expressing, but I was *filled* with *a great sense of peace.* And within the week, God showed me the truth concerning being born again and taught me to say 'Specific Prayers' which I had never known to pray before this time!

Well, finally at age 29, I did have that assurance and life has been so livable knowing that according to His Word, I am His, He is in me! Thereby, I declared—rather I shouted and clapped my hands and danced around my little kitchen shouting: "I am a Christian—I am a Christian" and as I did that, joy just flooded into my heart! I finally realized that the confession of faith is not: "I am a Christian"—but rather—"Jesus Christ is Lord!" I had been making that profession always; though at that time *I was a baby carnal Christian,* not knowing who I was! I have learned to lean on Him in a whole new way that seemed not possible when I thought of Jesus as outside of me or only beside me or with me.

I have prayed and asked the Lord if I might just write of visions, and not share of this experience as I just have, but it seems that the Lord would have me include this portion of my life. (I added this about that evil vision especially, for I shared this with someone just yesterday and it really made him sit up and take notice—so that I was able to then have his captured attention turn on to his need for deliverance and salvation! Also as I have written, I realized that this *was* my second—life-saving vision!) God loves to turn evil into good! Thank You Holy Spirit, 'Hound of Heaven' for leading me into this 'Life-saving deliverance'!

Word of Knowledge Visions!

During my teenage years, I often had what I now know were brief different sorts of visions that were part of what is known as the Word of Knowledge. I would see a scene in my spirit and just know what was going to take place in the next few minutes of time, and it always took place exactly as I had 'seen' it!

The most important vision in my life, is the one of Jesus that I have just told you of. This was the *most important happening of my entire life, my spiritual birth! The second* most important happening of my life, was the illumination of my spirit by the Baptism of the Holy Spirit and those visions that helped me to understand what prayer in the Spirit is all about! Marriage and the birth of our four children are the third most important happenings in my life! Birth, how important birth is to Our Heavenly Father! I suppose the birth of His only Begotten Son has been one of the most important happenings to God, *and then, secondly,* all *who have become His children by their re-birth experience in Christ—our Wonderful Redeemer!*

The Birth of a Song of Visions!

This 'Song concerning Visions' came to me in the morning as I was Worshipping God in the Spirit with a Song in Tongues. I was just playing my autoharp wanting to 'Feed Him a Little Cake' of morning adoration and praise to begin the day in the one of the 'best ways' I know of, that a day can begin. As I sang, I was encouraged once more to write the Visions! These words encourage us to look! That is the Essence of Vision, to have the *desire to 'see'* and then to ask Jesus, or the Holy Spirit, or our Father in Heaven—to give us these Supernatural Visions. And we can understand from the words of this song, that it is pleasing to our Lord that we 'look, and desire and ask in order that we receive!

I want to encourage you just now by telling you how Ruth Heflin began to 'see' in vision. Her friend, when first saved, had wonderful visions of the Book of Ezekiel which helped her to understand Scripture. Because of this, she kept encouraging Ruth to seek for visions. Ruth continually responded by saying, "The Lord has given me so much, including the bringing forth of the Prophetic Word, I don't think I need to have visions."

Her friend said to her, "But Ruth, don't you see 'pictures' in the Spirit as you are prophesying?" Ruth realized that she did, indeed see 'pictures' and took the matter to the Lord in prayer. The Holy Spirit led her to begin to 'seek' to have visions. She did so, and when last I heard Ruth preach in Israel, she was encouraging us to seek for Visions also. Just before the Lord took her home— she shared that *she was 'seeing' the Lord Jesus in vision every day!* I wanted to give you her Testimony that you would more readily be encouraged to receive and understand the Song the Lord gave me which speaks of–seeking and receiving vision!

'Visions of God'—a 'New Song'!

Visions, the visions of God are given, for the benefit of man.
Visions of God are given, to unfold His Heavenly Plans.

Visions of God are given, for the hearts that long for more!
Visions of God are given, to show the entrance to the 'Door'
The 'Door' of the Heavenly Home, the place where the saints abide,
Visions of God, are calling, on the 'Wings of the Eagle' to ride.
To see the Heavenly Home, the wondrous home of the Bride!
Visions of God will show you, the streets that are golden and wide!
See the place of eternal bliss, O Loved one don't chance that you'll miss
The Palaces above, 'Mansions of Glory' filled with His love.
Visions of God will show you, the Palaces filled with such peace,
The Abodes of those abiding in Jesus, the Carpenter has promised us these!
Open your eyes to the visions, of the things that this world cannot see.
They are open with clarity of vision, come look now, for that is His plea!

For Clarity

As I speak to you of visions, I remember that when I have been involved in meetings with those who worship and know to sing in the Spirit, with minds stayed on the Lord—these are the times when we find ourselves having many visions that speak to us as a group! In fact, in our meetings in the 'House of Prayer'—in Israel—there was always a time given at some point in the meetings to encourage all of those who have had visions or a 'Word from the Lord' to share them with everyone in the meeting. What joyous times we have had in the sharing. The Holy Spirit guides us and over and over we realize a message coming forth through the sharing in which we realize new love for one another and a deeper appreciation for the leadings of our Lord into the waters of revelation that bring joy, and a better understanding of the issues that we then need to pray about.

Sending up the 'Jew-Els'!

I have been praying and asking the Lord to remind me of the visions He would have me write about. I remember now that during the daily morning gathering in the 'Ark' of the End-Time Handmaidens in Jasper, Arkansas, I saw in spirit, that while we were singing in Worship using the Unknown Tongues, the Words were coming out of our mouths as many-colored jewels and were going up to heaven where they were being woven into our Eternal Garments! (These were the Jewels, of the Jew-El, Jesus, our Lord and our God!)

A Vision in Church during Worship…"Shush!"

As our Church Choir began to sing, the beautiful anointing that God has blessed them with was present. I closed my eyes in Worship and suddenly I 'saw' the heavens opened and Jesus standing there in an attitude of listening. I then realized that a huge crowd was gathered behind Him and they too were listening! Knowing that I was having a wonderful vision and would shortly share it with the congregation for their benefit, I said within, "Lord, is there more?"

To my surprise and great delight He whispered: "Shhh…we are listening!" I shared this when the choir was finished singing. Vickie, our Choir Director, went 'ballistic' with JOY! This is just one of the beautiful benefits of seeing and sharing visions!

'The 'Fist' of God'!

My sister Carly was several months pregnant with her only daughter, Reba. While taking a walk around the Calvary Pentecostal Church in Richmond Virginia, she stepped around a corner unfamiliar to her. Suddenly, three large black dogs, Doberman Pinchers, began to snarl and run toward her menacingly. Not knowing how or where to escape, she cried out: "Jesus!" She was amazed to immediately have a vision! She says that it was like a panoramic movie! She saw a gloved fist, (like a cowboy's hand) and in it was three leather straps that were extended around the dogs' necks, holding them back! The fist then took the dogs and turned them into the opposite direction and Carly continued her walk, while thankfully praising the Lord for this 'provision vision'!

A 'New Day' for Haiti!

Recently I received a call from my friend Gerry Yusko. She had just come across some notes she had taken concerning a trip to Haiti in November of 1999. Dianne Clark, Lillian Righi, Betty Peace, Beverly Ramer, Gerry Yusko and I, had gone to Haiti to Minister with 'GLOW' (*God's Love for Orphans and Widows)*, a newly established ministry under the direction of Rev. Betty Snyder. She and her husband had ministered for years in Haiti in the 'Mission Possible' Ministry.

After coming upon her notes, Gerry heard many times in the recent news, the slogan being repeated by the Haitians: "A New Day for Haiti!" She reminded me of a vision I had just before and during that trip which included those very words! Let us pray for the fulfillment of that vision!

The Sunday before our trip, while in church, Betty and I were being sent forth with prayer by our Pastor. Hands were laid on us, and I was slain in the Spirit. While I was lying in the Spirit, I spoke aloud the Words given me, "A New Day for Haiti!"

As soon as these words were spoken, a vision began of four men, who though they had no wings, seemed to be angels. I saw only the back of their head and shoulders. They were robed in white garments similar to choir robes. With arms extended forward, each had a long silver trumpet in his hands, but the trumpets were not being blown.

Later, in the community of Grand Godi, in Haiti, during a gathering outside of the new, unfinished church built by the 'Glow' Ministry, our group was praying.

Together, we were redeeming the land from the bloodshed and violence and voodoo done there in times past. We did this through taking communion, and sowing into the land portions of the communion elements, as taught us by Gwen Shaw, the founder of End-Times Handmaidens. (One can read of this tremendous area of Ministry in her booklet: "Redeeming the Land" $5.00 Box 447 Jasper, Arkansas 72641)

Just as we were finished ministering and the prayer ended, Lillian, who had *not known* of my exclamation the preceding Sunday shouted with a loud voice, "A New Day for Haiti!" The moment this remark came out of her mouth, the vision of those four with the silver trumpets began once more, but now they were blowing their trumpets!

This was the first and only time that I ever had a progressive vision! That is, as we left the spot where we were praying, entered a bus and were returning to the ministry of 'G.L.O.W.,' I kept seeing those angels continuing to blow their trumpets while we were traveling down the road.

Then the vision changed and I saw on the right side of the bus, in the sky, a choir of women singing 'Hallelujahs' and then on our left side, across from this choir, a chorus of men were singing the same. Suddenly, in front of the bus I saw Jesus! He was so large, He filled the sky and I saw Him wrap His arms around the map of Haiti and draw it and the Haitians to His Heart. There He was, hugging the map of Haiti to Himself, and I saw Haitians gathered together against His Breast, along with the map! This loving picture ended the vision!

Later, we went to Port Au Prince to see and pray for the White House, the Presidential Government Building of Haiti. We were unable to get beyond the high gate surrounding the Palace.

As we, just six little lady believers from America, were standing outside of the gate praying, a feeling of inadequacy and smallness came to me. Just as I felt this inability, I was startled to see in vision, once more, the four angels! They were standing now, inside the gates, on the grounds, blowing those trumpets toward the Palace! As we left the scene, I had the sense they stayed on there a-blowing!

All of this took place in November of 1999. The Word says Hab. 2:3, "Though the vision tarries, wait for it, for it shall surely come to pass!" I understand that concerning some personal visions, they must be held on to and believed for in order that they come to pass, but this vision and the beginning of its fulfillment teaches me that, concerning visions that are prophecy given of God, they *must eventually* come to pass! The Holy Spirit is teaching us, line upon line, and precept upon precept. I am so happy also to hear of the wonderful ministry being done there by the Trinity Broadcasting Network!

When I called Gerry and read this portion to her, she was reminded of a terrible situation that had been taking place on the property just adjacent to the Church of Grand God when we were there. An old man lived in a shack there and he spent his time trying to cast spells, promoting 'cock-fighting,' and being and doing many things of which a follower of Satan is capable. Shortly after our ministry of redeeming that land, the shack was torn down and that old fellow was never heard of again! I hope Salvation became a part of his life! Thank You, Holy Spirit

Gerry's Three Visions!

While Gerry and I were remembering and sharing, I thought of the three visions that she had previously shared with me. I asked her to repeat them. As she began, the Lord had me quickly write them down. I share them now as they have elements of teaching and then they show expressions of the love and tenderness of our God!

The Pain of Baby Matthew's Home-going…Comforted.

The first vision: On Thursday, Gerry had just buried her little thirteen month old son Matthew. Just now, two days later, it was Saturday, and the next day was Easter Sunday. She knew that once more there would be the baptism of infants at the church she attended. She wanted to go to church but was fearful that as she saw other infants baptized, the memory of the baptism of Matthew just the year before would be too painful for her to bear.

She knew Matthew was with the Lord, but didn't know how to handle this burden in her heart. She knelt beside her couch and prayed simply, "Lord, I'd like to go to church tomorrow, but the babies are being baptized and I don't know if I can bear it."

Suddenly, a vision began. She saw Jesus standing in front of the pulpit in her church. He was wearing a beautiful white robe and His Hands were out-stretched toward her. He spoke in a very calm voice: "My Peace be unto you!" This took away the fear and as she went to church the next day, the memory of her Lord's Words and the vision sustained and comforted her. She didn't see Matthew in the other babies as they were baptized, but rather as just babies, and from that day onward, she never had pain when she saw other babies. Truly, Jesus' Words are Spirit and Life. He had given her His Peace through a vision! (I have just completed putting together Gerry's Booklet called 'Matthew' 'God's Gift'. It is available if you write me. It is such a tender story of God's Love and Care at this painful time of baby Matthew's Home-going!)

The Lurking spirit is overcome by the Blood of the Lamb!

The second vision had to do with Gerry's husband Joe. He came home from work one day and startled her with his words: "I'm not going to live to see my first grandson!"

Their daughter-in-law was six months pregnant. Joe's father had died before his first grandchild was born and Joe felt this was his destiny also. At first, Gerry was busy about her day and just pushed his words aside, with the remark, "Oh Joe, that's crazy!" She was not taking him seriously. Joe became quiet, but later he wanted to get out the Insurance papers as he truly felt he wasn't going to live. As Joe persisted in this statement, Gerry realized his earnestness and fear.

Later when she went to bed, remembering Joe's words, she prayed and spoke her faith that Joe would not be taken in death before his time. She sensed that she was to begin to plead the blood of the Lamb over him. As she repeated this over and over a vision began.

She was looking into a long dark hallway. Suddenly she saw a sinister look-ing figure appear. He wore a long topcoat with a hat pulled down over his face. He reminded her of an evil character in a detective story. This figure was lurking near a door. He was waiting, and then he would slowly walk down the hall, but again and again he would return and was waiting, lurking at the door. Gerry once again pleaded the Blood of the Lamb Jesus, and suddenly the figure disappeared. Upon awaking the next day, Joe felt his old self once again and had no more fear of an early death.

This happened twenty-five years ago, as that is the age of his first grand-son, Michael! Gerry was thankful for this vision, as it made her realize that the feeling that Joe had was real, and that the *figure in the vision was death* and his intention was to take Joe's life before his time! The evil one had planted a lie in Joe's mind and was trying to receive an evil harvest. Thank God for the Blood of the Lamb, the knowledge to apply it, and *the wonderful communication of Visions!*

'Behold He Comes!'

The third vision that Gerry had was a wonderful blessed one, again, of Jesus. She saw Jesus standing upon a cloud and thought of the song, "Days of Elijah" and the line of the song, "Behold He Comes, Riding on a Cloud!" It was as though He was just standing on a shining cloud and as it moved, the Lord Jesus just glided with it!

This made her think of the Scripture found in Revelation 1:7, "Behold He cometh with clouds; and every eye shall see Him, and they also which pierced Him; and all kindred's of the earth shall wail because of Him. Even so, come quickly Lord Jesus. Amen." Did this vision speak to Gerry that He would come in her lifetime?

I feel to end this portion with the Words of the next verse: Revelation 1:8, "I Am Alpha and Omega, the beginning and the ending, says the Lord, which is, and which was, and which is to come, the Almighty!"

'A Vision of the Cross'!

Years ago, I read a story in the Guidepost Magazine concerning Grace Armstrong, a young girl who was dying of tuberculosis. Her family took her to Florida, literally to be able to die in a warm climate. As Grace sat in a little Methodist Church in Florida, she sighed within: "Lord, if only I knew that you really existed, I wouldn't mind dying." Suddenly on the bare cross above the altar, she had a vision of Jesus hanging there in agony. His head was bent down, and as she stared transfixed, Jesus lifted His Head and looked straight into her eyes! Her body was completely healed in that instant! This story had a wonderful ending and I never forgot it.

Years later, in 1973 on my second trip to Israel, every place I went, I kept seeing the Catholic Crucifix, the replica of the cross with Christ hanging on it. Not being a Catholic I questioned the Lord about this. I wondered why I was seeing this special cross seemingly everywhere I looked! I received no immediate answer

A few weeks later while sitting in the South Hills Assembly of God Church, here in Pittsburgh, I looked up at the bare cross hanging above the altar, and once more remembered the constancy of my seeing the Crucifix while in Israel. I asked the Lord about this once more, and was reminded of the story of Grace Armstrong. I thought of her vision of Christ and the complete instant healing given her when He looked into her eyes.

Suddenly it occurred to me that seeing and meditating upon a Crucifix certainly does not put Christ physically once more upon a cross…Our Glorified Savior is in Heaven at the Right Hand our Father. But, seeing Him there in my mind's eye; remembering His agony, borne gladly, for our sakes, does a work in my heart that can be done in no other way! This has become for me His Way of strengthening my heart to do His Will…whatever that will may be! I know that the Hebrew word for looking, is 'gazing intently' when it speaks of the serpent being lifted up in the Wilderness on the brass pole when the Israelites sinned and needed healing and received such when 'gazing intently' upon that which was a symbol of our Christ's Suffering in taking every vile sin upon Himself in our place. I can never sing that song with a casual quick beat…"If I be lifted up I will call all men unto Me." I know this speaks of our Lord's Crucifixion!

This song from my collection of songs called: 'Living Waters Flow: Doxology of Praise' came to me as I was worshipping the Lord. It shows what I meditate upon as I receive the Sacrament of Communion. It is a song that is to be sung just before a melody God gave me for Isaiah Chapter 53, which gives us graphic descriptions of our Lord's Passion on the Cross of Calvary.

'Verbal Visions'—that is, Songs given during Worship—to the '*inner*-eye and ear gates'!

'Come to the Shepherd'

Come to the Fountain crystal clear, drawn from Immanuel's Side.
Water and Blood flowing mingled down, Food and Drink for His Bride!
Come now oh come His little ones, see from this viewpoint His Side.
See Him feed His little Lambs, this Son who is His Father's Joy and Pride!
Eat and drink this Special Food, Pure undiluted, satisfying.
You will be nourished at His Side, come now rejoice His Blessed Bride.
Come to the Shepherd, the Savior of Mankind!

And this is the song the Lord gave me concerning the Crucifixion of Christ, our Passover Lamb;

'O Lamb of God'

O Lamb of God, Perfect Lamb of God, wounded, bruised for my redemption.
Broken, battered bore the pain, for my rebellion, for my iniquity,
Spent His Blood upon that tree, purchased eternal life for me.
He saw my helplessness, He said: "Father, I will go,

Take her sins upon Me, that our love she may know."
O Glory, glory Precious Savior, cared enough to die for me,
Suffered agony for you and me…Spent His Blood upon that tree!
Praise His Name! Forever praise His NAME!
Thank You, Lord, for visions and the direction to write of them; may they be a blessing to all!

Chapter Fourteen

Spotlight on the Royal House
of the Lion of Judah!

S uch an unheard of thing, that God, who created the universe, would become flesh and tabernacle among men through His only begotten Son. And then that He would allow that Son to take our sin upon Himself and die in our place that we might have access to His Father and life eternal. And then that this wonderful God would send His Spirit to council and comfort and dwell within us? These facts are almost beyond our understanding! But that is just what Father God did in answer to His Son's prayer in John 17:17, "Sanctify them through thy truth, thy Word is Truth." (KJV)

For those of us who have received Jesus Christ as Savior—God has sent His Spirit into us, birthing us in the Spirit that we might be Children of God. God the Father sent His Spirit *upon* us who have been baptized in His Spirit that we might be set apart unto Him! He poured the Holy Oil upon us that we might be anointed—as members of a chosen people, a royal priesthood, a Holy nation of kings and priests unto God Himself. We are Living Stones, being built up into a Spiritual House. I Peter 2:9–10 says, "But ye are a chosen generation, a royal priesthood, an holy nation, a peculiar people; that ye should show forth the praises of him who has called you out of darkness into his marvelous light; Which in time past were not a people, but are now the people of God: which had not obtained mercy, but now have obtained mercy."

Rev. 1:6, "And has made us kings and priests unto God and his Father; to him be glory and dominion for ever and ever. Amen." I Peter 2:5, "Ye also, as lively stones, are built up a spiritual house, an holy priesthood, to offer up spiritual sacrifices, acceptable to God by Jesus Christ."

We are Living Stones, being built up into a Spiritual House.

He gave us the Heavenly Fire with which to offer up the Spiritual sacrifices that is the fruit of our lips giving praise to His Name, Hebrews 13:15, "By him therefore let us offer the sacrifice of praise to God continually, that is, the fruit of our lips giving thanks to *his name.*" (KJV)

When I ask the question, "Lord, what is the 'fruit of our lips'?"

He answered: Isaiah 57:19, "I create the fruit of the lips; Peace, peace, to him that is far off and to him who is near," says the Lord, "And I will heal him." He creates the words, puts them in our mouth, and gives the interpretation of them. These words are part of the vehicle for bringing Christ the remedy, through His Holy Spirit, into any situation.

These words of Isaiah are repeated in Ephesians 2:17, "He came and preached peace to those who were far away and peace to those who were near." (NKJV) Hebrews 3:6, "But Christ was faithful as a Son over His House, who's House we are, if we hold fast our confidence and boast of our hope firm until the end." We, with Christ in us are of the House of Judah! We have received the Jewish Messiah, Christ the Anointed One of God, and have become Spiritual Jews. Romans 2:28–29 says, "For he is not a Jew who is one outwardly; neither is circumcision that which is outward in the flesh. But he is a Jew who is one inwardly; and circumcision is that which is of the heart, by the Spirit, not by the letter; and his praise is not from men, but from God."

We see in the Old Testament that the only people permitted to have the Holy Spirit come upon them for service as Priest and Prophet and King were those of the seed of Abraham, the friend of God who had made covenant with Him. One had to be a member of the twelve Tribes. This is still a pre-requisite. Thank God that we can be a Tribal member through our Lord and Savior Jesus Christ, Jeshua Ha Mashiach—Jesus the Messiah, the Anointed One! He was a Jew born in Bethlehem of the tribe of Judah. Shockingly, many do not seem to realize that Jesus was and *is* a Jew!

Hebrews 7:14 says, "Our Lord descended from Judah. He is called the Lion of the Tribe of Judah." Hebrews 7:17 reads, "He is called a Priest forever after the order of Melchizedek." This is part of His more excellent Ministry. Hebrews 8:6 says, "But now hath he obtained a more excellent ministry, by how much also he is the mediator of a better covenant, which was established upon better promises."

We, who are priests in the house of God, are to offer up Spiritual Sacrifices by *Fire*. For this service the heavenly Fire–Tongues - was given foremost!

Offerings unto our God—made by Fire—are not now made by Priests of Judaism!

But as Priests unto God—we can and are shown that we may or should do so!
The book of Leviticus is the book that Moses wrote to teach the Levites the commands of the Lord and how to specifically follow them. In the 23rd Chapter, when giving the particulars of the set, or appointed Feasts of the Lord, it is stated *over and over* that the *priests* were to *make an offering unto the Lord by*

fire! If in no other way *we might draw the Jew through jealousy,* as we are told to do, by performing this priestly obligation! We are now privileged to do this, if we ourselves truly understood this mystery and would be obedient to perform it, it could have marvelous results perhaps leading to the sooner fulfilling of the eleventh Chapter of Paul's letter to the Romans!

Since 70 A.D. these offerings by Fire—have been unable to be made by the Priests of Judaism! But—since 33 A.D.—when the veil of the Temple was destroyed—those who know and love Jesus and have Him residing within— have the privilege of going boldly into the Holy of Holies through the veil of His torn flesh as recorded in Hebrews 10:19–20, "Therefore, brethren, since we have full freedom and confidence to enter into the [Holy of] Holies [by the power and virtue] in the blood of Jesus. By this fresh (new) and living way which He initiated and dedicated and opened for us through the separating curtain [veil of the Holy of Holies], that is, through His flesh…" TAB We are privileged—therein—to offer up our sacrifices by the Fire of the Holy Spirit— the Tongues of Fire given in the Baptism. All of this has been explained in the Chapter on the vision of the Song in the Spirit! See Chapter Three: The Revelation! The Vision of Worship and Song in the Spirit!

We need to learn not only how to minister as priests on behalf of others, but also how to function in this office unto the Most High God! For this marvelous privilege, the Tongue Language and prayer and song in the Spirit are the chief elements, akin to the Incense offered by fire in the Holy of Holies by Aaron.

Understanding our 'Jewish-ness' because of our position in the Body of the Lion of the Tribe of Judah, Christ, our Great High Priest, gives us a new healthy respect for the whole of the Bible. We begin to see that this Book deals with *our* history. That the Old Testament, written by and for the Jewish people in the Hebrew language deals with *our* ancestry, we become 'kin' to the prophets and poets, the builders, the heroes and heroines.

As well, we see the villains and cowards. We begin to understand our weaknesses and strengths and how to better deal with them as we study this history of the root into which we have been grafted. We begin to assimilate the Psalms and Proverbs of Jewish writers into our own lives and it is well that we do so, for this is part of the purpose for which the Sacred Book was written.

The reading of these two thirds of the Bible gives us a better understanding of the other third, the New Testament, the Covenant which our Lord cut through His Blood. Mark 14:24 says, *"This is my blood of the covenant,"* and Luke 22:20 reads, *"This cup is the New Covenant in my blood which is poured out for you."* This New Testament was written almost completely by Jews who had been nurtured on the Old Testament and then had received this Jewish Messiah,

Christ Jesus, as Lord. It is called in Hebrew: 'Ha Brit Ha Da'shah' The Cutting in Blood, of the New Covenant; it was inaugurated by our Savior in His Body on the Cross!

Zachariah chapter 12 and the eleventh chapter of Romans assures us that the *whole House of Israel* will one day be born again into the House of Judah and become spiritual as well as physical Jews. Remembering the words of Peter and our Lord in the New Testament concerning our priesthood helps us to see the importance of researching the instructions and patterns given to Moses in the Mount concerning priestly duties and obligations. Not that we should in any way go back into rules and regulations that were *the shadow of the good things to come,* but rather that we should study the pattern to further learn how to minister thereby in the Spirit.

Studying the Song of Solomon helps us to begin to understand our Ministry unto the Lord as the Bride of Christ. Of the Shulumite, He gathers His Myrrh with His spices, eats His honeycomb with His honey, and then invites His friends to drink abundantly. Song of Solomon 5: 1, Young Man: *"I am here in my garden, my treasure, my bride! I gather my myrrh with my spices and eat my honeycomb with my honey. I drink my wine with my milk." Young Women of Jerusalem: "Oh, lover and beloved eat and drink! Yes, drink deeply of this love!"* (NLT)

Our Lord Jesus said that He was sending the Holy Spirit to be our Teacher as well as our Comforter and Guide. We know that there is not any jealousy in the Godhead. The Father and the Son and the Spirit are One. They are co-equal. We know that throughout the whole of the Bible we see the several different administrations of each. The Spirit brooded over the waters and brought forth. The Father gave His Only Begotten Son. Jesus the Son of God gave His Life a ransom for many. As we explore those things that are specifically of the Holy Spirit as recorded in the New Testament, we further learn from this Teacher sent by our Heavenly Father. Hopefully we will begin to understand more about the Language of Tongues—that were sent along with the Teacher—the Spirit of the Living God of Israel. "Holy Spirit, guide us."

The Gifts of the Spirit that have been given in the Baptism of the Holy Spirit are to be used in our ministry as Kings. As we look into the scriptures concerning the different offices, it helps us to better understand these offices and how better we may serve in them. Hopefully, we will begin to see the necessity of stirring up these 'Hot Coals' of Ministry by using the Tongue of Fire, given in part for that purpose.

Right here I feel is the absolute placing of the writing I did just last evening and this morning concerning the entire Chapter of Isaiah 53 and the Scriptures that speak of its partial fulfillment in the New Testament.

The one time no words came to me, I had a melody running through my spirit for two weeks and finally I said: "But Lord, You haven't given me any words!" He said: "Isaiah 53". Oh, it is so beautiful, the entire Chapter, written to be sung in a minor chord, and Alice Twitchell sketched the drawing of a bare branch sticking out of the ground with a crown of thorns hovering over it with blood dripping from the thorns of the crown! It is so powerful!

Last night I felt the absolute leading to write the Isaiah 53 Chapter from my New International Version of the Bible just before going to bed. Hmmm… very strange!

This morning as I awakened I wanted to re-write it from my New King James Version. Instead, I saw my Amplified Bible sitting on my table and as I read from this version, I was struck with the *powerful witness* of the *New Testament scriptures included* that showed the *fulfillment of the* Old Testament Scriptures! I must now re-write the entire portion, with those scriptures added. Because of length requirements and therefore brevity, I must just replace another chapter of my book for I realize that Isaiah 53 is the most wonderful Chapter of the Bible telling of our Lord Jesus Christ's Crucifixion, and since my book pleading with Ishmael to return to the God of his Father Abraham also speaks to Isaac with that same desire, and is included in this publication, 'Isaiah 53' must now be included from the Amplified Bible!

Thank You Holy Spirit; this will probably be the most important portion of my entire library of booklets! Also, because I could not fit my Essays on 'The Fear of the Lord' and 'The Wrath of God' into this book, 'Isaiah 53' and the poems on 'Hell' and '9–1-1, A 'Wake-Up' Call?…Nay an Emergency' should go a long way in helping today's reader to 'wake-up' to the 'Hour' that we are living in *right now!* It is 'High-Time'…to *repent* and *do all possible* to get right with God and be *'ready' for our Lord's soon return!*

Isaiah 53! (The Amplified Version of the Bible)

Isaiah 53: verse 1 "WHO HAS believed—trusted in, relied upon and clung to—our message of that which was revealed to us? And to whom has the arm of the Lord been disclosed?" [John 12:38–41;] [Rom. 10:16]

[John 12:38–50, 38 "So that what Isaiah the prophet said was fulfilled, Lord, who has believed our report and our message? And to whom has the arm (the power) of the Lord been shown—unveiled and revealed? 39 Therefore, they were unable to believe, For Isaiah has also said, 40 He has blinded their eyes, and hardened and benumbed their [callous, degenerated] heart—He has made their minds dull—to keep them from seeing with their eyes and understanding with their heart and mind and repenting and turning to Me to heal them. 41 Isaiah said this because he saw His glory and spoke of Him. 42 And yet [in spite of all this] many even of the leading men—of the authorities and the nobles—believed and trusted in Him. But because of the Pharisees they did not confess it, for fear [that if they should acknowledge Him] they would be expelled from the synagogue. 43 For they loved the approval and the praise and the glory that come from men [instead of and] more than the glory that comes from God.—They valued their credit with men more than their credit with God. 44 But Jesus loudly declared, The one who believes on Me, does not [only] believe on and trust in and rely on Me, but [in believing on Me he believes] on Him Who sent me. 45 And whoever sees Me sees Him Who sent Me. 46. I have come a light into the world, so that whoever believes on Me—who cleaves to and trusts in and relies on Me—may not continue to live in darkness. 47 If any one hears My teachings and fails to observe them—does not keep them, but disregards them—it is not I who judges him. For I have not come to judge and to condemn and to pass sentence and to inflict penalty on the world, but to save the world. 48 Any one who rejects Me and persistently sets Me at naught, refusing to accept My teachings, has his judge [however]; for the [very] message that I have spoken will itself judge and convict him on the *last day.* 49 This is because I have never spoken on My own authority or of My own accord or self-appointed, but the Father Who has sent Me has Himself given Me orders what to say and what to tell. 50 And I know that His commandment is (means,) eternal life. So whatever I speak, I am saying [exactly] what My Father has told Me to say *and* in accordance with His instructions." [Deut. 18:18, 19.] [Isaiah 6:9–10]

[Deut. 18:18, 19, "I will raise up a prophet from among their brethren, like you, and will put My words in his mouth; and he shall speak to them all that I command him. And whoever will not hearken to My words which he shall speak in My name, I Myself will require it of him."

(This was spoken to Moses—every studying Jew knows this, of which I am one! *gmcg)

[Romans 10:16, But they have not all heeded the Gospel; for Isaiah says, Lord, who has believed (had faith in) what he has heard from us?]

[Isaiah 6:8-12, "Also I heard the voice of the Lord, saying, Whom shall I send, and who will go for Us? Then said I, Here am I; send me. 9 And He said, Go, and tell this people, Hear and hear continually, but understand not; and see and see continually, but do not apprehend with your mind. 10 Make the heart of this people fat, and make their ears heavy, and shut their eyes; lest they see with their eyes, and hear with their ears, and understand with their hearts, and turn again and be healed. 11 Then said I, Lord, how long? And He answered, Until cities lie waste without inhabitant, and houses without man, and the land is utterly desolate, 12 And the Lord removes His people far away, and the forsaken places are many in the midst of the land."

(This took place historically from 586 B.C. and then again in 70 A.D. until the late 1880's and then was restored officially on May 14,1948 A.D., and then again Spiritually June 6, 1967 A.D.!)

Continuing on with the Chapter and verses describing the Crucifixion of our Lord Jesus Christ:

Isaiah 53: 2–4, "For [the Servant of God] grew up before Him like a tender plant, and as a root out of dry ground; He has no [royal, kingly pomp] form or comeliness that we should look at Him, and no beauty that we should desire Him. 3 He was despised and rejected and forsaken by men, a Man of sorrows and pains, and acquainted with grief and sickness; and as one from Whom men hide their faces He was despised, and we did not appreciate His worth or have any esteem for Him. 4 Surely He has borne our griefs—sickness, weakness and distress—and carried our sorrows and pain [of punishment]. Yet we *ignorantly* considered Him stricken smitten and afflicted by God [as if with leprosy]. [Matthew 8:17]

[Matthew 8:17, "And thus He fulfilled what was spoken by the prophet Isaiah, He Himself took (in order to carry away) our weaknesses and infirmities and bore away our diseases.]

Isaiah 53:5–6, "But He was wounded for our transgressions, He was bruised for our guilt and iniquities; the chastisement needful to obtain peace and well-being for us was upon Him, and with the stripes that wounded Him we are healed and made whole. 6 All we like sheep have gone astray, we have turned everyone to his own way; and the Lord has made to light on Him the guilt and iniquity of us all." [I Peter 2:24, 25]

[I Peter 2:24, 25, "He personally bore our sins in His [own] body to the tree [as to an altar and offered Himself on it], that we might die (cease to exist) to sin and live to righteousness. By His wounds you have been healed. 25 For you were going astray like [so many] sheep, but now you have come back to the Shepherd and Guardian (the Bishop) of your souls."]

Isaiah 53:7–9, "He was oppressed, yet when He was afflicted He was submissive and opened not His mouth; as a lamb that is led to the slaughter, and as a sheep that before her shearers is dumb, so He opened not His mouth. 8 By oppression and judgment He was taken away; and as for His generation, who among them considered that He was cut off out of the land of the living for the transgression of my [Isaiah's] people, to whom the stroke was due—stricken to His death? 9 And they assigned Him a grave with the wicked and with a rich man in His death, although He had done no violence, neither was any deceit in His mouth." [Matthew 27:57–60;] [I Pet. 2:22, 23.]

[Matthew 27: 57–60,] "When it was evening, there came a rich man from Arimathea, named Joseph, who also was a disciple of Jesus. 58 He went to Pilate and asked for the body of Jesus, and Pilate ordered that it be given him. 59 And Joseph took the body and rolled it up in a clean linen cloth used for swathing dead bodies, 60 And laid it in his own fresh [undefiled] tomb, which he had hewn in the rock; and he rolled a big boulder over the door of the tomb and went away.]

"[I Peter: 2:22–23," He was guilty of no sin; neither was deceit (guile) ever found on His lips. 23 When He was reviled and insulted, He did not revile or offer insult in return; [when] He was abused and suffered, He made no threats [of vengeance]; but he trusted [Himself and everything] to Him Who judges fairly.]

Isaiah 53:10–12, "Yet it was the will of the Lord to bruise Him; He has put Him to grief and made Him sick. When You and He make Him an offering for sin [and He has risen from the dead, in time to come], He shall see His spiritual offspring, He shall prolong His days, and the will and pleasure of the Lord shall prosper in His hand. 11 He shall see the fruit of the travail of His soul and be satisfied; by His knowledge of Himself [which He possesses and imparts to others] shall My [uncompromisingly] righteous One, My Servant, justify and make many righteous—upright and in right standing with God; for He shall bear their iniquities and their guilt [with the consequences, says the Lord]. 12 Therefore will I divide the spoil with the mighty; because He poured out His life unto death, and He let Himself be regarded as a criminal and be numbered with the transgressors, yet He bore [and took away] the sin of many and makes intercession for the transgressors—the rebellious." [Luke 22:37]

[Luke 22:37, "For I tell you that this Scripture must yet be fulfilled in Me, And He was counted and classed among the wicked (the outlaws, the criminals); for what is written about Me has its fulfillment—has reached its end, and is finally settled."

Messiah was to be raised from the dead
Psalm 16:10. Old Covenant
New Covenant FULFILLMENT: Acts 2:22–32; Matthew 28:1–10; Mark 16:1–8; Luke 24: 1–9; 44–48; John 20:1–31; I Corinthians 15:4–8.

Messiah now at god's right hand
Psalm 110:1. Old Covenant
New Covenant FULFILLMENT: Mark 16:19; Luke 24:50, 51; Acts 2:33–36; Hebrews 10:12, 13.

Messiah is to come with the clouds of heaven
Daniel 7:13,14. Old Covenant
New Covenant Parallel: Matthew 24:30; 25:31; 26:64;
Mark 14:61–62; Acts 1:9–11; Rev. 1:7.

Messiah is to sit on the throne of david
Isaiah 9:6,7. Old Covenant
New Covenant Parallel: Luke 1:32,33.

Messiah is to reign over the entire earth
Psalm 72:8, 11. Old Covenant
New Covenant Parallel: Philippians 2:9–11; Hebrews
1:8; Revelation 11:15; Rev. 19:11–16.

Note: The preceding are only some of the many Old Testament prophecies of Messiah that were fulfilled in the New Covenant. These were copied out of the New Covenant Prophecy Edition (NIV) International Bible Society Colorado Springs, Mexico City, Herrijunga Nairobi, Hyderabad, and Bangkok and given to me by a Nun in the Chapel on the Mount in the Galilee Area, when visiting there in 2004. Thank you Jesus!

Chapter Fifteen

Duties of the King using Gifts
of the Holy Spirit!

Our Lord's Title, Lion of Judah, speaks first of His being a King. He has made us to be a nation of kings. This *Wonderful, Counselor, Mighty God, Prince of Peace, Everlasting Father, Son of God, Lamb Slain,* has gone on High and obtained a *More Excellent Ministry!* And now He is commissioning and equipping and making available to us, through the Baptism of His Holy Spirit, the *Gifts* of the Holy Spirit. The Ministry Gifts of the Spirit are now available to us as given to each by *His* choice. Kings are to take authority over dominions and principalities, bringing deliverance. Kings feed the Lord's sheep and have teaching ministries. They minister unto others by preaching the Gospel. Kings pray and lay hands on the sick for healing. Kings minister the baptism of the Holy Spirit.

Thank God for Kings. Specifically, Kings are involved in caring for the whole house of God through ministry unto the people. Let's catalogue and explore the Gifts of the Spirit that we can begin to have a better understanding of those Gifts and how they are to be used by Kings! These are found in I Corinthians 12:7–11. Teach us Holy Spirit.

The Word of Wisdom is not only the ability to be wise as promised for the asking, in James 1:5, *"If any of you lacks wisdom, let him ask of God, who gives to all liberally, and without reproach and it will be given to him."* And then the wonderful wisdom from above spoken of in James 3:17 *"But the wisdom that is from above is first pure, then peaceable, gentle, willing to yield, full of mercy and good fruits, without partiality, and without hypocrisy."* but rather the 'Word of Wisdom', gives an understanding, just a Word as it were, from God out of His whole paragraph, concerning His program and plans! This Word is given by revelation!

Example: Just after the great happening that took place in the upper room, Peter stood and declared that this was the fulfillment of the Prophecy found in Joel 2:28–32. Peter knew this by the Word of Wisdom. He did not confer with the others before he made this proclamation. Acts 2:14–16, *But Peter, standing up with the eleven, lifted up his voice, and said unto them, Ye men of Judea, and all ye that dwell at Jerusalem, be this known unto you, and hearken to my words: For these are not drunken, as ye suppose, seeing it is but the third hour of the day. But this is that which was spoken by the prophet Joel.*" And Peter continued on quoting and speaking prophecy to the hearers. He was telling them things that he could have known by no other means than by the Word of Wisdom being in operation through his lips as his understanding also was being illuminated that very hour!

The Holy Spirit gave him the understanding that *'this was that'!* That this happening on the Day of Pentecost was God's Program being carried out as given in the Book of Joel!

This Word of Wisdom can be given through a vision, as seen in Acts 10:11–48. Peter was put into a trance and given a vision that showed him, as he declared in verse 28, that he should not call any man impure or unclean. This was God's *New Program for the Gentile Nations* shown to Peter. In reviewing this portion of Scripture, we see that while Peter was *still speaking*, the Holy Spirit came upon all who were present and heard the message and they began to speak in Tongues!

The Holy Spirit *does not interrupt Himself, but He does interrupt His servants*—as displayed or affirmed to in this passage! (Indeed the speech through Tongues by *the Lord of the Church* should not be considered an interruption). Can we not rather see this happening as a confirmation that the unknown Tongues are the Word of the Lord? That they are the Audible Spoken Word of the 'Christ in us' as we yield to this speaking of *mysteries unto God?* Paul writes of this in I Corinthians 14:2, "*For he that speaketh in an unknown tongue speaketh not unto men, but unto God: for no man understandeth him; howbeit in the spirit he speaketh mysteries.*" (KJV) All of this ministry is by the moving and empowering of the Holy Spirit!

Too often men and ministries have called for 'perfect timing,' meaning that the utterances of Tongues and Interpretations and Prophecies are to be given *just at specific times,* rather than honoring *the utterances themselves—since they are of the Holy Spirit—as* being *the very specific time!* So often, such stipulations lead to silence when the Holy Spirit desires to speak—but must find those who are willing to receive rebuke for what is considered disobedience by others. Too many Churches go for weeks on end without any 'Messages in the Spirit' as a result.

The Word of Knowledge is a supernatural revelation concerning a person, place or thing in the past, present or future. It is given by the Spirit to aid us in ministering clarification and or comfort and exhortation sometimes having to do with a long forgotten or suppressed or hidden incident. An example is found in Acts 5: 1–11, when Peter questioned Ananias concerning that which was conceived in his heart. Peter knew that Satan had filled his heart to lie to the Holy Spirit. He knew this by the Gift of the Word of Knowledge. Peter knew by the same gift the intents of the heart of the wife of Ananias. In the book of Acts, this Word (foreknowledge) was given concerning that which was to take place in Paul's life when in Rome!

The Gift of Faith is similar to, but different than the *'measure of faith'* given to every man to profit withal spoken of as in Romans 12:3, "For I say, through the grace given unto me, to every man that is among you, not to think of himself more highly than he ought to think; but to think soberly, according as God hath dealt to every man the *measure of faith.*" With the Gift of Faith, one has *no doubt whatever,* but rather acts as the Holy Spirit leads. With this gift in operation, one doesn't say within: "What if I pray and nothing happens?" One just *knows,* and so this often has the Word of Knowledge combined with it.

Example: Acts 3:4–8. Peter said, "What I do have, I give to you. In the Name of Jesus Christ the Nazarene, walk!" Peter was exercising the Gift of Faith that has no doubt whatsoever!

Gifts of Healing: The word is plural - *Gifts.* Does this mean that the other Gifts would many times be in operation to bring about the Healing such as the Word of Knowledge—knowing supernaturally the specific cause of the sickness—or the Gift of Faith as in the example above? It certainly speaks of that Gift mentioned in Mark 16:18, "Whereby those who believe will lay hands on the sick and see them recover." Another example would be the healing that took place by the cast shadow of Peter in Acts 5:15, and the release from tormenting spirits that brought healing in Acts 5:16.

An example of this combination took place as a Minister was praying for the Gift of Healing for one that was blind. I was given to know by the Word of Knowledge that this one was diabetic and that this was the underlying cause that had to be addressed.

The Gift of Miracles: speaks of that which takes place which is not according to the norm. All of the above mentioned healings are miracles. The difference sometimes has to do with the element of time. Most often, a miracle is that which happens immediately—while healing often takes place over a period of time. Usually a miracle is thought of as having to do with transformation—water into wine—the sea becoming calm at the Word of Jesus—the raising of the dead. All of these took place after Jesus was baptized by the Holy Spirit. Peter performed the Miracle of Resurrection by the Gift of Faith. In Acts 9:40, he said, "Tabitha, arise!"

The Gift of Prophesy: This is one of the vocal Gifts. That is, one speaks when *moved* upon by the Holy Spirit. It is given to the Body of Christ for correction, instruction, building up, comforting and or to give foreknowledge. Acts 21:10–11 gives an account of a Prophet named Agabus forewarning Paul that he would be bound hand and foot and given over to the Gentiles when in Jerusalem. This prophecy had the Word of Knowledge in operation. Also the use of the belt was a prophetic sign. Being given the Gift of Prophecy does not necessarily mean that one is a prophet. A message in Tongues with an Interpretation is considered a Prophecy.

The Gift of Discerning of spirits: Acts: 16:16–18 gives the account of Paul being bothered by a woman who was possessed by a spirit of divination. She said very spiritual sounding things, "These men are the servants of the Most High God, which show unto us the way of Salvation." She brought her masters much gain by soothsaying. She could foretell things before they happened. Deuteronomy 18:12 tells us that divination is an abomination in the sight of the Lord.

Many become involved with this spirit by seeking information through the false methods by which it operates—fortune-telling—astrology charts prognostication—and so forth. For the most part, men and women do this ignorantly in a search for the True Supernatural Powers of God. Those seeking in false places will open their lives up to evil forces. Divination is the *Imitation* of the Word of Knowledge.

Paul had the Gift of Discerning of spirits. In Acts 16; 18 Paul said to the spirit, *"I command you in the Name of Jesus Christ to come out of her."* And the spirit of divination came out that very hour. The ones who were making money through the operation of this spirit were not happy about the deliverance. And neither will those making money through evil gain be happy when we minister by casting out evil spirits. Nevertheless, we must minister and thank God for the authority to do so!

The Gift of Divers or Various Kinds of Tongues—the Holy Spirit sometimes gives a Tongue in a language that is known to a listener. After singing in the Spirit over a radio broadcast I was told that I had been singing a wonderful message of God in the Iranian language. God is so faithful, I have just returned from a trip to Israel where I attended a DVD filming by Jay Rawlins and bought his book *Fishers & Hunters* by Jay and Meridel, his wife. In it I read on page 46—of a persistent thought that came to Meridel several months before their trip into Russia while in prayer. "Meridel, I will give you the Russian tongue if you believe Me. I want you to speak to certain of My people." This was spoken into her spirit by the Holy Spirit!

While in Russia she was observing a man on a subway train who was looking so tired and dejected and as she observed him the Lord spoke to her: "Speak now!" It was a command. Meridel was frightened to do so, until the Lord spoke again: "Now!" came the firm command. Meridel opened her mouth and out came a Language of the Holy Spirit! The gentleman lifted his head and turned in amazement and brightened into a smile and began to speak rapidly as though in answer. She picked up the conversation, not knowing what she was saying. Tears rolled down his tired face and a peace came upon them both. It was a supernatural happening. His face shone like an angel as he left the train.

Several times she was ordered to "Speak". And one of those times I was sitting across from her and saw her speaking to a woman. The one sitting next to her burst forth in tears and gave every indication of having been spoken to in her native language. As I was observing this wonderful happening, I affirm that indeed, the woman behaved as though she understood every Word, responding happily in Russian!

Then further on page 53 Meridel speaks of a letter that was given to Brezhnev, composed by the tour leader—Ruth Heflin and in it was given the Scripture concerning the release of the Jews: Isaiah 43: (6a), "The Living God has commanded, 'I will say to the North Give up.'"

Just days later arriving in Israel, the Headline in the Jerusalem Post was: "To satisfy world opinion, 300,000 Jews will be released in the next decade!" Between 1972 and 1982, 300,000 Jews were released from Russia! And I, dear reader, am the one who delivered that letter!

Ruth came to me and asked if I would go along with a young man and show him where the Communist Party Headquarters Building was, as we had just had it pointed out to us that morning. I pay no attention to directions and was at a loss as to where we were when we saw the building. I told Ruth that I didn't think that I could direct him, but she brushed this off with: "Oh you can do it!"

I had offered her my coat in which were sewn the pockets for the Bibles I had brought in from Finland. When she ignored my protests, I thought, "Oh, she doesn't want me to direct him, she just wants an opportunity to have my coat be used by someone." Now how to make a long story short?

The one thing I had remembered was that when Ruth asked the tour-leader that morning, how to get a letter to Brezhnev, she had told us to address it to: The 'Social Secretary of His Excellency Brezhnev'! We finally found the building after mistakenly arriving first at the Gum Department Store and I gave up a panicked prayer of: "Please Lord, show me where the building is!" I then spied Russian flags and we arrived and went *into* the Communist Party Headquarters Building.

Even as we were walking in I remember thinking: "Lord, what are we doing going into this building?" I had thought to meet someone there on the outside to give them my coat!

Once inside a soldier (who had been mentioned in a vision before we went on the trip as one who would be helpful…appeared). We were asked for our passports and Jim, the young man carrying the letter, looked worried and asked if we should give them up. I said confidently: "Lets give them to him; it will be alright"—(and wondered where that speech out of my mouth came from!) Now, the young man who was to deliver the letter forgot what to say and so I replied to the inquiry concerning our visit. "We have a letter for the Social Secretary of His Excellency Brezhnev!" He looked cautiously at two plain-clothes detectives and He directed us to another building and walked us there. I remember thinking as we entered that second building: "Oh Lord, if I had not read of Daniel and the lions den, I would surely be getting 'antsy' at this point! But Lord, this is enough!"

A man appeared and asked what we wanted: Again I had to repeat the official sounding greeting concerning the letter. He angrily answered: "I can't take the letter; there are 'letter-bombs' being distributed! You must make an appointment with the embassy!" This would take weeks! I answered impor-tantly, with much 'Holy-Ghost' authority in my voice: "We haven't the time! We have to fly out of Russia tomorrow and this is a very important letter that must be delivered today!" He hesitated and then said grumpily: "Alright, give it to me!" Surprisingly, Jim said to me: "Should I give it to him?" And I answered—as though I were an ambassador for the United States: "Give it to him!" (We are ambassadors for Christ!) Jim reached into his breast pocket and handed the letter to the agent. He received the letter in a manner that said he really didn't want to take it; and didn't know why he had agreed to do so. We courteously turned and left.

When walking back to Hotel Russia the adrenalin rose up in us and we almost cried as the tension of the realization of actually being in the Communist Party Headquarters Building hit us and we laughed instead of crying, with relief.

For me, the book *Tortured for Christ* by Richard Wurmbrand was fresh in my mind. Reading it just six weeks earlier was my reason for being in this situation this day. With tears pouring out of my eyes, I had said: "O Lord, how do you get those Bibles into Russia?" This trip was His answer. And I was aware that we were walking on the heads of those below who were impris-oned under the streets of Moscow! Just as Meridel in her book said she had seen in vision and did not understand until later and was reading: *The First Guidebook to Prisons and Concentration Camps in the Soviet Union* written by Avraham Shifrin, describing the detention cells that are beneath railway stations and under the main squares of cities. Bantam Books, available at P.O. Box 32, Zikhron Ha'akov, Israel

When I arrived at my hotel, I was exhausted! I lay on my bed and refused to get up when a knock came at my door. I thought it was my room mate who could get the key at the main desk that was on each floor, I was just too tired to move! The knock came again and when I didn't answer, suddenly the door opened and a man crawled into my room on his hands and knees and proceeded to use a screw-driver to 'jimmy' open a panel on the floor in the door-jam, and while removing a tape he looked up and realized that I was in the room, lying on my bed. He scooted backwards quickly and was out the door! I didn't even get off of the bed. I had had it with espionage and just wanted to sleep!

One thing more, while Velma and I were enjoying ourselves having tea and pastry in a little city of Suzdal the next day, Ruth was sitting in her room waiting for a reply to her letter. But mine was the room guarded all day as they mistook me, for Ruth!

On the Day of Pentecost, this was the way TONGUES were used. There were 120 gathered (Acts 1:15) praying when the Holy Spirit fell in that magnificent outpouring that took place, when the Day of Pentecost was fully come! Acts 2:4, *"And they were all filled with the Holy Ghost, and began to speak with other tongues, as the Spirit gave them utterance."* (You see, it is the Holy Spirit who gives the utterance…speech…and what other can the Holy Spirit speak but the Word of God) Acts 2:5–8, *"And there were dwelling at Jerusalem Jews, devout men, out of every Nation under heaven. Now when this was noised abroad, the multitude came together, and was confounded, because that every man heard them speak in his own language. And they were all amazed and marveled, saying one to another, Behold, are not all these which speak Galileans? And how hear we every man in our own tongue, wherein we were born?"* So then, the miracle was not one of hearing, but rather the 120 were speaking in known languages that they had never learned, *for the benefit of the hearers!*

This has happened many times in modern times. I love the story I have heard of the little Polish woman who gave a message in perfect Hebrew with words that greatly impacted a Jewish Rabbi. He was astonished, and convicted of the truth of Christianity when he became aware that this woman knew not one word in Hebrew!

Also, when one gets serious and begins to speak in tongues frequently and fluently, many different dialects and languages can be brought forth and emerge from ones lips. The Lord knows the needs of the people. We don't have to know. We need only to open our lips and pray in the Spirit. Intercession in this way is most effective and can be done as often as we will do so!

Paul says in I Corinthians 14:2 that when one speaks in Tongues, no man understands him. Do we see by this that the Gift of Divers Tongues, and the manifestation of Tongues used in speaking mysteries unto God, though akin, are two different utterances. One utterance—spoken in a language unknown to the speaker—is spoken in the known language of another present for the spiritual benefit of that one—while tongues in private are for our benefit in building up our faith according to Jude verse 20. And we are the first beneficiaries! We are building up our faith, and entering into His Rest. We are refreshed! And then, tongues equip us to minister as priests, first unto God and then on behalf of others in intercession, even as Jesus, our Great High Priest in cooperating with us, does His part in bringing about the answers and blessings to those for whom we are praying. The Lord has shown me that as often as we speak or sing in the Spirit, He is busy taking the language, on the 'Wings of the Wind' to those who understand the language proceeding out our obedient mouths using our spiritual iPods!

The Gift of Interpretation of Tongues: I Corinthians 12:10…to another is given the interpretation of tongues: This Gift is of much worth especially as the Body of Christ is gathered together worshipping and adoring the Lord and seeking more of Him. As this Word comes forth it is as 'fresh hot bread' out of the oven. The Gift of speaking in Tongues that precedes an interpretation—first of all alerts the Body of Believers—"attention everyone—the Lord of the Church wants to bring you a special Word for today—be quiet and 'pay attention'!" It also alerts the one who has the Gift of Interpretation—to begin to listen within for the message that they are about to broadcast! The Tongues being spoken clears the air of demonic forces—with those 'Singing Swinging Laser-light Swords' flying around—and charges it up electrically—preparing the hearers for the prophetic message. This answers in part the question, "Why Tongues and Interpretation at times—rather than just prophecy?"

I Corinthians 14:13 states, *"Wherefore let him that speaks in an unknown Tongue pray that he may interpret."* We see in this statement first of all that we are to pray for this interpretation when we or others are used to bring forth an audible message in Tongues while gathered together as the Body of Christ, for this is the context in which Paul was speaking throughout the fourteenth chapter.

Also many have taken this Scripture and applied it personally, privately. That is, they have considered a matter with their understanding and then have prayed in the Spirit using the language of the Spirit, tongues, and then have believed for and received the interpretation. The Holy Spirit honors this use of tongues and it is a wonderful way to receive direction. As a Nation of Kings, we are thereby tapping into the Heavenly Realm to learn better how to properly Reign in conjunction with our 'Code of Ethics and Law,' the Bible.

Also note that when Paul asks the question: "Do all speak in Tongues" and the inference in the answer is no—this is speaking of the Gift of Tongues in operation as we are gathered together as the Body. He has just been speaking of the Body Gifts. Not everyone has the Gift of Tongues and Interpretation in this light—for bringing forth a message from the Lord of the Church to His awaiting Body—but, the manifestation of the Spirit, the original bringing forth of Tongues is available to all. Everyone should speak in this Heavenly Language, else we would not be instructed to do so in Jude 20 as well as in Ephesians 6:18...praying with all prayer and supplication *in the Spirit!* This should really make those without the Baptism of the Holy Spirit to desire to ask for this Marvelous Experience that they be not *speechless* in the *Supernatural Language!*

Chapter Sixteen

Activities of Priests—after the Order of Melchizedek

Results of 'Thrusting Forth' the Hand, a Power-filled Weapon!

Now I want to share here a few instances where the 'swirling' or *thrusting forth of the open hand'* have brought blessing of deliverance to me, at least and those with me, since this Word from the Lord was given! (Chapter Twelve: 'Fasting for a Change!' 1970 First Extreme Fast) But first, a vision which helps to illuminate our understanding!

During our morning worship and prayer time in St. Louis, Missouri, at the Millennium Hotel, during the 30th and last International End-Time Handmaidens Convention in July of 2005, I had a vision. I was singing in the Spirit with my hands lifted and 'swirling' in Worship when I saw 'rings' of light going upward and widening just as one sees the rings on a pond when a stone is thrown into it. The Word of the Lord came: "As you Worship me in this manner, with Song in the Spirit, it ascends straight up to the Throne creating an area of 'Open Heaven' above you!" He gave me the sense that this 'swirling' of lifted hands along with the Tongues of Worship ascending upward, cleanses the air waves, dispelling those evil wicked rulers and powers of darkness, frustrating the spiritual forces of the evil 'prince' of the power of the air, in the heavenly realms mentioned in Ephesians 6:12. The Lord let me know that even as this was done through a group of Worshippers, so it is done when just one is worshipping in the Song of the Spirit, with hands lifted in worship! This 'swirling motion' is also as a 'wave offering' unto the Lord, which was one of the duties of the Priest in the Old Testament! Exodus 29:27–28, speaks of the heave offering and the wave offering and the breast offering and the peace offering. I believe that our lifting up unto the Lord of our arms involving our shoulders and hands and heart and strength and minds—stayed on Him, are as pleasing offerings to our Lord God!

Protection in America when using our authority as Priests!

While here in America, an enormous angry woman, known for her violent temper was hurriedly coming toward me and a friend, with violence on her tongue and 'murder' in her eye! Instantly, without thinking, I thrust forth my hand in her direction and said with the authority that the Lord puts into our speech: "You will not touch me!" She stopped in her tracks, looked shocked, turned and meekly walked off! This took place years ago, and since that time, she has never threatened me again, but rather has gone 'out of her way' to be friendly!

This same Action, in Israel!

And then, in Israel, during an attack by a man who tried to steal my friend Marilyn's purse, another friend, Patsy Carol, tackled him and thwarted his efforts. We then turned and saw a group of men coming at us threateningly. I thrust forth my hand at arm's length and forcefully spoke in Tongues. They stopped cold in their tracks and looked at us blankly. We walked hurriedly away in safety. Of course we know that Angels were protecting us as we always claim the Scripture: "The angel of the Lord camps round about those who fear Him, God, and delivers them!"

Deliverance in the Kidron Valley

I remember also while walking, taking a 'short-cut' across the Kidron Valley in Israel, to my home on the Mt. of Olives. A yellow stray dog began snarling at me. I ignored him until he came close enough to snap at me and grab the hem of my trench coat.

I thought to myself: "Hmm, he's not 'fooling around'!" I turned, thrust my hand out at him and spoke loudly in Tongues. I will never forget the results! He stopped in his tracks and his face had the appearance of one who has run into a glass window! While he stood there transfixed, I hurriedly walked away, safe in the care of the angels who were encamped 'round about me'! Note: My part in the rescue *was to use the weapons of the authority and the Language given me through the Baptism of the Holy Spirit!*

In China

And again, while in China, after slipping the last of several hundred Gospel Tracts into bicycle baskets and mail boxes and other places available, at 1:00 a.m. a police car drove up beside us. A soldier and three 'plain-clothes' detectives stepped out; confronted my two friends and myself, waving an 'unlawful' tract in our faces. Their menacing expressions and gestures indicated that we should get into their cars and go with them to the police station. I immediately thrust out my hand toward them and loudly spoke a 'volley of Tongues'! To our relief and joy, their expressions changed drastically and the same 'dumbfounded' expression that I have come to know and appreciate appeared on their now stunned faces! God spoke to me that this action and Tongues 'disarmed' them!

While they stood there speechless, I stood and lifted my arms to Heaven and sang in the Spirit using Tongues, the Heavenly Language! The anointing came upon me in power and I went to the first detective and placed my hands on his chest and spoke in Tongues. I did the same to the other two. All three just looked at me unable to compose themselves. Their expressions were 'blank'! When I then went to place my hands on the soldier, he backed away crying: "No" "No". He grabbed the tract and ran away. We stood there for another hour, while they politely checked our passports, used their camcorders, and coaxed us, through an interpreter on a phone to please come to the police station. The soldier never re-appeared!

I haven't yet written the story concerning what happened next, at the police station and then later back at the Hotel. I have done so concerning my arrest in Moscow for 'smuggling' Bibles. That story is found in my booklet: "New Freedom, Stay Free!" But I must relate to you the amazing incident that took place when we were finally returned from the Police Station to the Hotel at 4:30 a.m. that morning. It had nothing to do with Tongues, though as I think of it, what I had to say finally may have been an interpretation of the Tongues, which the Lord put into my song and speech, in the Spirit, earlier that evening with the Detectives!

Rather than being allowed to return to our rooms we were ushered into a large Conference room. Seated at a head table were 5 soldiers. They had medals on their chests and gave off the impression of being 'high-up' in the military. They also must have all understood English, because of what happened after another hour of questioning us.

We were seated at a large Conference table, facing the Officers. As they continued the same line of questioning that had been put forth at the Police Station, my friend Elizabeth—another in our group, also arrested—repeatedly spoke with her Slavic accent the only thing that she had said repeatedly in the Police Station: "God loves China, God loves the Chinese people!" For my part I tried to answer the questioning as I had at the Station, by saying things that I felt were a witness for Christ. The brother that had accompanied us in our 'tracting' said little, but was quiet and respectful.

Finally, after an hour of what seemed to be just 'going in circles' I thought within: "This is getting us no-where—I have to change my approach!"

I spoke up and said with feigned 'heated' irritation: "We are American Citizens! Your Premier just visited America, and President Clinton put him up in fine accommodations! (Our trip took place in 1998.) He 'Wined and Dined' him Royally! And this is how you treat us!"

Suddenly, all five Officers jumped up from their seats and rushed into the foyer!

I clasped my hands to my cheeks and thought: "Oh Lord, now my big mouth has done it!"

After just a few moments, one of the Officers returned—took Elizabeth's hand into his, patted it and said kindly: "Now Missy, you may go to your room."

He then turned to me, took my hand in his, patted it and said: "Now Missy, you may go. You may go to your room and rest!" We were on the train back to Beijing before the morning was out. We were given no fine, nor were our Passports marked negatively in any way. Praise You Jesus! And thank You for showing us what Prayer in the Spirit can accomplish!

Patterns given to Moses show us the way!
Scriptures that enlighten us as to what is taking place in the Spirit!

Sons of God in the natural may have some difficulty in relating to Jesus in the role of the Bride. They need not have this hesitancy, for there is neither male nor female in the Spirit. We all, men and women, are a Royal Priesthood unto Him. We are Priests after the order of Melchizedek, if you please, Hebrews 5:9, *"And being made perfect, he became the author of eternal salvation unto all them that obey him; called of God an high priest after the order of Melchisedec."* And Hebrews 3:6, *"But Christ as a son over His own house whose house are we, if we hold fast the confidence and the rejoicing of the hope firm unto the end."*

We are part and parcel of this Royal House of Christ of which, He is the Great High Priest! In the second part of this scripture, the 'if', should certainly motivate us to the obedience of *holding fast* to our Lord. We are keepers and participants in the service of the House of God. We are *Living Stones* in His *spiritual house,* and as such are to offer up spiritual sacrifices, acceptable to God by Jesus Christ. Hebrews 13:16, *"But to do good and to share, forget not, for with such sacrifices, God is well pleased."* The one sacrifice does not do away with the other, we are to do both.

The pattern given to Moses while on the Mountain in Sinai is shown to us in part. In Exodus Chapter 28, Aaron and his sons were to be clothed with

Holy Garments for glory and for beauty. A breastplate, an ephod, a robe, a coat, a miter, and a girdle were to be put upon Aaron, and linen breeches were to be put upon him and his sons. A plate of pure gold engraved with the words, *HOLINESS TO THE LORD*, was to be put on his forehead. They were then to be anointed and consecrated and sanctified that they could minister unto God in the Priests' Office. Moses was to pour Oil upon the head of Aaron to anoint him.

Our Lord Jesus was stripped of every garment and had a crown of thorns put on His forehead that *we might be clothed with priestly garments of righteousness*. After His ascension, He sent the Holy Spirit *upon* us that we might be anointed and consecrated and sanctified, that we might have the privilege of ministering unto God in the priests' office through the Baptism of Holy Oil being poured upon our heads.

Exodus Chapter 29 speaks of a portion of bread being put in the priest's hands and then being *waved* as an offering unto the Lord. And then the breast of a ram was to be waved and then the shoulder was to be heaved. These were to be *Peace Offerings* unto the Lord. Do we not see in these that we are to take the Living Bread of the Word into our hands and read and then to lift up our hands unto the Lord in a wave offering and bless the Lord?

As He blesses us in return out of Zion, our hands are filled with anointing and waves of blessings go out in all directions from the hands that have Christ in them and the Spirit upon them! The breast speaks of putting our whole heart into our ministry unto Him and the shoulder speaks of serving Him with all of our strength. As we minister unto the Lord in Worship in this way, we find ourselves becoming part of the *heave offering*. This is the way to enter into the rest of the Lord and find Perfect Peace. We give of ourselves in Worship and He responds by anointing our heads with fresh Oil and our cups run over!

The Lord told Moses to take certain amounts of principle spices of myrrh, cinnamon, calamus and cassia and to make of them an oil of holy ointment compounded after the art of the perfumer, and with it he was to anoint the Tabernacle of the Congregation. This would sanctify the vessels of service. It was to be Holy anointing Oil throughout their generations. He was also to take sweet spices, stacte, onycha, and galbanum, with pure frankincense, and make of them a perfume, salted together, pure and holy. He was to beat some of it very small and put it before the testimony in the Tabernacle of the Congregation, where the Lord would meet with them. This is where we see the type of our Lord Jesus, the 'Rose of Sharon' and the 'Lily of the Valley' beaten down on the hammer and the pestle' of the cross, to become the Incense that comes up before the Lord, out of our 'bellies' as we worship in the Spirit. Hallelujah!

Upon man's flesh the Oil could not be put nor could any of the perfume be made for or put upon them. The Oil and the perfume were to be unto them: Holy for the Lord. Exodus 30:22–38.

In Leviticus 9:21–24, *"Aaron waved for a wave offering before the Lord, as Moses commanded. Then Aaron lifted up his hand toward the people and blessed them and came down from offering of the sin offering, and the burnt offering, and peace offerings. And Moses and Aaron went into the tabernacle of the congregation and came out and blessed the people; and the glory of the Lord appeared unto all the people. And there came a Fire out from before the Lord, and consumed upon the altar the burnt offering and the fat, which when all the people saw, they shouted and fell on their faces."* Lev. 10:1–2 reads, *"And Nadab and Abihu, the sons of Aaron, took either of them his censer and put fire therein, and put incense thereon, and offered strange fire before the Lord, which he commanded them not. And there went out fire from the Lord, and devoured them, and they died before the Lord."*

In Exodus 30, Aaron was to make an altar to burn incense upon and was to put it before the veil that is by the ark of the testimony, and was to burn thereon sweet incense every morning and every evening. He was to burn per-petual incense before the Lord throughout his generations. He was to offer *no strange incense* on the altar.

This bears repeating: Our Lord Jesus is the 'Lily of the Valley' and the 'Rose of Sharon!' The petals of the flowers are ground down to make a portion of the incense to be offered up to our Father. Jesus fulfilled this necessity through the grinding down of the pestle of the cross. The cross also supplied the ingredient of myrrh given him as a baby to foretell or foreshadow His suffering! This, the agony of being bruised, rejected, despised for our iniquity is spelled out in detail in Isaiah 53. Our Lord became for us the sin and burnt and peace offerings.

Ours is not the cumbersome ministry that Aaron had to be involved in, but rather we are obligated as priests to minister on behalf of others in intercession. And then we have the glorious privilege of ministering unto God Himself in the offering up of the morning and evening sacrifices of sweet incense.

As we understand that Christ Jesus Himself *is* this precious incense and sweetness, it gives us great pleasure to open our mouths. And then, by using the *Tongue of Fire*, the *Prayer Language of the Spirit*, we offer up unto God the Savor that is so pleasing to His Nostrils. We could call this Perfume and Fragrance: 'Essence of Jesus'! We are ministering the sacrifice—the fruit of our lips, given in Holy Spiritual Song. Can we realize that some who have followed after the Lord in love and obedience in bringing forth the Heavenly Perfume become as the Golden Censer in His Hand, and He, the Great High Priest, can waft them back and forth among the nations, spreading the Blessed Fragrance and draw-ing many to His Precious Side as He ministers Himself through them?

The lesson concerning Nadab and Abihu help us to understand the gravity of Priesthood Ministry. It helps us to understand that God sent the *Unknown Language,* the *Tongues,* as the very fire from heaven that was to light the sacrifices. We are not to use the energy of man to 'stir up' the Gifts that are in us through the laying on of hands. We are to use Tongues. Nor are we to use our *native language* in an effort to light the incense. Everyday language is fine for expressing thanksgiving or praise. It is a perfume that is pleasing to the Lord in that capacity, but it is a savor that we use also on others, on ourselves, on our possessions…"I love you, I love blue, I love shoes, I love this, and I love that." It is a common perfume and is not to be used for worship of the Almighty. Our everyday language is fine for praise and thanksgiving. It is our best perfume in the natural. But for the service of Worship, He has given us the Heavenly Fire and the Heavenly Fragrance, His Spirit and His Words, and His Son!

Without the Baptism of the Holy Spirit, we cannot minister unto God fully as a Royal Priesthood ought, for we have no Holy Fire with which to ignite the sacrifice! We can bring our offerings of thanksgiving and praise through the gates and into the courts. We can even have the boldness to enter the Holy of Holies by the Blood of Jesus, by a new and living way, which He hath consecrated for us through the veil, that is to say, His Flesh. See Hebrews 10:19–20.

But until we have been equipped from on High with a Tongue of Fire, we are not prepared verbally to offer up the Holy Perfume by Fire as did Aaron. We have only the common words of our *own* understanding and these are not a Holy Perfume used only unto God. We are limited when we have only our native tongue. We cannot speak mysteries unto God in this language. We can minister in the capacity of priests unto the House of God as Levites, but not unto God Himself, as fully as only the Holy Spirit can prepare us to do. We are limited in the area of worship, when we possess only our native language. God is a Spirit and must be worshipped in spirit, and in truth. John 4:23–24, *"But the hour cometh, and now is, when the true worshippers shall worship the Father in spirit and in truth: for the Father seeketh such to worship him. God is a Spirit: and they that worship him must worship Him in spirit and in truth."* II Corinthians 3:17, *"Now the Lord is that Spirit: and where the Spirit of the Lord is, there is liberty."* (KJV)

Do we realize also that as we bring forth 'Living Waters' from our inner wells, that this Water invisibly washes our feet from the 'soil' of daily life? This prepares us, as our Lord prepared His disciples for their 'walk in the Lord'. And then as we send up these fragrant 'waters' they become 'cloudy steam' unto our Father. He then blesses by sending down the 'oil' that anoints the entire congregation truly preparing them to be His Congregations!

We can pray for our brothers and sisters and for the needs of the world around us. We can worship to the utmost of the depth of our hearts, and that is a beginning, but still we need the fire to light the incense. I am not speaking to you of something that *YOU* cannot have. God is no respecter of persons. Ask Him for a Baptism by His Spirit just now and receive His Holy Spirit anointing, empowering, illumination *upon yourself!* This will make of you a better witness for our Lord Jesus Christ and His Gospel! Acts1:8; *"But ye shall receive power, after that the Holy Ghost is come upon you: and ye shall be witnesses unto me both in Jerusalem, and in all Judea, and in Samaria, and unto the uttermost part of the earth!"* You just can't help being a better witness, with a new boldness, and we know that this is the desire of every loving heart to whom Jesus has given 'new birth'!

Chapter Seventeen

'First Love' and Ministry in the Garden!

In Song of Solomon 4:10–5:1, our Lord says that the smell of the ointments of the Bride is better than all spices. Why so? She ministers to the Lord using the Heavenly Fragrance and adds to the Words the Precious Melody of Song in the Spirit. She hears from Him that her lips drop as the honeycomb and that "honey and milk are under her tongue." She is called a *Garden Enclosed.* This is His way of acknowledging that her pleasant fruits are for Him alone. A spring shut up and a fountain sealed, again acknowledgement that the Living Waters flowing from her well are for *His enjoyment first!* (Note: Remember— Tongues are for no man—must not ever be used toward any but Almighty God in Worship—how-be-it—the Holy Spirit does direct us to use Tongues when ordering demons to vacate and in intercession on behalf of others and in private 'building-up' of ones own faith.) But the 'Song in the Spirit' is chiefly 'for His ears alone' expressed in Worship! Of course—all may enjoy the sound of it and the resulting pouring out of Anointing Oils from Heaven, (Zion)! All of the Brides are to join in singing this Anthem, this 'Sacred Song'!

This Wonderful King tells the Bride that her plants are an orchard of pomegranates, which speaks of the Priesthood Ministry. She has lain prostrate at the feet of her Lord, listening as did Mary of Bethany, touched the hem of His Garment and knows that the fruits are full of seed—which makes for a delicious drink of refreshing for herself—and the tinkling of the bells is as the Inner Sound of His sweet Voice.

He mentions the pleasant fruits, camphor, with spikenard, and saffron, calamus and cinnamon with all trees of frankincense, myrrh and aloes, with all the chief spices. Again, in her garden are the ingredients with which to make the Holy Anointing Oil and the Sweet Incense. He calls her a Fountain of Gardens. She brings forth the waters as required of the Bride when Eleazer goes searching.

Jesus calls her a Well of Living Waters and Streams from Lebanon. This is the one who *sings to the Well within* and brings forth the Mighty Geyser, the

Pillar of Cloud. She is the Tabernacle and her mouth is the 'door' from which the Pillar of Cloud issues, and from which the Lord whispers within her heart and gives to her direction through the Word of Wisdom and blesses her eyes with Visions to accompany His Words.

And then Father God smells of that Cloudy Pillar that emits the Fragrance of His Son, and condensates the Cloud, causing a gentle rain to fall upon all of the ground surrounding the Bride! Is this the greening of *Ha Eretz,* the Land of the Promise?

"Awake, oh north wind; and come, thou south; blow upon my garden that the spices thereof may flow out. Let my beloved come into his garden, and eat his pleasant fruits." Song of Solomon 4:16. The North winds of adversity are given that she be strengthened as she in quietness and confidence waits upon Him.

The warm South Winds are the moving of the Spirit wafting the spices unto Him. Do the South Winds speak also of a baptism of fire, the chastening and purging, which brings us into conformity to His Will, that we may be more fully used of Him? Or are the South Winds those warm ones that waft in blessing as she is pleasing Him? Either way, she is blessed with His presence and attention! What a blessed ministry that we may feed Him with words of love and then actions that back up our arduous commitments.

Could we apply this Scripture not only to the ever present - the warm winds that coax forth and the cold winds that instruct - but also project it to apply to the time mentioned in Habakkuk Chapter 3, that begins when He revives His work in the midst of the years, and the prayer is that in wrath He will remember mercy? Teach us Lord. Nevertheless, she is determined—in His Strength—to rejoice whatever befalls in that time period.

God came from Teman, the South. Is this the place of the Garden? And the Holy One (came) from mount Paran. Selah. His glory covered the heavens, and the earth was full of His praise. And His brightness was as the light; He had horns coming out of His hands; and therein was the hiding of His power.

The Horns speak of power, strength, invisible rays of light, the spiritual swords, the flames in the pitcher. The clay vessel broken, we are the vessels of clay written in the palms of His hands, our Gideon—*the*—Mighty Man of Valor. The Tongues in us are the flames in the pitcher. See II Corinthians 4:6–7, *"For God, who commanded the light to shine out of darkness, hath shined in our hearts, to give the light of the knowledge of the glory of God in the face of Jesus Christ. But we have this treasure in earthen vessels that the Excellency of the power may be of God, and not of us".* We are the 'pitchers' voluntarily ready to be broken—if and/or when necessary!

As we blow our trumpets, our vocal shofars—our voices go up before Him in Worship—as priests of the Most High God after the order of Melchizedek—

sending up 'High Praises'! He blesses out of Zion, sending down the anointing which fills us to overflowing with His Spirit's power!

And as that overflow of the Spirit comes out of our hands and our feet, those invisible rays of light come forth as spiritual laser beams, the pure white light, the Word that is the creative energy of our God! These rays of anointing are 'flying' out in all directions! And as we go singing—and at times 'swinging' in the dance—those Tongues issuing forth as *'Singing Swinging Swords'* are dispelling—taking up serpents—routing the invisible powers of darkness. The Scripture takes place—before Him went the pestilence, and burning coals went forth at His Feet—in us!

This is one spiritual application of Habakkuk 3:3–5. *"God came from Teman, and the Holy One from mount Paran. Selah. His glory covered the heavens, and the earth was full of his praise. And his brightness was as the light; he had horns coming out of his hand: and there was the hiding of his power. Before him went the pestilence, and burning coals went forth at his feet."* The Christ in us is going forth as we endeavor as John the Baptist to decrease and prepare the way for 'His Coming'—while He increases!

This reminds me of the promises in Psalm 149:7–9. "To execute vengeance upon the heathen, and punishments upon the people, to bind their kings with chains, and their nobles with fetters of iron, to execute upon them the judgment written - this honor have all his saints. Praise the Lord!" In Mark 16:17–18 the Scripture says, *"These signs shall follow them that believe, in my name they shall cast out devils. They shall speak with new Tongues; they shall take up serpents, drink any deadly thing and it shall not hurt them. They shall lay hands on the sick and they shall recover."* All of this is because of God's power flowing out of anointed hands, when the faith for such is present and exercised! (The Bride goes forth in 'Army Boots'!)

The Tongue of fire is the *'light-switch'* for unleashing the electrifying power of the Holy Spirit that dispels the darkness of the evil one. Tongues go forth as guided missiles that know just where the evil things are that need to be bound and cast away, that healing and deliverance may be brought about.

The rest of chapter three of Habakkuk deals with God's doings during this time when the earth is cleaved with rivers and the mountains tremble and the sun and the moon stand still in their habitation at the light of His arrows and the shining of His glittering spear.

"Though the fig tree shall not blossom, neither shall fruit be in the vines, the labor of the olive shall fail, and the fields yield no meat. The flock shall be cut off from the fold, and there shall be no herd in the stalls. Yet will I (the Bride) rejoice in the Lord, and will joy in the God of my salvation. The Lord God is my strength and He will

make my feet like hind's feet. And He will make me to walk upon mine high places, to the chief singer on my stringed instruments."

All of this is a mystery, and yet for the first part when we worship with bridal love, the Lord blesses out of Zion with an anointing that revives the Christ in us and His power does come out of our hands in blessing even as His did when He was here on earth. He promised that the evil one would be ashes under our feet as takes place when burning coals go forth at the feet of the Christ in us. *(The evil one has retaliated with imitation; making mockery of those who spend most of life, lighting up and burning little white paper candles (cigarettes) to his domain, while filling their lives with ashes!)* (See 'Fiddle-Sticks' further on.)

Concerning the end of the chapter, only the brides who have learned to worship Him and thereby be filled with the anointing will be able to rejoice and joy in their beloved at such a time of desolation. Because of that, they will have hind's feet, (be sure-footed following Him) and walk upon their high places, (His elevating and promoting) Glory!

Song of Solomon 5:1 reads, *"I am come into my garden, my sister, my spouse; I have gathered my myrrh with my spice. I have eaten my honeycomb with my honey. I have drunk my wine with my milk. Eat, oh friends, drink, yea, drink abundantly, oh beloved."* She feeds her King. He is satisfied and blesses the friends inviting them to eat and drink. The Pillar of Cloud is received, smelled of, and then is made condensate—the latter rains that make the desert places blossom and bloom are sent down as showers of blessing! Revelations of the Lord are given along with a new understanding of His Word.

I have learned that when we join hands—somehow this increases—multiplies—the anointing resident within us. Then as we lift our voices in Worship Songs of the Spirit—songs of assents that *concentrate upon Him*—ascending into Songs in the Spirit—using Tongues—a perfect order of Worship takes place! This flows and blesses and feeds Him, and when He then responds by sending the Anointing down upon us, we become filled with an overflow of the Spirit, and we find ourselves being bathed in the Glory of God!

We cannot keep ourselves, then, from profusely thanking and praising Him, which leads to an overwhelming desire to clap and dance and shout as His Glory lifts us above all mundane circumstances! It really has to be 'felt to be telt'! (A Pennsylvania Dutch expression—telling it all!) When He blesses back, many petitions are tended to before we need ever state them. We begin to see that He hears before we call, and as we call, not with grumbling, complaining, whining, nor even crying, but with true Worship, He is answering—and has answered—already! Most needs do not even have to be expressed. We know that He lives in our praise! (Psalm 22:3; NLT) *"Yet You are holy, the praises of Israel surround your throne."* (This praise from Jesus lips expressed while He is on the cross is unimaginable that it could be expressed and spoken by any other than Himself!)

In the 17th chapter of Luke verses 7–10 we are shown our duty. (Jesus speaking) *"When a servant comes in from plowing or taking care of sheep, he doesn't just sit down and eat. He must first prepare his master's meal and serve him his supper before eating his own. And the servant is not even thanked, because he is merely doing what he is supposed to do. In the same way, when you obey me you should say, 'We are not worthy of praise. We are servants who have simply done our duty.'"* Feed the King first—tend to His needs first as dutiful and proper servants. Oh, how much sweeter to see the same service in the relationship of bridal love, rather than from duty or obligation. Or again as the prophet Elijah said to the widow, in essence, *"Feed me a little cake first."* I Kings 17:13. All thy needs will then be tended to. See how beautiful our Lord Jesus is to us. Certainly we are as widows—having nothing in and of ourselves. But now that we have Christ Jesus in these vessels, we are as the Cruz of oil that never will be empty, but rather will always have enough to be and to give light.

With the Holy Spirit upon us as a wedding garment thrown over our shoulders, as was the way of God's marriage of Israel, His wife, in Ezekiel 16:8; *"And when I passed by and saw you again, you were old enough to be married. So I wrapped my cloak around you to cover your nakedness and declared my marriage vows. I made a covenant with you, says the Sovereign* LORD, *and you became mine."* He, the Almighty Creator of this universe and everything in it—in such sweet display of humility as leaves us in wonderment—has chosen to elevate us to the chosen place of being called His Bride!

HIS WELLSPRINGS WITHIN!

Along with the increased power in witnessing, there came into my life a new awareness of what God had saved me *to,* or *for!* I knew what He had saved me from - an eternity of darkness apart from Him; in a state where the worm never dies and the fire is never quenched according to the Words of His own dear lips in Mark 9:44. And I knew why, because of His great love shown in the Father sending His only begotten Son - John 3:16. But that for which He had created me, I had here-to-fore little awareness of—other than that I was to lead others to salvation through Jesus by the Holy Spirit, through the sharing of the Gospel.

I knew that Revelation 4:11 says, *"You are worthy, O Lord our God, to receive glory and honor and power. For you created everything and it is for your pleasure that they exist and were created."* (*This* Scripture teaches us 'Why we were born'!) But I somehow felt that—us being created for His Pleasure—would apply in heaven, when we will see Him face to face. I had no idea that this fellowship with God, other than in the capacity of the Holy Spirit being my Helper, Comforter, Teacher and Guide, could and should begin right now down here on earth.

I had not realized that He, the Lord God, our Creator, had a need, a desire that only *we* could fulfill. His great heart, whose love we can never completely fathom, is longing for us to love Him in return—to the depths of our capacity. I Corinthians 13:5 tells us that love seeks not its own, that is, true love will not stop loving if love is not returned. Love just keeps right on loving; but to have the emotion of love returned is one of the purest joys known to man, and—probably—to God also! I knew that Scripture said that we were to love God with all the heart, and with all the understanding, and with all the soul, and with all our strength (see Mark 12:33). But somehow this came across to me as a love that was more of an attitude of respect or of gratitude, which of course it is, but the Holy Spirit showed me that it was far more!

My Experience of a New Depth of Love!

I had a *strange experience* just a few months after my Baptism in the Holy Spirit, when I took a trip to California. I have already written of this trip in which I found myself with a new capacity for witnessing, but I have not written of something else that took place. I shall try to express it now. I was in the home of my cousin Lorraine, sharing with her about Jesus. Her husband, David, came home while we were sharing and I continued talking about Jesus. I asked David if he knew Jesus and he assured me that he certainly did and that he had been born again for quite a long time. As he shared his love for the Lord, his eyes shone and I was struck by the beauty of his blue, blue eyes! I mentioned this to Lorraine. "Lorraine, your husband's eyes are beautiful!" She agreed.

I didn't stay long and as I was leaving, I was surprised to see a picture of Jesus on the wall in their foyer. As I looked at that picture, I exclaimed, "Lorraine, no wonder I liked looking at David's eyes, he looks just like Jesus!" She smiled and agreed and we said our goodbyes. I didn't mention this to Lorraine—but just now to you, dear reader—a curious thing was taking place as I was repeatedly telling David of the blueness of his eyes. He had a knowing grin, displaying a dimple in his cheek, and his expression gave the impression that we had a wonderful secret between us! Now David was unaware of what his face was expressing, and I know that it was not flirting, nor lust of any kind. I have seen and experienced these emotions before, and I knew that this was not that - but I didn't understand or 'know' what it was!

Two weeks later, home in Pittsburgh, I am enjoying one of my dearest pleasures - the break a mother can take when raising four children. I slipped down into a warm tub full of bubbles, with a good book in my hands and let myself just soak!

My book, 'Come Away My Beloved' by Francis Roberts, was a book of prophetic writings. It was a gift given me by Velma, the one who had led me into the Baptism of the Holy Spirit just two months before. When she presented it to me, she said, "This is the kind of book that you can read by just turning anywhere - it doesn't need to be read consecutively. I know you will enjoy it!" And she was certainly correct. I had picked it up and read many chapters and had underlined many places, but I had not yet read *the very first chapter!*

Well, dear reader, here I am immersed in soap bubbles up to my neck, relaxing and finally reading the first chapter entitled 'The Call of Love' and I quote, "O My beloved, abide under the shelter of the lattice—for I have *betrothed thee* unto Myself, and though ye are sometimes indifferent toward Me, My love for thee is at all times as a flame of fire. My ardor never cools. My longing for thy love and affection is deep and constant."

I read that far and I thought, "Lord, this is too personal, these words are too intimate." And I had thought, up until this time, even the hymn "He's all I need" was a little too personal. I continued to read.

"Tarry not for an opportunity to have more time to be alone with me. Take it, though ye leave the tasks at hand. Nothing will suffer. Things are of less importance than ye think. Our time together is like a garden full of flowers, whereas the time ye give to *things* is as a field full of stubble." (Hmmm)

"I love thee, and if ye can always, as it were, feel my pulse-beat, ye shall know many things the knowledge of which shall give thee sustaining strength. I bare thy sins and I wish to carry thy burdens. Ye may have the gift of a light and merry heart. My love bower is the place where ye shall find it, for my love dispels all fear and is a cure for every ill. Lay thy head upon my breast and *lose thyself* in me. Thou shalt experience resurrection life and salvation shall be opened within thee." (This is what it means to 'lay our head upon His Breast? It means to 'lose ourselves' in the Lord? Well, it is about time for me to fully discover what this invitation means. I had gotten that Word of Prophecy from Mother Heflin while living in Israel, but up until this very moment, I never really understood fully what it meant! I know that I have 'lost myself in Jesus' over and over. And especially in these times, the interpretations of the Songs in the Spirit are received. Oh Lord, thank You for Your precious 'Times of Illumination' that help us to understand You better!) (Forgive me dear reader for interrupting your trains of thought as I was telling you of my discovery in my tub—full of bubbles—the tub that is, not my head!)

I said, "Lord, this sounds like an intimate love letter." (Which it was)! I read the first chapter over once more and then began to remember a strange conversation that I had mulled over in my mind as I was hanging up clothes in the basement that morning. It was something that Nancy—my friend who was the first to sing in the Spirit, on that wonderful day when almost all of the women present in her home, received the Baptism of the Holy Spirit—had said.

She said, "I loved Bob—her ex-husband who had been unfaithful to her with her former 'best friend'—with all of my heart, and my wedding day was my most precious memory—but the joy I experience during our meetings when we are worshipping Jesus is more important to me than my wedding day!"

In the tub now, remembering how strange that had sounded to me, for some reason made me think of the other strange happening—when David Noah, cousin Lorraine's husband—had smiled at me as though we had a wonderful sweet secret! As I was remembering his look and the depth of the blueness of his eyes, all of the sudden I was looking into a face on my bathroom door, and with a start, I realized that I was looking into the Face of Jesus! And then something more registered! Suddenly I realized that I...that I...oh, I couldn't even express it, it seemed so wrong—but finally I said in truth, "Oh, Jesus, I'm *in love* with You! I'm not allowed to be in love with You—am I? Oh Lord, forgive me, I didn't mean to fall in love with you, but...Oh, I rebuke you Satan...Lord, forgive me...Jesus...*I am in love with You!*" And wonder of wonders, each time I repeated that expression: "I love You," I felt the warmth within my heart that I had come to know was the confirmation of the Holy Spirit, so I said it again and again. Each time I repeated that new unbelievable phrase, I felt that confirmation each time, as though He were answering me: "I love you, beloved!"

By the time the water was draining out of the tub, I was saying, "Lord, you know how I share everything I learn, Oh Lord, please, if this is not of you, please help me!" And then as I was drying, I thought, "Lord, what is this going to do to my love for everyone else?" (By the next morning as my daughter came up the steps from her bedroom, I looked at her and wanted to say: "He loves you, love Him back!")

That night, I crawled into bed with a pen and paper, and as my husband lay sleeping beside me, I began to write. My letter went something like this:

"I'm in love! I am more deeply in love than I have ever been in my life, and I am allowed to be! I am in love with my Spiritual Bridegroom, and I am His Virgin—if you please, Bride!" As I expressed my love to Jesus in this way, I felt as though something deep within me, in the wellsprings of my being, was being fulfilled.

In my teenage years, I had been caught up in a love for one that I had no business being in love with, and every time I was tempted to remember and think of this one, I had to resist it, suppress it and push it down, away from me.

This was a terrible bondage that took me years to overcome, and I only overcame it when I learned how to give it to Jesus, in confession…*specifically*…but here for the first time in my life I had found the One that my heart yearned to love fully, and I have found that He desires this love of me and it is so deep, *it is worship!* As I expressed this love to Jesus, I felt warm and cleansed and free! I felt wholeness and a completion that I had *never known before.*

Suddenly it dawned on me as I was writing. "Lord, this is what every heart is yearning for. We want to express love more than we want to receive it, and so often we give this *depth of love to another,* and *it is not for them, it is for You!* And so they—the one to whom we give this misplaced love—mistreat it, don't know how to handle it, don't know how to be jealous of it as You are in the right way (guarding and protecting it), and so we turn from them and *transfer* this love to another person, or another thing! *We were created with a desire to Worship built into us!* The Word says in Revelation we were created to give You pleasure."

These are the reasons that all over the world men and women are giving themselves to sticks or stones or bowing down to graven false images. Or making a thing of worship out of their automobiles, or education, or hobbies, or best girlfriend, or boyfriend—of the same sex perhaps—or even their children or mates!

"Lord, our world is crazy, because even our religious institutions, even Christian ones, are not understanding that when the Word of God tells us *to love You first* with all of our heart and soul and mind and strength, you are calling upon us to love you *first,* with all that is within, which is really what WORSHIP is all about!"

This is the *first love* that Christ is calling us to in the letter to the Church of Ephesus, Rev. 2:4, "Nevertheless I have somewhat against thee, because *thou hast left thy first love."* When we learn to be obedient to this command of yours, You then give us the capacity to love everyone else *more* than we could have without loving You first, and in the right degree to the depth of our being! "Oh Lord, if only we can learn to *transfer* over to You these unsatisfying actions, of putting our love in the wrong places! We so often transfer our attention and yearning over to another that isn't You! We can be healed and satisfied and made whole by You. If only, we will transfer our first, greatest capacity for love, over to You, our first love…with all of our hearts, souls, strength and minds!" This is what is meant by the admonition to *Worship!* And the Lord God is the *only one* that we are to worship!

Now, I know that I did not write all of this that night, but I have learned to express this new understanding in the way that I have just done, as best as I know how. (*Shortly afterward when I heard the men's singing group known as the 'Camarons' singing, "I'm in Love with Jesus," I was thrilled that I finally understood their proclamations!)

This is what happened as a result of my new understanding of being *in love with Jesus!* The very next day, I went to our weekly prayer meeting. These meetings, we had continued having ever since the first one when our whole group received the Baptism! That day as the meeting began, Velma said, "Someone has something special to share with us today!" I looked around and waited. Again she repeated her statement.

Nobody seemed to have anything special to offer, so hesitantly I said: "Well, I have something, but I'm not sure that I am to share it!"

Velma replied, "Oh yes, that is it! Tell us!" So I took out the letter that I had written the prior evening.

As I began to read my letter of declaration and discussed the reality of being allowed to be in Love with Jesus, and the possibility of transferring all of our love to *Him first,* Velma began to weep! I didn't understand this at the time, and I will tell you just a little later what the weeping was all about, as I was to learn later. I can't remember much of the rest of the meeting except Velma's tears and the fact that our prayer group seemed to receive favorably all that I tried to express of my newfound revelation.

A few days later, Jayne—a cousin of the one who had the meeting in her home—we had our meetings at our different homes each week, which helped to keep everything new and certainly exciting—came to me and said, "Grace, Carolyn tells me that you shared something in this week's meeting that I need to hear."

As I shared with her, I now realize that the Lord gave me the Word of Knowledge - though I didn't recognize it at the time. I said, "Well, Jayne, it's like this: Here is Pastor Brown, who loves the Lord (with all of his heart that he knows to love Him) and he is a good man, doing all he should, but his wife isn't that interested in the things of God as he is. Then there is Pricilla. She is the Choir director and she also loves the Lord, but as things are, her husband is not interested in coming to Church, so she goes alone and just enjoys the Lord and fellowship with the saints! Now they both have their eyes looking up at the Lord, but one day their eyes are drawn to notice each other in a special way and a new love begins to bloom—one that will take their attention off of the Lord—and on to one another. They both know—as soon as the bloom becomes a full flower, that they should not be allowing this in their personal gardens, but the desire to give and receive love is so strong—and they haven't yet learned this new revelation! Too bad; Satan has been allowed to use their flesh and natural inclinations, to lead them 'up the wrong garden path', to get their eyes on one another, the creature, rather than our Creator.

"Now, when they are made to realize that it is really Jesus that they can be in love with—are allowed to be deeply, fully in love with—and they transfer this love to Him, they can *immediately* be freed from bondage to that which they know is wrong, and can come into a new liberty and a new joy in expressing all of the love that is in the depths of their being to Jesus, and they will be more than loosed and delivered and healed emotionally!"

Suddenly Jayne began crying and said to me, "Are you sure Carolyn has told you nothing about me?"

I frowned and said, "What…what are you talking about?"

Jayne replied, "I'm the choir director; I fell in love with the Pastor, and that is why I have come here, to this city, to get away from that situation!"

I said, "Well, great, Jayne, the Lord wants you to do just as I have said. Transfer all of that love to Jesus. Realize that you are allowed to be 'in love' with Jesus, and give Him your whole heart! Fall in love with Him! You know that we often transfer our love, from one person to another, and you can do this just now." We prayed together and she left my home behaving as though she had a new lease on life!

In another instance, as I shared this message with a new group of people just a few month later, I kept noticing one woman in particular. She was beside me and as I was speaking, I put my arm around her shoulder, for she was weeping profusely as I spoke and couldn't seem to stop crying. When I had completed this new revelation that I have just shared with you, the Pastor, who was in charge of our gathering said: "Let's stand in a circle and pray."

They did so—I prostrated myself on the floor, because I was so aware of a heavy anointing that came as I shared, and I did not want to see appreciation in the eyes of anyone—and besides that—I was overcome also! While they were praying a Word of Prophecy came forth, "I have released you from your captivities; go and be as My Hands and My Feet in this world and minister one to another!" (Unknown to all—this was a confirmation of that exact Word that had been given to me previously!)

The next day, I asked the Pastor about the little woman who had been weeping. He answered: "You will never know how the Holy Spirit ministered to her through the message that you shared!" "She was in love with her own sixteen year old son! She had birthed him out of wedlock. Her life was spent on caring for him, and then she *had tried to commit suicide* two times—because she didn't know how to be freed of an *inordinate love* for him that had developed over the years! You showed her how to be free with that message that the Lord gave you! What a marvelous and necessary ministry!"

Well, just a few months before this, again at Syracuse, where I was given the awesome revelation concerning Tongues and the misconception of them as being poison in the Body of Christ, I was also given the Words, out loud in my heart, first in Tongues and then in English, "I have anointed you to preach deliverance to the Captives!" At that time, I had responded, "Lord, how can I preach, I'm a woman! (This was my Baptist teaching.) And Lord, who are the captives?"

When I heard this Word once more after sharing the revelation of 'being in love with Jesus,' I began to realize that this is a special message! One that truly can bring deliverance to many 'captives', with hearts given in the wrong direction - to the wrong people, places or things! Rather, we should give our hearts and all that we are and possess to the Lord God Almighty. He created us and loves us more than we can ever know and certainly deserves to be loved in return. We need to give Him as much as is in our poor power to respond and give; if only we know to do so—out of the depths of our beings—out of the 'well-springs' of our lives!

By the way, going home from this meeting the next day, Velma revealed to me the reason for her crying that day that I first shared this message. She said, "The Holy Spirit confirmed in my heart the truth of the message you shared. I was in love with a man in the same way. He also is a Christian and I had left Canada to get away from the love I had for him as I knew that it was wrong." She said, "The very day you shared this, I called him, made arrangements to meet him and shared with him all that you had spoken! He agreed that this was the answer and we both have been set free and have learned to Love Jesus with a new wonderful Bridal love!" She concluded, "I am so thankful that the Lord has given you this deliverance message!"

So dear friend, reading just now, do it! Transfer any inordinate loves in you life over to the only One who can truly receive and handle the deepest love from the wellsprings of your being. Deep calls unto deep at the noise of His Waterspouts - Brides, calling out in lovesick adoration to Him alone to whom this depth of love belongs! And his billows of love will flow all over and cleanse you and give you the greatest meaning and fulfillment in life. You will truly be made whole!

A Deeper Love than ever before possible!

I began to love Jesus more deeply than I had ever been capable of loving anyone else in my whole life. I was glad that the Scripture told me that this is the way that it should be. For this depth of love amounted to worshipful adoration and if I had given it to any other than the Lord God, I should have been guilty of idolatry. I love Him to the very depth of my being, and expressing it to Him makes me realize that *this* is what I had been created for. To love, worship, revere, praise and adore my Savior. The more I express this love for Him, the happier I become. Even now as I write this and tell Him once more of my love for Him, I fill up with His joy. This is His response to my expression of love for Him.

I discovered that I desired to serve Him now, not out of a sense of duty or obligation, or even the thanksgiving which I had previously felt, but rather out of devotion and a desire that sprang from that joy of loving Him to this new depth of my being. I found myself searching through the Word to find everything I could that would please Him.

I had discovered, as did Paul, that above service, above ministry, above sacrifice and even obedience, that *love* of Him, and others—this expression of love toward our Savior, really does ignite a new depth of love for others! This is one of the greatest benefits! And this new depth of love fulfills all of the law including the law of love, which is a giving of self to Christ first and then, we are enabled so much more fully—to give to others!

With this newfound expression of love toward the Lord filling me with a joy that I cannot describe with words, I wanted to cry out to my children, my friends, all who would listen, "He loves you, love Him in return—'fall in love' with Him!" I know this probably sounds so strange—even maybe weird—but it is a *truth* that helped me to understand more fully, more clearly, what Worship really is. I know it has made the most 'life-changing' difference in me. It has enabled me to put Him—Jesus—first, and think of Him first, above everybody and everything else in life! I remember my Amy saying to me as a teen-ager— "You mean you love Jesus more than me?" I answered; "Honey, we are supposed to love Jesus best, but that just helps me to love you even more than I could, if I put you above Him!" "You will understand this more—when *you* put Jesus first in your life!" Sadly, I learn, that often, those who don't put Jesus first, become angry with those who do!

The wonder, that He who created the universe with a word is pleased, yea, desires this expression of the first love from our hearts and lips, is almost too overwhelming for us to grasp - but its true! The only thing that He cannot give to Himself is our companionship, our fellowship, our love, and the fruit of our lips, expressing the worship of our hearts. He creates that fruit, according to Isaiah 57: 19. But we must express it and give it in order for Him to receive it! Remember, He *declares* in the Song of Solomon 2:14; (KJV) *"O my dove, that art in the clefts of the rock, in the secret places of the stairs, let me see thy countenance, let me hear thy voice; for sweet is thy voice, and thy countenance is comely."* "Sweet is your voice, and sweet the sound thereof." It may sound to you like a rusty tin can scraping against the curb, but He implies: "Your voice is sweet, let me hear it!"

David was a man after God's own heart. He had not only the fear of the

Lord - reverence and respect which is clean, bringing wisdom - but David fervently *loved* God, and expressed it to Him. He praised God. He tried to express in words and song, how great, how magnificent, how worthy to be revered and honored, but most of all, how *loved* He was, by David. David's days and nights were filled with meditation in God's Word. His mind was stayed on God.

Oh, should we not cry with David even now, "How great Thou art, how wonderful, how strong, how magnificent how wise, how tender, how brave, how gentle. Oh, you alone are our Rock, our Hiding Place, our Strong Tower, and how wonderfully comforting to be covered over with your Wings, even as a chick protected by its mother. How wonderful to be a lamb guided by so great a Shepherd. What a wonderful Husband thou art." Isaiah 54:5, *"For thy Maker is thy husband; the Lord of hosts is his name; and thy Redeemer the Holy One of Israel; The God of the whole earth shall he be called."* What a wonderful Protector and Savior. No wonder Isaiah wrote, *"For unto us a child is born, unto us a son is given, and the government shall be upon His shoulder, and His Name shall be called Wonderful, Counselor, the Mighty God, the Everlasting Father, the Prince of Peace!"* Isaiah 9:6. He is the greatest!

LOVE GIFTS AND GETTING TO KNOW HIM!

The Lord began to bestow upon our Bible Study group gifts that weren't listed in I Corinthians chapter 12. To some He brought forth the Gift of Music, with the ability to compose words and music—rather for myself, I just write down what I hear in my spirit. . To others He gave songs in the night. (One song—'Dispelling the Gloom' was given me this way—as I have already shared but it is so strange and wonderful it bears repeating!)

My sister Carly reports that when she was a barber, when cutting the hair of restless children, she hums this song and mothers are surprised to see their children immediately behave!

Others of our group found that they had new capabilities for writing poetry and essays. Nancy heard a word of prophecy that her hands had been anointed with artistic ability. She was to purchase art supplies, and as she did so, she found herself able to draw and paint lovely pictures of flowers with intricate detail and beauty!

As surprised as we were with these new abilities, we were not nearly as thankful as we should have been, for with our limited vision of Him, we wondered, "Why Lord, what does this have to do with leading others to Jesus?" We were always fearful that the time spent with these talents would take away from our time of leading others to Him and studying of the Word. Such wondering has a tendency to rob one of the pure enjoyment of just simply receiving a love gift bestowed because the One giving it loves us, and He loves to make us happy, and is just seeking to show us that love.

We were told much later, through a Word of Prophecy, that music put together by the Master with an anointing of the Spirit upon it many times has the power to reach man to a depth that words alone may not go.

This softens and opens one that the Word might then reach them, and be sown in good soil. The same Word was spoken concerning the love of Jesus shining out of our eyes and smiles. I suppose that this would apply to beauty in art and poetry also. *Every* gift bestowed by God, if used to His glory, will result in further blessing.

The Lord did not reveal these things to us when first He gave. He was bestowing beautiful gifts upon us, gifts more precious than jewels; and He was doing it out of love, even as a bridegroom bestows gifts upon His bride. He wanted us to see this facet of His love. This love of our Jew-EL! This is love of the Bridegroom for His Bride.

We need not have feared that using our talents would take away from leading others to Christ. As we used these gifts, with minds stayed on Him, we learned to spend hours alone with Him, painting, praising, writing, compiling music - even better, worshipping - and adoring and listening to Him!

He became truly our dearest Friend, the One that we took most of our joys, our triumphs, our hurts, and our large and small sorrows to before we took them to any other. And we found that we then did not have to take them to another. You know, in the first telling of anything lies the excitement of the telling. Repetition takes the edge off of the telling, unless we are discussing Him and His Word.

We reap from this sowing more energy, more joy, more love, more wisdom, and more vision. And this, in turn, makes us better witnesses than had we neglected this most important ministry unto Him, which truly results in ministry unto ourselves, for we can't 'out bless' Him. As we minister unto the Lord, He ministers unto us. And isn't this the desire of the Bridegroom?

This jealous God whom we serve desires a loyalty that can only spring forth out of love. This love that is so deep it is worship! This depth of love was created in us for Him alone. He alone knows how to handle such love. He is fiercely jealous of it, and if we will give this love to Him, He will respond with such tenderness, such gentleness, such respect and care that we will be completely fulfilled spiritually. He alone knows how to respond to and handle such expressions of love. He will keep it pure and undefiled if we but give this worship to Him, to whom it belongs. We will not be drawn after false doctrines, after inordinate love of things and others into idolatry, but will learn to love others in a deeper way with a purer love, in the proper measure, second only to the love of the Lord as Scripture requires!

Gathering together with other body members to praise Him and listen to Him, where the power of His anointing can be felt as in no other way, is one of the most thrilling experiences of life. If you don't feel this way, you haven't experienced—the Anointing! Ask the Lord to take you to a group who has! There you can: 'Get into the Waters'—first to the ankles, then to the knees, then on up until you 'launch out' into the deep, and swim in the Anointing!

In these latter days as He is gathering His people and purging them and drawing them into a deeper closer unity of oneness in Him, we will before His second coming see the fulfillment of His Church, without spot or wrinkle, being gathered unto Himself as a Body of total commitment, one to another, as well as to our Lord and Savior Jesus Christ. And it will be a power-filled, strong, pure, burning witness, His Body, His Church, His Bride. Daniel 11:32 says, "But the people who do know their God shall be strong and do exploits." Hallelujah! I want to be in that number.

Chapter Eighteen

Healing, Deliverance and Direction accomplished, Through Prayer and Travail in the Spirit!

Cancer is Defeated!

The year was 1983. I had just met my dear friend Betty Peace on the 4th of July, and she and I were driving home to Pittsburgh from Ashland, Ohio, where we had just been involved in Ministry with the 'Guardians of Joy'. Lila Aldenderfer, their secretary, had invited me to minister at a 'Brush Arbor Gathering.' The date—never to be forgotten was July 26, 1983.

The minister who had loaned Pete and Cass Twitchell the tent for this ministry, had just the night before given Betty a Word of Knowledge, "I see dark shadows all around this area," and he motioned in a circle the whole trunk of her body.

Betty replied, "Well, God is healing me from cancer." She was speaking what she had learned of claiming victory through faith in the Word of God.

"That's good," he answered, "God is going to completely heal you. You are going to feel a heat come over your body, and a tingling, and then a peace and you will be completely healed by the Power of God!" I was so surprised; I had just met Betty 3 weeks before and knew nothing of any cancer in her body!

Betty was stunned. She had just recently received the Baptism of the Holy Spirit and was brand new to such things as the Gifts of the Spirit, and the Word of Knowledge just given to her. I was shocked! I also was skeptical, only because of the exactness and length of prophecy that this minister was bringing forth, not only to her but to others. Later I had to ask the Lord to forgive me—every Word that was given this night was fulfilled in the lives of those friends of ours who were prophesied over.

The next day, July 26, while driving home, Betty began to speak to me concerning a woman who had brought problems, distress, confusion and misery into her life for the past 25 years. Just as Betty began to speak, I had a vision of this woman as a child of about three years. I saw the expression on her face and knew in the Spirit that she had just been sexually molested. Instantly my heart and spirit were filled with compassion for this woman. I said, "Betty excuse me, but I must pray in the Spirit!"

I turned my face to the door and began to pray in Tongues. The Spirit of Travail came upon me. I prayed and cried audibly allowing the Tongue of the Holy Spirit to flow through me, as the depth of *His* compassion, *remorse and regret,* filled me. This went on for what seemed like hours. The spirit of the prophet is subject unto the prophet, "The spirit of a son of God is subject unto the Spirit of God!" I would not quench the moving of the Holy Spirit in my vessel on behalf of this woman - in spite of the fact that I knew that this action and these sounds coming from me were a shocking happening for my new friend Betty!

Just before we reached the Fort Pitt Tunnel leading into Pittsburgh the Spirit of Travail lifted and I composed myself. As we exited the tunnel and started across the double-deck congested bridge, Betty looked over, saw and commented on the huge 200 foot high fountain located at the Point of the Golden Triangle Three Rivers, State Park. Being a little 'country girl' she had heard of the Fountain, but had never seen it. She exclaimed in awe, "Oh, that's the Fountain I have heard about!"

I had been at the site of that Fountain when it was being built and began to tell Betty about it. Velma Clate, the woman who had led me into the Baptism of the Holy Spirit, and Sister Gus, a Catholic Nun, and myself had taken the Autoharp and gone to that spot to pray and sing in the Spirit in a desire to dedicate it unto the Lord! We had learned that not only was it located at the juncture of three rivers, but was also being fed by a 4th *Hidden River!*

To my way of thinking, this Fountain was symbolic of that Huge Fountain of Living Waters that could come forth from the 'gathered' Bride of Christ, go up into the Heavens as a Fragrance unto our God, and be poured back UPON all flesh as a gentle rain—as spoken of in Joel 2:28, though all *will not receive* Him, Salvation, nor the Baptism of the Holy Spirit! Previously I had seen such a Fountain in vision, except that it had been a huge Fountain similar to 'Old Faithful' in Yellowstone National Park. This vision had come in response to a question I had asked of my Heavenly Father. This took place when my Pastor had been admonishing us, saying, "We are wells, let's get the 'logs' out of our wells that the Rivers of Waters might flow!"

I said, "Father, if I am a well, I am not a farmer and don't have hands, how can I get the logs out?" Suddenly I had the vision of a huge geyser, and the Lord spoke in my heart! "Take the Oil of the Spirit that I have poured out upon you. Put it under the Living Waters within and strike it with the Tongue of Fire. Get the Waters so hot through Worship in the Spirit that they will come out of your belly as *Steam* and will *push* out all of the logs!" (Rather like steam pressure.) My husband Larry was a Steam Fitter and he tells me that steam is called, 'live water!' He said that you can take a fifty year old pipe, corroded on the outside, but it will be shiny, 'whistle-clean' on the inside, for almost nothing can withstand steam pressure! Oh, if only I could help Christians to hear and understand the larger *Vision* that the Lord has given me concerning Worship in the Spirit using Song in the Spirit. This was my prayer the day of that *private Dedication Service of the Fountain* there at the Three Rivers Point in Pittsburgh, Pennsylvania, by the three of us!

While I was sharing all of this with Betty, suddenly she cried out, "Oh, I have to pull over, I can't stand the pain!"

Startled, I said quickly, "You can't pull over on this Bridge, Betty!" I saw the pain etched on her face and heard the agony in her voice. Realizing that the Fire of God was in my hand because of the intensity of the travail and the *speaking of Tongues in prayer* that had just taken place, I reached over and laid my hand on Betty's head.

Immediately she pulled at her collar trying to get some relief, and cried out again, "Oh, I have to pull off the road, *I can't stand this heat!*"

I admonished her once more, "You can't pull off—we are on the bridge!" And then, just as quickly as it had all begun, it was all over! Betty felt fine and relaxed. After 25 radium treatments and 2 cobalt implants resulting in constant bleeding and the inability to take even a potato chip into her mouth without running to the bathroom sixteen times a day—as she later related to me, *Betty was completely healed!* The bleeding stopped—along with the pain and distress! When examined weeks later—no cancer could be found! Thank You Jesus!

She told me that when the pain had come in the Van, it was so intense; it reminded her of the gutting of a chicken. In the days before tidy super market packaging of meats, we had to buy our chickens live; decapitate them and pull the insides out! It was called 'dressing them!'

I believe that this pain was caused by the Hand of God tearing away from Betty a spirit of cancer that had even entered her entire lymph system. Or, rather, perhaps, because of the sound and situation of travail and Tongues of the Holy Spirit coming forth, the spirit of cancer could not stand such prayer and tore itself out of her body. Remember that Jesus commanded a spirit to "Come out and *not to tear the one being freed!*"

Betty said that the heat which followed the experience of pain was of such intensity that she felt as though her whole body was on fire! This all took place 26 years ago and my dear friend Betty Peace lived long enough to see her twin girls of five years—at that time—complete high school and college, which had been her prayer. She became an ordained minister in 1986. She lived a full life, making her first Missionary trip to Mexico with Rev. Mertis Stamps. Also, she made 14 Missionary trips to Honduras with her good friend Reverend Thelma Oney and two trips each to Haiti and Israel. She also became the Executive Director of Young Adult Handicapped, Inc. for 13 years! All of this took place after deliverance of cancer, *through the blessing of prayer in the Spirit accompanied by travail.* Praise the Lord forever!

Since this experience, I believe that *many* cancers are caused by an evil spirit from the *evil one.* Satan is no gentleman. He is filled with hatred and is out to destroy whenever and whoever and however he can. We are filled with compassion and sorrow when we see little children, especially, afflicted with this devilish malady.

We see also, that distraught emotions brought on by constant upheaval, torment and mental unrest can cause enough stress to open us up to this enemy. Other times we might be tempted to nurse feelings of hatred and un-forgiveness. These attitudes can then be a *Route* that opens the door to the *Root of Bitterness,* which the Word of God tells us, can defile the whole body. We are told to guard against this by forgiving others as we would have them to forgive us.

This brings us to another avenue of this problem - how do we forgive? Betty has told me of her experience concerning this issue of forgiveness. She said that when she became a Christian, she realized that according to the Word of God, she had to forgive this person. She would say the prayer, "Lord, I forgive her." All was fine until another evil act was done by this one. Again, Betty would say a prayer of forgiveness.

Finally, after repeated incidents of meanness done against her personally and Betty's resulting prayer of forgiveness—in exasperation one day (when this one had tried to drive her off of the road with her automobile) she exclaimed, *"Lord, I can't forgive her!* I have tried and tried but I just can't forgive her!"

The Lord spoke in her heart, "You can't, but I can. Are you willing to let me forgive her *through* you?"

"Well, yes Lord", was her answer. After this the un-forgiveness seemed not to enter her heart when nasty incidents took place. She would cry out, "Lord, help!" and the cry was as one lost at sea in a life-raft and didn't mean "Grow me wings to fly out of here, or strength to row," but meant, *"Lord, You do something!"* Betty found herself instead, praying for this one's salvation rather than continuing to be angry!

How Gracious is our Lord! It was after this that the Holy Spirit used a heart's attitude of forgiveness, Jesus' strength in our weakness and, Tongues and travail that Betty's deliverance from cancer was accomplished! The woman who caused the trouble that Betty was speaking of has since received Jesus as Savior, when we took her to an Evangelist's meeting! Praise and honor and glory to our wonderful Redeemer!

Mental Relief Sought & Found!

I have heard a noted psychologist say concerning patients who have been baptized in the Holy Spirit *but are not using* their Prayer Language—that if he can encourage them to speak in the Heavenly Language for three hours, they can be totally restored and once again lead productive, happy lives, even after years of therapy that had no lasting results.

The Holy Spirit Directs!

Oral Roberts said that when He was led of the Lord to begin a University, he and his dear wife Evelyn—who has since gone on to be with our Lord—spent six hours, praying and travailing in Tongues! At the end of this time, when they felt that they had 'prayed through,' the Holy Spirit gave them the whole plan of how to begin the wonderful University of ministry that they established at that time

'Ray' is delivered from Stroke!

A Missionary to Guatemala named Rafael fell to her kitchen floor in the beginning of an apparent stroke. The Lord spoke to her, "Ray, pray in the Spirit!" (I always enjoyed that He used her nickname!) Again the Spirit spoke, "Ray, pray in the Spirit!" As she finally responded and began to speak in Tongues, she was restored well and whole and was no more troubled with any seizures! (It must have been a demonic spirit troubling the Missionary at this point in time.)

The Crooked Made Straight!

Years ago, upon seeing a man almost doubled over, being led into our Christian Book Store by one who brought him for prayer, my sister Carly burst forth in what one could call a 'Volley of Tongues.' That is, her voice became almost as the 'Screeching of an Eagle,' and as a result of this 'Outburst of Tongues in the Spirit', the man straightened up, stood tall and erect, and was well after years of this infirmity! (This sounds like the work of a 'troubling spirit' again!)

His Lungs are healed!

This same sort of 'Prayer in the Spirit' was said for a brother, Mack Peace, Betty's husband, who had for years been unable to breathe properly. He had Sarcodosis and scar tissue in his lungs, and was so weak he was unable to work any longer. While she was here visiting from California, Carly prayed for him in this manner repeatedly for the next two weeks! Every time she came into their home, she would place her hand firmly against Mack's chest and go into a powerful 'Volley of Tongues!' Mack was completely restored. He quickly regained his strength and still, many years later, enjoys excellent health. He goes from morning to night, chopping wood, cutting grass and running his household. All praise and honor and glory to our Wonderful God! We give thanksgiving, for the Power resident in His Heavenly Speech, and the laying on of hands by those who believe in such.

The Spirit of Profanity is Released

A Catholic gentleman gives this testimony. He loved to hear the Tongues spoken, especially in Song in the Spirit, but try as he may, couldn't seem to pray in the Spirit. He had asked for the Baptism of the Holy Spirit, eight months before, but hadn't received his prayer Language. Also, he couldn't seem to control his habit of swearing, using profanity. He was told to seek the 'Giver' rather than the Gift, but wasn't satisfied that he couldn't speak in Tongues. He then went to a Monastery for a weekend Retreat. This would be his first attendance and he was so happy. But when it came time for him to receive the Eucharist (communion), it would be his first time to receive not only the host (bread) but also the wine.

As it became time to do so, he said within, "I am a 'tea-totaler', I can't drink that wine." He said: "The Lord spoke in my heart and said, "Is that My Blood?" I replied, "Oh, yes Lord." As he drank the communion wine, he felt heat, as of a sword going down his chest, and before he realized what happened, he burst forth in Tongues! He has never used profanity since. This gives us much to think about—right?

Follow His Roadmap!

Almighty God, the Creator of this Universe, is an Awesome God, and if we will begin to follow His Roadmap as Written in His Holy Bible—will rebuke the fear of man, and rather obey His Holy Spirit, so much more could be done to cleanse Planet Earth and bring about true Holy Unity and Love between Christians, which should result in us being able to win lost, hurting people to our Beloved Lord Jesus Christ! Help us, Lord, to open our mouths and bring forth the Living Water, in the Spirit! Amen!

God's Wonderful Holy Spirit!

He came upon the face of the waters, brooded and brought forth upon this earth a habitation for us. He didn't need one. When He came upon Samson, that man's strength was unequaled. He came upon Saul when Samuel anointed him with oil and he was turned into another man and prophesied. A double portion of Himself was poured upon Elisha and even his bones in the grave caused life to be restored. He came upon Sarah in her old age and put life in her womb. As well He did for Elizabeth the mother of John the Baptist. He came upon Mary and brought forth the Savior of the world.

John declared of Jesus that He was the Lamb of God who takes away the sin of the world. He then immediately declared that this One upon whom you see the Spirit descending and remaining—is the 'One who *baptizes in the Holy Spirit'*. The ministry of Jesus was spoken of as baptizing in the Holy Spirit—rather than of healing or deliverance or miracles or of raising the dead. This baptism, through the Gifts and Fruits of the Spirit, equips His people to minister in all of these preceding ways. Christ's Ministry began when He returned in the power of the Spirit from the wilderness into which the Spirit had driven Him, and proclaimed, *"The Spirit of the Lord God is upon me."* Luke 4:14–18.

The Word tells us not to grieve or quench the Holy Spirit. He spoke to the early church—through a Word of Prophecy, we realize—and *said, "Set apart for Me Barnabas and Saul for the work to which I have called them."* Acts13:2. He is Lord of the Harvest.

Does this not help us to understand why we should seek this baptism and walk very softly about the subject? This is Holy Ground. We must never forget that in Matthew 12:31–32 Jesus tells us, *"Wherefore I say unto you, all manner of sin and blasphemy shall be forgiven unto men; but the blasphemy of the Holy Ghost shall not be forgiven unto men. And whosoever speaks a word against the Son of man, it shall be forgiven him; but whosoever speaks against the Holy Ghost, it shall not be forgiven him, neither in this world, neither in the world to come."*

There is no jealousy in the Godhead. Jesus promised to send the Holy Spirit to teach and comfort. I know that the Holy Spirit teaches us while we are in that position alone, of having Christ *in us*. He shows us Jesus and convicts of sin and righteousness and judgment. He teaches us the Word. But, oh my, the wonderful further teaching concerning the anointing He shows us when He comes also *upon us!* He teaches us concerning the *Gifts of His Spirit* and the *Fruit of His Spirit* and the *Tongue of His Spirit* and *Worship in His Spirit* and *in His Truth!*

Closing Prayer!

Holy Spirit, Comforter and Teacher, you have revealed that the misconception concerning Tongues is a poison in the Living Body of our Lord Jesus Christ, the Church. And that a body *cannot* get well until the poison is drained out of it. Our Father, let this pen of a ready writer be as *Your Tongue,* bringing *clarity and proper conception of Light.* Bring *healing to Your Living Body.* Use your Words as a *surgeon's scalpel to cut away* misunderstanding and misconception. *Lance the snake-bite!* Draw out the *venom. Heal the wound.* Clear up our vague, foolish, imperfect understanding of Your perfect gift. Cauterize with Your Fiery Sword, as the *visions* and the *Revelations* and the Word of Wisdom that You have given - spoken, written and visualized, are shared.

Lord God of Israel, forgive the *misuse* of that small member of Your Body—the tongue. Use Your Light on *Tongues* Lord, to *overshadow* and to bring forth *new life* and cause these *Waters of Life—the Living Waters—to extinguish the fires of satanic rubbish!* Release Your Body from the *stroke* caused by *poison-pens* dipped in the shallow wells of *mis*understanding. Frustrate the works of darkness. Cause us to see Your Word in new Light.

You have given us Your Words - spoken and written. They are power-filled vehicles of service and deliverance! Apply eye-salve that we may see in the Spirit the totality of what is ours, and then the 'how to' of their use!

Through the Baptism of the Holy Spirit, You have *anointed and clothed and equipped* us to be *Priests* in the Holy of Holies for the service of *Worship.* You have chosen us to be your *Brides.* You have made us to be *wells* with the ability to bring forth *Living Waters.* Oh Lord, use the revelations in this book, given by Your Holy Spirit, through the Word of Wisdom, to teach us how to function properly in these privileged positions!

May Living Waters flow in such a fountain of fullness that we shall be en*light*ened and will desire and de*light* to bring forth from *our* fountains? 'Deep will then be calling unto deep' at the noise of Thy 'water spouts'. And singing unto spiritual wells the waters will *spring-up!* And together the *Body of Christ,* being bathed in these *Healing Waters* and receiving 'steam cleaning', shall go forth as a *Bride* from her chamber, having made herself ready without spot or wrinkle, singing and dancing unto her *Beloved,* longing for *His return!*

And then, as Rebecca of old, His Bride *will* draw *water. She will bring forth for her Heavenly Eleazer, the Holy Spirit a Mighty River of Living Waters.*

These waters will flow for even those who have not power to draw for themselves—because that they have not understood and received the Baptism of the Holy Spirit that enables them to draw forth *these* Waters.

May we see the desert places blossoming and blooming as a result of this *Water.* And with the blooming of the desert, may the Fig Tree Israel, also receive a greater abundance of *new life!* When this takes place can the longed-for appearance of our Beloved Jesus, our Messiah, be more than just moments away?

Oh Holy Spirit, Beloved Comforter, Wonderful Counselor, Most Patient Teacher, guide us into *all Truth* concerning Living Waters and their *flow.* In these closing hours of the 'Age of Grace', when the enemy has come in like a flood, raise up Your Standard. Bring forth! *Flood* Your people with a greater awareness of the Supernatural Powers of these Waters to cleanse and remove the ravages of any deadly deluge! Give please, a clearer understanding of the Cleansing Healing Properties of these Waters that may flow from the Inner Chambers of the Holy of Holies that are within us. The result being, that we will not be able to keep our mouths—the doors of Your Tabernacles—shut! But rather, we will *pour forth* the Prayer, the Song, and the Worship in the Spirit, through the use of the *Unknown Tongues,* those Living Waters—that are in the Deep Wells of our 'Inner Man'. Amen.

'YE KNOW HIM'!

By Walter L. Wilson, M.D.

This work, no longer published, has been so important to my 'Walk in the Spirit' that I feel that it needs to be brought to the attention of every believer. I have just returned from the 100 year Centennial Celebration of the Azusa Street Revival in Los Angeles CA and learned that there are 600 million souls world-wide who have received the Baptism of the Holy Spirit! I am so thankful that because of books like "Good Morning Holy Spirit" by Benny Hinn that we think and know so much more of the Holy Spirit—and yet—we still hear Christians speaking of the Holy Spirit and referring to Him as 'It' or "Something told me"—as though He had no Personhood—thus I am extra pleased to include this Chapter from Dr. Wilson's little booklet!

What, or who is the Holy Spirit to You?

John 14:15–17, "If ye love Me, keep My Commandments; And I will pray the Father, and He shall give you another Comforter, Even the Spirit of Truth whom the world cannot receive, because it sees *Him* not, neither knows *Him; but ye know Him;* for *He* dwells with you and shall be in you." (KJV)

In many Christian circles little reference is made to the Holy Spirit and only an obscure place is given to Him in public ministry, personal life and private conversation. He is often referred to as "It" and treated as an influence, or a power, or an indescribable, intangible something.

On one occasion, a lady who was a prison worker in one of our great cities, *reproved me for a message I had given concerning the exalted place the Spirit must have in the life of a believer.* As she talked with me concerning the matter, she referred to the Spirit quite a number of times as "It." I listened patiently for some indication that this friend *knew the Holy Spirit as a Person,* and *loved Him as a Person of the Trinity.*

When it became evident that she did not have this knowledge of the Spirit, I said to her, "May I have an imaginary conversation with Mrs. Price, who is sitting on her porch down the street a little way?" She gave me her permission and I began as follows:

'His Name is not 'It'!'

"Mrs. Price, I am happy to tell you that Mrs. Schwartz came to the conference. *It* came last Monday morning and *it* has stayed all week. I asked *it* if *it* was saved and *it* said that *it* was." At this point my friend looked around at me *greatly astonished* and said "I cannot understand why you would call me '*it*'!" I said, "Pardon me, but you have interrupted my conversation." I then continued this imaginary visit with Mrs. Price, saying: "I asked *it* to tell me how *it* was saved, and *it* replied, "I believe that *It* died for me at Calvary and that *It* bore my sins away by shedding *It's* blood for me on the Cross." My friend was *so shocked at my references to Christ as "It"* that she turned to me *in great indignation* and said, "That is blasphemy! How can you refer to our Lord Jesus in such a way, and why are you doing it?"

Of course this reaction is just what I wanted and at once I called her attention to the fact that she had been referring to the Holy Spirit as *"It"* during our entire visit together. This brought to her heart the *revelation, which I had hoped she might receive.* Her face blanched with fear and she said, "O God, please do not strike me dead for insulting the Spirit as I have done." Then turning to me, she said, "I see clearly that the Holy Spirit *has never been a real person to me,* but here, and now, I acknowledge Him as my God, my Lord and God's Gift to me." This state of mind exists among many of God's people. [The excerpt continues.]

'My Personal Testimony' (Walter L. Wilson)

The first seventeen years of my life after meeting the Savior were years of much Bible study, much activity and *no fruit.* Teachers had instructed *me to not speak to the Holy Spirit in prayer nor commune with Him about the work of God but to go to the Father with every matter.* The bareness of my ministry and the lack of results in my service was the cause of no little sorrow and regret.

One day the Lord graciously sent across my path a man of God who said to me, "What is the Holy Spirit to you?" I replied that He was one of the Persons of the Godhead. This servant of God answered that this was a true statement but did not answer his question, "What is the Holy Spirit to you, *what does He mean to you?"* This inquiry produced *a deep heart searching* and I replied, **"He is nothing to me at all.** I know who He is, but *I have no personal relationship with Him."* My friend assured me that *my life was barren* and *my ministry fruitless because of this neglect.*

I had been treating the Holy Spirit as *a servant of mine.* I would ask Him to come and help me when I would teach a class. To be more explicit, *I really asked the Father to send His Spirit to help me.* This left the Spirit as *a servant subject to my call and request.* He was never more than an agent of the Godhead to serve me whenever I felt His need and *asked the Father* for His ministry.

The message, which this Christian brought to my heart, roused within me a great desire to *know the Spirit and to serve Him successfully.* I had a fear, however, of doing the wrong thing and felt that *perhaps the Father and the Lord Jesus would be offended* if I should go directly to this Spirit about any matter.

About this time, the Lord very graciously sent a devoted minister from Chicago who brought a wonderful message on Romans 12:1, "I beseech you therefore, brethren, by the mercies of God, that ye present your bodies a living sacrifice, holy, acceptable; unto God, which is your reasonable service." (KJV)

Having finished his address on the subject, he leaned over the pulpit and said, *"It is the Holy Spirit to whom you are to give your body. Your body is the temple of the Holy Spirit and you are in this passage to give it to Him for His possession. Will you do this tonight?"*

I left the service deeply impressed with the thought that no doubt *here was the answer* to my deep need and the *relief from my barren life.*

Upon arriving home I went to my study, laid myself flat on the carpet with my Bible open at Romans 12:1. Placing my finger on the passage, I said to the Holy Spirit, "Never before have I come to *you* with myself: I do so now. *You* may have my body, my lips, my feet, my brain, my hands and all that I am and have. My body is *yours* for you to live within and I receive *you* as my own Personal God. I shall see *your* wonderful working in my life and I know *you* will make Christ very real to my heart. I thank *you* for accepting me for *you* said the gift is 'acceptable.' I thank *you* for this gracious meeting with *yourself* tonight."

Upon rising the next morning I said to my wife, "This will be a wonderful day. Last evening *I received the Holy Spirit into my life as my Lord and gave Him my body to use for His glory and for the honor of the Lord Jesus.* I know He will do it and He will use me without a doubt." She replied, "If anything unusual happens today, call me on the phone. I will be anxious to know."

About eleven o'clock I had the joy of phoning home that the Spirit had spoken through my lips to the hearts of two young women, sisters, who had entered my office *on business. Both of them trusted the Savior.* This was the beginning of new days of victory, blessing and fruitfulness, which have continued since that time. *I ceased to neglect and ignore this gracious Person who had come to live with me.* Now He was free to use me in His service for the glory of the Lord Jesus. Your days, too, will be transformed and your life made fruitful if you will give to the Holy Spirit the place He should have in your life. [All of this and eight chapters more are included in my booklet: "Ye Know Him" Write me at my home: Grace McGonigle # 8 Hill Top Drive, Finleyville, PA 15332 Phone: 724–348–5317 e-mail: gilah2000@yahoo.com]

(Myles Monroe's new book: *The Most Important Person on the Planet* should make for marvelous reading! Of course this Person is the Holy Spirit of the Living God!

'Fiddle-Sticks!'

TIME: PRE-POLLUTION ERA
AGENDA: MEETING OF THE BORED
PLACE: LOWER CHAMBERS, 'SMOKEY ACRES'

Shabby Claws: (Satan): "He gave them miracles—it only made them demand more of the same! When they realize His ability to do anything, they just demand each a miracle of their own before they pledge allegiance to Him!"

"Let's not use that 'Miracle' approach, it only makes them more aware of my weaknesses. They're not worth that much bother anyway. Hee…hee… hee…I'm saving my 'Miracles Mirages' for a really 'Big Bang" at the closing of this age!"

"I've gotten plenty of mileage already, convincing them of my lies—that they 'evolved' from apes! Who but fools would ever believe such ridicules claims?"

"They see a tiny seed spring forth into becoming a tree, and a little baby being born in 9 months—fully formed and with eyes and ears and a brain and a heart and yet—they believe that they themselves evolved from an ape!"

"Incredible! They believe any of my ideas, if I just make them sound full of knowledge—'puffed-up'—(a lot of 'hot air') and, or sophisticated,* you know they mistakenly think that word means dignified."

"Let's see now, they do a pretty good job of hurting Him for me when they are least aware of it. I'll tell you what, fellows, let's work on that angle. Let's be '*super subtle*' in this new campaign."

"Let me think…Hmmmm, they're always hearing that idle hands are the Devil's workshop. Let's make them think that their hands are busy—while, oh, this is too good—I mean bad, while they are actually doing something useless!"

Pontius: "Oh, fiddlesticks!"

Shabby Claws: "Pontius, will you stop using that nice language! And don't ridicule my ideas! You had your chance, and you flubbed it! You should remember how my subtle hand trick worked on you." "I wash my hands of this whole matter."

"Indeed…that was a really 'bad deed', I commend you!"

"Be quiet now and let me think. Yes, that's it. Let's conjure up something useless to occupy their hands with, while…oh, wouldn't it be a horrible joke on them, (and especially on Him) if we could give them something to do that would really be harmful to them; to their bodies, without them even realizing it, for years and years…maybe even decades and decades."

"Well now Judas, I know that's only twenty kilograms of a second, but not to them. After all, how much really is 30 pieces of silver down here? Be still now, though, that was, '*Supertanic*', what you did with just a kiss. I delight in fouling up the lips! Hmmm, how can we do something more to foul up their lips?"

"Now, boys, here is what we will do. Barabbas, you get the Book out, you know I can't stand to get near that thing—what? Well, I'm not much different than most of them who ignore it, only my reasons make sense!"

"Heh, Heh, Heh, wasn't that a victory, remember how hard we worked to get them to take that accursed Book for granted? I think we might have to get that campaign under way again. It's not really necessary right now, though, most only use their Bibles for a 'coffee-table' decoration, let's get back to this other business."

"Let's see, never mind getting the Book out—I can quote it perfectly! Though, of course, more often than not I misquote it. He-he-he…they rarely know the difference!"

"They are so dumb about its contents; I get ages of mileage out of "Hath God said?" Poor old Eve taught me the effectiveness of that method! We ought to name one of our concoctions after her! I just suggested to her: "Take into your mouth that which will make you wise—and will let you see into another realm—and become as a god! She sure 'swallowed' that 'line'—hook and sinker'!"

"Oh I get such glee, just remembering the scene! I think I will use that later to introduce things I'm brewing up with names such as: 'angel dust'—'miracle weed'—'crack'—'pot'—but now back to this other thing."

"I have to get them used to putting wrong things into their mouth, as I did with Eve, before I can get them to put things into their veins."

"That wretched Book tells them "The life is in the blood"—I bet I can get them to 'mess- up' their blood by putting foul things into themselves, even through the different openings of the body—oh I'm getting excited thinking about it! But wait—let's get the beginning process started somehow!"

Shabby Claws: "Pontius! Will you quit that? Stop using that nice language!"

"Nero, stop blowing that smoke around, you waste more time down here than anyone! Nero, ah-hah, that's it! Let's make them waste as much time as you do, they can blow smoke around—they will be wasting their breath—they'll be wasting their time! But how can I get them to do that?"

"Hmm—where there is smoke, there is fire. How true. (I love—humph—that is I—relishes that expression). Wouldn't it be nice if we could give them something that would burn with fire—you know—sort of symbolic of my domain—like *burning little candles to me?*"

"Well, I know it sounds ridiculous, but I bet we could sell them on burning little candles—and that would cause smoke, (you know how I enjoy a smoky haze); it keeps out that wretched pure light. Hmmmm"

"But a candle burns too slowly—and doesn't make near enough smoke, and then too, a candle might make them think of that one they are not supposed to hide under a bushel! There I go again. Who mentioned that Book? It's bad enough hearing Him say something like that!"

"A little paper torch—hmmm? How could we get them to do anything that silly? Maybe we could get them to blow on the torch, and, no—the other end—that's it!"

"We could get them to *suck* on the torch. Oh, I know it sounds fantastic, but you know, they are born with the desire to suck! They put their thumbs into their mouths (wretched habit), those brats drive me nuts with their innocence and I rarely get an idea from one of those little ones, but there it is!"

"Oh, this is *HELL*-er-ific! I can't wait to get his idea under way. We can have them start out with a little paper torch, and maybe we could—hmmm—yes—fill them up with something to make them resemble little candles."

"Oh, I know they won't think of them as candles, but to me the irony of the symbolism will be so be-*UGLY*-full!"

"That's the best of it. Fill them up with something which seems harmless; maybe a little 'habit forming-something' full of deadly slow-working germs—my kind of suicidal germs—this is *my* concoction. I'm going to make this a *Blaster-Piece!*"

"We'll put in some irritation and misery and suffering and agony and even death! Ah-hah—this is one up on Him!"

"Oh, I know all of that will be foul-tasting, but they will get used to it. By the time they catch on it might be too late. Oh, I like this almost as much as our 'witches brew.'"

"They won't stagger, so maybe we can keep it subtle enough to convince them that their sucking is sophisticated; they're so dumb, I told you, they think that's a nice word"*

Shabby Claws: "Pontius, if you say 'Fiddlesticks' one more time! Wait! That's it Pontius! 'Fiddle Sticks'! Let's call them '*Fiddle Sticks*'! No, that would give the whole project away. We mustn't let them know that 'Fiddle Sticks' is our 'Christening Name' for this satanic 'baby'!"

"Oh, there I go again! We mustn't let them know that Fiddle Sticks is the official name of our new nightmare. Take my name—Beelzebub Satan, Lucifer 'Lucky Strike'"

"They are constantly saying: 'Good Luck' to one another. They mean it for good, not realizing they are honoring me using one of my 'nick-names'! 'Luck'—'Lucky'—'Luci'—all is derived from my official name, Lucifer!"

"Maybe use my name backwards—'Live'—since I am coaxing and tempting them with all of my toys. And if they succumb, before His Representatives get to them, they will have to live with me in Eternal Death! Hee, hee,hee—where the worm never dies and the fires are never quenched!"

"He told them that—hoping to draw them away from me. Maybe you can come up with a few nicknames—'butt', 'reefer'. Ah, you boys work on it. That's all for today!"

"This is really bad for a morning's work, hey? Remember our motto, 'Keep it subtle', and oh, yes, check the Book if you want to; I don't think He mentioned anything about this. He is always giving those punks more credit than they deserve and He actually expects them to use the good sense His Father gave them."

"Why He bothers at all with them is more than I can see. Well, I'll just have to go on trying to show Him that they aren't worth His having said 'no' to me."

"Are they, Pontius" "Are they, Judas?" "Are they, Barabbas?" "Hee, Hee, Hee, I just delight—(Oh, that's a good one—"Gotta 'light', buddy?")

"I just delight to see you fools cry!"

*Sadly, most believe that the definition of Sophistication means, dignified. But see the true definition in: (The American College Dictionary Random House, New York 1956)

*The definition of *sophistication:* Deceptive, misleading; impairment or debasement, as of purity or genuineness; a subtle tricky, beguiling, but generally fallacious (false) method of reasoning; to mislead or pervert; specious; pleasing to the eye but deceptive; false notion; logically unsound. *Satan is a sophisticated sophist!*

Specifics: How to be freed from 'Fiddle-Sticks'...and other Suicidal Seductions!

The 'Mini-Skit' 'Fiddle Sticks' that I have just shared, is of course, speaking of the terrible addiction of smoking. I realize that I would be doing a terrible injustice to you who are reading if I do not share the wonderful way in which the Lord led me into the 'power of deliverance' from this vice! This testimony will also teach how to be delivered of: inordinate evil imaginings—of alcohol and of other drug addictions. This will be a lesson on the power of 'specific prayers' and how to apply them! If followed, they can completely change your life! I have shared these experiences over the years and have seen so many being benefited as they hear—and do!

Just after the day I discovered that I was indeed a Christian *according to His Word* I was standing at my sink peeling potatoes. While peeling I was discussing with myself the anger I was feeling concerning one of my neighbors. In the middle of this discussion I remembered that I was a Christian and so I thought; "I'll pray about this!" I laid my potato peeler on the sink counter, sat down at my kitchen table, bowed my head and prayed. "Dear Lord, help me to be a good neighbor in Jesus Name, Amen."

I went back to the sink, picked up the peeler and proceeded to work. The conservation within became angrier than before I had prayed!

"Why doesn't she keep that German Shepherd tied up? Wait a minute; I just prayed about this and I'm still angry! I'll pray about it again, I'll persevere!"

I went to my table, sat down and prayed a second time. I said the same prayer but with more fervency.

"Lord Jesus, help me to be a better neighbor please Lord, Amen." I went back to the sink and was angrier still! I thought;

"What is the problem? I have prayed about this twice and I am madder than ever at her!" I wiped my hands and a third time went to the table, sat down and then *for the first time ever in all of my life*—I prayed a *specific* prayer. Instead of generalizing I said:

"Lord, the reason that I am angry with Sue is, she lets that dog of hers loose and it scares the children."

The Lord replied: "The dog never leaves the yard!"

"But Lord, the children don't know that!"

"They do." said He, "does Sue know Me?"

I was mortified with shame as I realized that I had been as petty as to be angry over a dog and Sue might be on her way to hell without me ever having witnessed to her.

"Oh Lord forgive me I cried. I'm sorry for being more concerned over a dog than her soul!" He forgave me. I went back to my potatoes happy. All the anger was gone. I was singing,

"Onward Christian Soldier." And I was thinking about how I could manage to speak to Sue about Jesus. I had just learned *the most important lesson of my life!*

The next day *I completely forgot everything* I had learned the day before. Again I was standing at that same sink. This time my mind was not filled with anger at my neighbor but rather I was meditating upon the experiences and the remembrances concerning another person.

In honest confession they were thoughts that I should not entertain but had done so for years and in fact seemed *powerless to dispel them from my mind!*. This is called the process of temptation when one is thinking wrong thoughts before one is even aware that they are thinking them. I was seeing mental pictures that should not be looked at. They could be called 'R' rated internal viewing! Seems I had a V.C.R. within and Satan was having a field day slipping in his video film whenever he wanted to and I seemed powerless to eject it! But this day remembering that I was a Christian I once more decided to pray about this matter.

'Same old prayer':

In my prayer, as I have said, *I forgot all that I learned the day before* and the prayer went something like this.

"Dear lord, please help me to be a good wife and mother and Christian in Jesus Name." There was *no mention of the film* I had just been viewing. My thinking up to this time was muddled by a statement I had often heard: "God can not look at sin!"—I can't find the 'proof' scripture to 'back-up' this statement, but if He can not look at sin, I certainly would never think of making Him look at mine, by telling Him in prayer all that I had been thinking and remembering.

I knew I should not be thinking these things, so anytime that I went to prayer about this problem I more or less swept the bad thoughts aside and would *never think of sharing them with the Lord,* knowing that He knows all about everything anyway—so I couldn't figure out how He couldn't look at sin!

Of course this was a very wrong precept and I never received Victory with this plan—but I just didn't know any better!

After my prayer, I went back to my sink and Satan pulled out all of the stops in *glorious panoramic Technicolor*. I felt so defeated, until suddenly, I was overwhelmed with shock! I remembered the 'Battle-Plan of Victory Prayer' that I had been taught concerning Sue and the Dog just the day before! When I remembered the specific rhetoric of specific prayer I thought:

"Oh No, how can I tell the Lord all of this?" And if you think it would be agonizing to tell your sweet little grandmother—or another, who held you in esteem—all of the things you were guilty of thinking—you can get just a glimpse of what it felt like to realize that I had to sit down and I 'tell it all' to the Lord.

I was so serious though to want to be delivered that I did just that! Remember now, up until this time I had in my arsenal of weapons against the evil one the prayer of Jesus.

"Get thee behind me Satan." He would leave *for about five minutes* and be right back. Sort of like 'time out for a commercial'!

True Confession!

For the first time in my life at age twenty-nine I knew to be specific and discuss all of my mental sin to the Lord. It went something like this.

"Lord, did you see what I was just imagining?" And I made myself tell Him everything I had just thought. The re-run was so painful. At first I tried to justify.

"Well Lord I just can't help myself. Lord, I can't help it that I fell into this imagining, I don't know why it started." Now—I knew the when and the how of it's beginning, but I didn't go into that! The Lord made no reply. I just confessed it all out—picture after picture—after picture and thought after thought!

Throughout this entire time, the Lord made no reply but I knew He was listening. He didn't condemn or have an attitude other than that of a good listener and my prayer went *from trying to justify my thoughts*—to just surrendering—and confessing—telling Him of all my guilt—*specifically*—something like this:

"Lord, I just know that I find myself remembering that curly hair and those piercing eyes and honestly, I can't help it, but the remembrance gives me pleasure." But knowing that it was wrong to entertain such thoughts—during this *disclosing of them to Him* who is altogether lovely and holy—my confessed memories suddenly, took on a whole new picture of 'cheapness'—of 'tawdriness'—of 'shoddiness'!

Having confessed my sins, specifically, I began to be *so sorry* that I had *ever* entertained them. In His audience, all that I was telling Him became stupid and disgusting to my own ears. My cheeks began to blush hot with shame and I truly wanted no more to justify or be involved with anymore of such 'thought life'. With tears of remorse streaming down my face I cried out to Him in repentance:

"Oh God, forgive me, Lord, please forgive me." *And He did!* Just as quickly as I asked, to my utter amazement, *the terrible weight of my sin was lifted off of my shoulders.* I felt light and free! I felt completely forgiven! I went back to my sink overjoyed with the lightness and freedom that I was experiencing! What a wonderful surprise. I was free and loved it. I went to my sink singing and happy. I was truly free! After fifteen years of bondage—not knowing how to get free—I had been captive all of those years!

Can I tell you that I was never tempted again to think what I ought not to think? No, but I can tell you something *better.* The very next time that I was tempted—about two hours later, for *the first time in my life,* I was aware of the *difference* between *temptation* and *yielding to temptation.* And I learned what to do about it! I realized that I John 1:9: had taken place in my life!

"If we confess our sins, He is faithful and just to forgive us our sins and to cleanse us from all unrighteousness." My confession—specifically— had led to repentance and then I was forgiven and cleansed of all of this unrighteousness!

But Satan hadn't given up, and the Holy Spirit allowed the tempter to 'try to ensnare me again' for the Lord knew that I would learn from this—to run to Him the moment I recognized that I was being tempted. I would be delivered—and then strengthened by the realization of the quick deliverance that came as I quickly turned to the Lord with: "Help Lord!"

Just hours later that very day I halted in my thought life and realized that Satan had slipped his film into my set and was trying to get me to review it. The *moment that I was aware* that there were wrong images crossing my mind, I remembered all that had taken place this wonderful morning of deliverance. It had felt like a load of bricks had been lifted off of my shoulders! I remembered the confession—the shame, and then—the release that came, when I confessed specifically—repented and asked forgiveness. I *did not want to have to go through that whole experience again!*

Instead of focusing in and getting a clear picture of what Satan was trying to have me see, and giving in to temptation—as I would have before this experience—I called out to the Lord. "Jesus, Help!" I didn't yield to the temptation! I stopped it cold by crying out to Jesus and He scrambled the channel and I could no longer see anything. Praise God He heard my cry and delivered me. The Lord then put His film into my internal V.C.R. and my thoughts became—Very Christ Related. I was singing and rejoicing in God my Savior!

Oh, before I go into the marvelous testimony of my deliverance from cigarettes and alcohol, I forgot to tell you—after weeks of learning of the power of specific prayer, I was enjoying great victory in staying free of the temptation that comes from evil imaginations. I learned to *'cast them down'* through *specific prayer* and *calling upon the Name of Jesus*, before they could get even a 'toe-hold'! And then one night while asleep I had a dream which was filled with all of the pictures, plus some, that I had ever imagined! In the past when this temptation in dreams would occur I would awaken feeling defeated and I would think:

"What is the use of trying to stay free while awake, if the evil one has the advantage of entering my dream state?"

But, upon awaking this time—I was first tempted to 'relive' the dream. But I remembered the agony of having to confess to my Heavenly Father if I were guilty of yielding to this temptation. I couldn't bear the self-disappointment and the disappointing of my Lord that this would cause so I dropped to my knees beside my bed and said. "Lord, I don't know how much of that dream was temptation and how much of it was yielding because I was dreaming, but here it is." I began confessing the dream specifics to Him.

I hadn't proceeded long when I felt within that the Lord would have me to discontinue—that I had passed the test—and that He was pleased. I *never* had a dream of this kind of temptation again concerning evil imaginations! Satan is not pleased if his actions cause us to drop to our knees, and run into our prayer-chamber with Father! Satan once more flees as we submit unto God—just as the Word promises in James 4:7-8, "So humble yourselves before God. Resist the Devil, and he will flee from you." "Draw close to God, and He will draw close to you!" What a wonderful escape method and reward!

As we see the Lord deliver so powerfully in one area of our lives—such as the vulnerable area of our thought life that the evil one apparently has access to—it makes us stronger in faith that Jesus can deliver in every areas of our life. It is as though the Lord—our 'Heavenly Potter' takes our little clay vessel and allows us to go into the oven of temptation and trial for He knows that when we discover, His Strength to deliver as we call upon Him to do so—our clay vessels are strengthened.

Clay Pots!

I want to say here that rather than be discouraged when I realized that

Satan was allowed to tempt me again, because that I had studied Ceramics, I saw the wisdom of God in allowing it! When one is making a beautiful vase through the art of Ceramics one is involved in working with a piece of 'green ware'. This is a gray *piece of clay* that has been molded into a shape. This green ware is very fragile before it is fired. One must be very careful that it doesn't break, just from the pressure of ones hands while cleaning it—by scraping and washing away the mold lines. So, this delicate object must be fired at 1200 degrees Fahrenheit, which strengthens it and turns the gray clay, white! Are you beginning to 'get the message' in my illustration?

Next, after glaze is poured into it and a design of some sort is put on it with another coating of glaze, it is then fired at 1800 degrees. Now it comes out of the kiln glazed and capable of holding water and is often very lovely to look upon. If one wants to further beautify this piece of art, a gold-fire at 2200 degrees is necessary and then to make it even more valuable and lovely a platinum fire of 2400 degrees is necessary.

This whole process is an illustration to me of what the Holy Spirit is doing in our spiritual growth, and I believe that it helps us to better see the 'working out' of the scripture found in scriptures such as II Timothy 2: 20–21, "But in a great house there are not only vessels of gold and silver, but also of wood and clay, some for honor and some for dishonor. Therefore if anyone cleanses himself from the latter, he will be a vessel for honor; sanctified and useful for the Master, prepared for every good work."

And especially do I see this process in II Corinthians 4:7, "But we have this treasure in earthen vessels that the excellence of the power may be of God and not of us." (For a great Bible Study on this subject search out the following scriptures: Isaiah 66:20; Jeremiah 48:11; Hosea 8:8; Acts 9:15; Romans 9:22–23; IThess.4:4; I Peter 3:7; and Revelation 2:27.)

During the next few weeks every time that I was aware of thinking what I should not, it didn't take long to realize such. In other words the temptation was not long in running, before the Wonderful Holy Spirit would nudge me and remind me of what was happening and I would cry out to the Lord again. "Help, Lord!"

When I asked the Lord to "Help", it was not with the thought that I wanted to have a little assistance with the furthering of my own strength or will (won't) power but rather I cried "Help" like a sailor out in the middle of the ocean alone in a life raft. When he cries "God Help Me", he is not wanting Jesus to grow him wings that he might fly to safety, nor for strength in his arms to row the vast sea to safe harbor. He is crying, "God, *You do something.* I am too weak. Be my strength!" And I find that this is—if not the only way to handle temptations—*my* wonderful powerful means of deliverance! *Before a beginning yielding to them* becomes overwhelming, and we find ourselves yielding fully to temptation. My great victory in all of this was to become aware of the *difference* between *being tempted,* and *yielding* to temptation.

I later learned how to be free from cigarettes and alcohol using that which I have just shared with you, the *specific prayer—which puts us in an attitude of leaning on Christ's Strength, rather on our own poor power of resistance!* Our bodies are not our own. We need to take care of them. They have been paid for with the Precious Blood of the Lamb, Jesus Christ of Nazareth! I Corinthians 6:18–20, "Run away from sexual sin! No other sin so clearly affects the body as this one does. For sexual immorality is a sin against your own body. Or don't you know that your body is the temple of the Holy Spirit who lives in you and was given to you by God? You do not belong to yourself, for God bought you with a high price. So you must honor God with your body." (NLT)

Now to tell you of the great victory of deliverance that the Lord Jesus afforded to me, after I applied the wonderful blessing of 'Specific Prayer' to the problem of cigarettes! After my deliverance from evil imaginings and remembering—I sat at my table reading my Bible four and five hours a day! I loved reading the Bible. While reading, as the saying goes, I 'smoked up a storm'! I did this partly because now, after years of 'giving up' in my own strength the smoking habit, I was more 'hooked' than ever, and partly as an act of defiance to those ones—who had been used to rob me through the years of the joy of the awareness of my salvation—by insisting that if I was smoking I could not possibly be saved!

This is like saying that the act of Salvation brings with it instant growth and maturity to new baby Christians. It doesn't work that way. Well yes—for some the Lord has given instant Miracles along with the Salvation Package, but this has been a bonus of blessings, not the 'norm'. So I was ready to blow smoke rings into the face of all of my former accusers as a way of saying. "I'm saved, saved, saved, and saved, in spite of my bad habits!" (Sadly, I had done this to a dear elderly Pastor who visited me, hoping to be a blessing to me. I did this partly to not be a hypocrite, as he visited me when I had a cigarette in my hand—and partly really hoping within that he would see beyond my smoking and be a true loving Christian in spite of my bad manners! He did pass my test—not reacting negatively, nor that he even noticed, and after my recovery I enjoyed having lunch in the home of Rev. Carl and Joy Boyer. We enjoyed watching the black-capped chickadees eating from the 'feeder' sitting on their dining-room window sill. This is a lovely memory concerning lovely Godly Christians!)

One day as I was sitting reading, smoking and praising and thanking my Lord for so great a Salvation and also for the wonder that He had shown me the way of deliverance from evil imaginings and memories, I was saying to Him:

"Oh Lord, how can I share with others how wonderful you are, and how greatly you are willing to deliver. I can't tell my friends and neighbors about my former thought life. It wouldn't be fair to my family. Lord, how can I show others how wonderfully you deliver?" And then I looked at that little 'white worm' of a cigarette that I was holding between my fingers. The attention drawn to the 'cig' at that time was enough. I knew it was the Holy Spirit pointing out the way! I continued looking at the cigarette and my conversation with the Almighty One went something like this:

"Well yes Lord, that would be a good way to show others, but Lord I really enjoy smoking them now!" Through the years of smoking and 'giving them up' I hadn't really enjoyed smoking, just seemed to need something to do with my hands while talking or thinking. But now I really liked the habit. But as I watched the smoke curl up off of the cigarette I knew that I had heard from God and I knew that what He had already shown me of the way of deliverance was so valid that I could apply it to this little 'coffin nail' and my Jesus would be Victor! I said;

"Alright Lord, take it away. Show me Your Strength!" Note: For the first time I did not say: "I will give it up." But rather I threw the burden of the act upon the shoulders of the Burden-Bearer of all Burden Bearers!

I put that cigarette *out* and *for three weeks* I had *no desire whatever for smoking!* Then one Sunday evening I had an argument with my husband. I ran from the room and went to my bedroom and sat down and I remember thinking *to* myself;

"How dare he speak to me like that!" I was very angry and the desire to smoke came into my mind. I remember sitting there 'stewing within'. I wanted to light up a cigarette and sit there and 'meditate' upon *my anger.* At the same time, I heard within a song that we had been singing in Church Choir. The words went: "Pray, pray, pray, pray." *I didn't want to pray! I wanted to be angry!* I mused on my anger a few moments longer and still the song persisted within: "Pray, pray, pray, pray".

"Alright I exclaimed" exasperatedly. I dropped to my knees to pray—but before I had even brought my hands together in an attitude of prayer nor formulated my prayer—to my *absolute utter amazement,* all the anger was *gone!*

I hadn't even prayed yet, only exclaiming in an exasperated way "Alright!" My obedience to the gentle prompting of the Holy Spirit, for He was the One singing within my spirit—was rewarded in a way that I could never have imagined!

Instantly, all the anger was gone! All of the desire for the cigarette was *gone!* I was free! Tears of gratitude streamed down my cheeks as I knelt there thanking the Lord! And I was absolutely 'hooked' from that moment—to this one, concerning the way of deliverance for me! And this is to run to Jesus every time that I am aware of temptation concerning anything. And I call upon Him: "Lord, show me Your Strength!"

I never from that moment, until this moment today have ever wanted another cigarette! I discovered that this 'way of deliverance' had been already given in II Corinthians 12:9, "My strength (the Lord's Strength) will be made manifest in (your) weakness." This scripture seemed like a mystery to me until I discovered that it was His strength that Jesus wanted to be displayed in my weakness. When I had tried deliverance in my own strength, I was a failure. The Scripture: Philippines 4:13 "I can do all things through Christ who strengthens me," became my 'joy-filled' battle cry!

That very hour, I arose from my knees and found that not only had the anger left, but I had a new love for my husband. I ran into the kitchen where he was seated, still looking angry. I threw my arms around his neck and kissed him! I saw the anger melt out of his face. I was *astonished!* Always before this, when we would argue, it would take days before we spoke again. We never seemed to be able to communicate and get to the root of the problem, and also, his angry looks frightened me into silence!

I went to the sink to finish the dishes praising the Lord for these new found victories! I thought to myself:

"I have to go to Church tonight and share with the children"—I was teaching 'high-school students'. It dawned on me that Satan wanted me to get angry—begin again to smoke—and then he would whisper into my ear: "How can you teach them anything, you are a hypocrite!"

"Lord Jesus, just because I dropped to my knees, even when I didn't want to, You honored my actions and taught me a new wonderful way of not only escape from the temptation of cigarettes but a new loving way of avoiding arguments with my husband!" Praise Your Name and the wonderful Power of the Presence of the Holy Spirit to deliver when we seek deliverance, His Way! You try it for yourself and see!

Now just here I must tell you though, of another problem I encountered with the **spirit** of nicotine! *You need to know this if you are to have total victory* in any area—not just in the realm of cigarette smoking. As I have said, I never again was tempted to smoke—*while awake!* I began to 'hate' even the smell of cigarette smoke! However, *years later*—after I received the Baptism of the Holy Spirit—and I realize now, that the Holy Spirit wanted to teach me concerning my authority and ability to cast out spirits—I began to dream that I was smoking!

These dreams were so real that I would awake thinking: "Oh Lord, why have I begun to smoke again?" I would feel such remorse, because the dreams were so real that I actually thought that I had begun to smoke once more. Then, for moments after awaking from such dreams, I would look for an ash tray, and it then took awhile for me to realize that *I had not begun to smoke again—that this had been a dream* and it was so real that I was amazed that this could be happening.

After several repetitions of such dreams, I shared this terrible problem with a mature Christian minister and she said:

"Grace, you are being bothered by a *'spirit of nicotine'!*" As I heard this I thought:

"Can this be?" And, "Imagine if spirits can have such influence as this, concerning smoking, think of what demonic power of evil they can cause, to be able to trouble us in this manner! And suppose it had been in another area of past sins—demons 'hanging on' or being able to influence us through dreams that are so real we think that we are actually guilty of committing them! This can cause the hopelessness which many times lead us into committing sin once more!"

Well, my friend immediately rebuked the spirit of nicotine and commanded it to come out! Once more I was free for years and years with never having a dream like this again. She did not think to command this spirit to not ever enter again, which is what Jesus did when He rebuked and cast out a spirit. I have not had a cigarette since 1963, thank God! But in this last year, I found myself troubled again by dreams of smoking. And once more the dreams were so real that I awakened and even spent days *thinking that I had once more begun to smoke.*

In wondering how it once more entered, I asked the Holy Spirit's wisdom. I then remembered going into the 'Eat and Park' Restaurant and because the 'no-smoking' booths were all filled, I agreed to go into a separate room where smoking was allowed. It smelled awful and I was too sickened to enjoy my meal! I left with the meal uneaten. Shortly after this, the bad dreams returned. I really believe that because I entered a room where smoking was allowed, the spirit of nicotine was actually invited to be in that room, and that is how I was once more troubled by this spirit! Please, think deeply on what I have revealed to you concerning evil spirits, and do not scoff. A large part of Jesus' Ministry had to do with casting out evil spirits of every kind.

My next discovery in deliverance was how to be free from the use of any alcohol. I felt that it was quite alright to have an occasional drink at home. Especially so, on a 'Holy'-Holiday! The thought patterns we have are many times, so strange. We use times of celebrating His Birthday or Resurrection or

Christmas, to 'toast' one another using that which His Word and our experience has shown to be so detrimental to good sound health and life habits. The problem being that too often a 'toast' leads to a 'roast' of our morals. As I have already said in the account of my second vision, (Living Waters, Flow—the Chapter Thirteen on Visions) the frontal lobes of our brain governing morals are the first to be numbed, making us vulnerable to immoral responses!

The Scripture in Proverbs: 23:29–35 says, "Who has anguish? Who has sorrow? Who is always fighting? Who is always complaining? Who has unnecessary bruises? Who has bloodshot eyes? Is it not the one who spends long hours in the taverns, trying out new drinks. Don't let the sparkle and smooth taste of wine deceive you. For in the end it *bites* like a *poisonous serpent; it stings like a viper.* You will see hallucinations, and you will say crazy things. You will stagger like a sailor tossed at sea, clinging to a swaying mast. And you will say, "They hit me, but I didn't feel it. I didn't even know it when they beat me up. When will I wake up so I can have another drink?" (NLT)

Proverbs 31:4, "It is not for kings, O Lemuel, it is not for kings to drink wine, nor for princes strong drink, lest they drink and forget the law and pervert judgment of any of the afflicted." (KJV)

We are Kings and Priests unto God, and I must remember that I have greatly erred in judgment under the influence of alcohol.

Why do we take even one drink; to stimulate appetite? If we need that in a land that is overflowing with good food in great abundance we may already be ill and need some other remedy. Thinking that we must introduce a drug into our systems in order to be able to relax and enhance the ability to converse is in error also. For too often this leads to excess and our conversation suffers thereby. Renewal does not come via the 'bottle'—only nursing babies can be benefited by these!

Are we surrendering to 'peer pressure', that wrong motive that we try to persuade our children they ought not to indulge? Romans 12:2, "Don't copy the behavior and customs of this world, but let God transform you into a new person by changing the way you *think.* Then you will know what God wants you to do and you will know how good and pleasing and perfect his will really is." (NLT)

I defended my 'right' to drink in moderation to any who would question. I quoted Paul's admonition to Timothy to take a little wine for his stomach. I referred to the Lord's turning the water into wine. And knowing the way of wine drinking personally and understanding the story in that light; I knew that one has no sense of whether wine is 'good' or 'bad' after one has drunk much at a feast. I was self-assured that it was real wine spoken of—intelligence doesn't call grape juice wine. Considering all of this I felt the Lord was not showing disapproval concerning my 'social drinking'.

And then one morning—a dear neighbor came to my door. Her daughter had gotten into trouble and she greeted me with this statement. "I have gone to all my friends and they have given me their advice. I know that you are a Christian and thought that I would come to you and see if you can give me some Christian advice!" I was so complimented. I wasn't even aware that she knew that I was a Christian.

I prayed and asked the Lord to give me wisdom to be able to help her. He must have for as I shared with her I gained her confidence and I know that she began to share with me things that she had not shared with the other friends. We ended our visit with prayer and she went away comforted.

That very evening I went to my other neighbors home, the home of my old 'drinking buddy'. Before I had more than two beers in me, I was disclosing everything that my trusting neighbor had gone on to confide in me! And her teenage son was nearby getting an 'ear-full'! Imagine! Even a heathen wouldn't behave like that!

The next morning I awakened and lay thinking of the happenings of the day before. Suddenly I remembered what I had done the night before.

"Oh no, Lord", I cried, "I didn't!"

"Yes", He whispered quietly, "you know you did!"

"Oh Lord, I couldn't have! How could I betray a confidence like that, and on just *two beers?*"

"She trusted me Lord. Lord, If I want to minister for You, I guess I can't drink anymore." He agreed.

"Lord", I prayed, "Take it away." Again, leaning on His strength, not my own.

For three weeks I had no desire for any drink. Then one afternoon, again at the home of Agnes, my 'drinking buddy', I was sitting on her patio when she brought out a tray on which there was a tall 'stiennie' of beer for the both of us. Up until this time I used to love to drink beer from these 'stiennie' glasses where I could see the two inch collar of foam and the sweat beads running down the sides of the glass. This was my favorite 'cooler' especially on a hot day—even though it doesn't cool one off, it makes you hotter—lemonade or iced tea is far better! Now this was a hot day in August.

I apologized to my friend saying that I was sorry that I hadn't told her but I was no longer drinking.

She replied: "Aw c'mon Kid, you can have a beer." "What are you, a Priest?" "Well, even the Priests are allowed to drink beer!" As she spoke I looked at the glass and it did look good! Just then as I looked and *was tempted by my eye and my flesh,* I heard within a paraphrase of the scripture from Proverbs.

My Wonderful Counselor, the Holy Spirit who is *always present at every conversation,* made me aware of His Presence there to help just then by putting in my mind, the Words, *"Look not long upon the glass as the sweat beads run down the sides!"* I knew that the scripture says: "Look not long upon the wine as it sparkles in the cup for at the end, it stings as an adder and bites like a snake." In other words, alcohol can poison the brain cells. That is why we have headaches after a drinking bout!

I laughed at the paraphrase and the humor in it and the laughter broke the temptation. I have never wanted a drink since. And a few times over the years when Christians have suggested that I have 'just a glass it won't hurt', the Holy Spirit reminds me that He has not changed the scripture and therefore neither should I change my response. "No Thanks!" How happy I am that His strength is made manifest in my weakness! And when His strength becomes mine, I am no longer in the former area of weakness. I am freed! And that is my confession!

The Alcoholics & Narcotics Anonymous Associations do a great amount of good for others with their '12 step' programs. But I wonder if the admonition to constantly speak the former addiction as a present reality is putting into speech the way of defeat because that there is *the power* of **life and death** in the *tongue!* The constant declaration stating that one is still what one has been delivered from seems to me to be 'self-defeating'! Perhaps addicts need to repeat this profession, because that the temptation has *not been eradicated;* but rather is being suppressed by the program and 'self-will' but perhaps not 'specific' prayer to Jesus. If so, then they *are* still addicts and I see in this the purpose of the negative confession of the addiction. They have not been completely delivered by Christ's Strength alone!

Could they begin to openly call upon Jesus Christ by His Name, rather than call Him—"Higher Power" in their confessions; could they then receive 'total deliverance'? Acts: 4:12, "There is salvation in no one else! There is no other name in all of heaven for people to call on to save them." (NLT) (This speaks of salvation in every area.) I ask forgiveness if I have misunderstood this part of the Programs, I certainly don't mean to criticize what has been such a blessing to so many. I have made these comments to have them be taken into serious consideration!

The scripture tells us to submit unto God, resist the devil and *he will flee from us.* The best submission I ever learned was to call upon Jesus as I have just shared with you. Again, I have found deliverance not in asking Jesus to strengthen me, but rather to BE my strength…to show me *His Strength.* This has been my path to Freedom! Later, I learned *after the Baptism* that I had the power to take authority over the evil one, but until that time in my life the lesson on specific prayer and leaning on His Strength were my bucklers…and still are!

Just before I was really made aware of my Salvation—before I was assured beyond a 'shadow of a doubt' concerning the 'life-changing' path of freedom and joy and growth, that this knowledge gives, and just before the lessons learned that I have just shared with you, I was invited to a prayer group.

I had just gone forth to the altar of a Church after the minister gave a 'stirring' presentation and invitation to be saved and 'surrender all'! Tears were running down my cheeks and as I approached the altar the pastor asked me: "Why are you here?" While wiping my eyes, I couldn't put into words any answer, but left that altar feeling that wonderful confirmation of the Holy Spirit that He is indeed within. I didn't know that 'this was that'—the confirmation that He was already in me—at that time—and that He was bearing witness to the Truth of His Presence. (*He Jesus, knew* what my prayer request was!) I also was wondering why the Pastor had not known to pray with me the prayer of Salvation. I thought that my tears and his invitation would give him a 'clue'. Years later when I asked him concerning this he replied, "Well, I didn't know if you wanted to bring a letter of changing to our Church, or be baptized, or if you wanted prayer for something else." Even as I write this, though his answer had me later irritated for years, I see now I must forgive him—he *was* unaware. Pauline Moore, a dear sister who is now with the Lord, and later became my mentor, stepped up and invited me to her prayer group. Feeling the presence of the Lord, I heartily agreed.

On Tuesday, I took my sister-in-law to the dentist and afterward she invited me to have a glass of wine. I had not learned all that I have just shared with you on deliverance, and so accepted. I had another glass and the effect of the wine led me to 'go looking for trouble'! I am ever thankful that 'trouble' was not at home. Friday came, the day of the prayer meeting. I thought, "Lord, there I was in Church on Sunday, 'surrendering all' and by Tuesday I was drinking and forgetting my surrender. How can I go to this prayer meeting?" I decided that because I promised to go, I would go just this once, and think of some excuse to not return.

There were just 5 ladies gathered in the home of Mabel Christopher. Within fifteen minutes of their opening prayer, I was down on my knees, confessing, not specifics, but rather of my *inability* to follow the Lord. I knew I was hopeless and shared this confession with them. Pauline gave me a book she had brought just for me. It was, 'The Burden is Light' by Eugenia Price. I loved to read Readers Digest Books and other literature that was uplifting, but this was the first book that I ever read, that was written by a Christian. I was completely unaware that there was specific Christian Literature!

I came upon one sentence in that book that completely shocked me and was the beginning of the opening of my spiritual eyes. The sentence was one that Eugenia had written of herself. "I went through a dark period of my life when I wanted to run back to the bar and to my old friends and say: "I didn't mean it, it isn't real, take me back!" Shocked, I thought: "She felt this way, and she was already a Christian!" I realized that I had expressed these same thoughts and believed that because I did so, that 'for sure' meant I was not saved! This was a 'breakthrough' for me! Just days later, I came upon the book and scripture that brought forth my deliverance! I discuss them in this next paragraph.

I am writing all of this in depth as best as I know how, because I believe that many are being held in bondage because of these same 'pockets of ignorance'. Many times we hear loving and concerned ministers of the Gospel giving the invitation for salvation by giving their listeners the following impression. "If you don't *know* beyond a shadow of a doubt that you are 'saved' and 'if you are not sure', you should ask Jesus into your heart once more. The inference being: "Ask Him again this time and *really mean it!* It might not have 'taken' the first time you asked!" We almost never hear the congregation being told, as I finally, at the age of 29 read in Billy Graham's book, 'Peace With God'…if you have ever asked Jesus into your heart, rest on the fact of God's Word, *that He is there!* When I read this I couldn't believe it! I thought: "This can't be so, I have asked Jesus into my heart over and over again, and still I am tempted." As I have said, I was convinced erroneously that this fact of being tempted meant that 'there is nothing new' here—same old 'shack'! "I must not be born again!"

The very next day I read in 'Letters to Young Churches' by J.B. Phillips… printed in 1956 and this was now 1963—this book I had 'lifted'—yes , I took it the year before, from a Presbyterian Church I had once visited and had not opened it until this day—and just now found on my bookshelf! I quote: Colossians 1:27, "For I am a minister of the Church by Divine commission, a commission granted to me for your benefit and for a special purpose: that I might fully declare God's Word—that sacred mystery which up till now has been hidden in every age and every generation, but which is now as clear as daylight to those who love God. They are those to whom God has planned to give a vision of the full wonder and splendor of His secret plan for the sons of men. And this secret is simply this: *Christ in you* Yes—Christ *in you,* bringing with Him the hope of all the glorious things to come." I read this—remembered reading the day *before, Billy Graham's statement: if you have ever asked Jesus into your heart, rest, on the fact of God's Word…that He is there!* I thought, I have asked Jesus into my heart maybe a hundred and fifty times!

Suddenly the truth of these two statements, one from the writings of Billy Graham, the other from Saint Paul, 'hit me'—penetrated my being with TRUTH! I leaped to my feet in surprise and shock and shouted there alone in my kitchen: "I *am* a Christian!" "I *am* a Christian!" I clapped my hands in thanksgiving and exaltation and joy filled my soul! Always before, when someone would ask me if I were a Christian I would answer: "I think I am or, I hope I am!" And the familiar answer would come that I had erroneously believed was truth! "If you don't 'know' you are a Christian, you probably are not, If you *are one*, you will know it!" There is was again—the affirmation of error that I had believed for so long!

Now, for the first time, I understood a revelation concerning the Scripture stated in Romans 10:9–10, "that if you confess with your mouth the Lord Jesus and believe in your heart that God has raised Him from the dead, you will be saved. For with the heart one believes unto righteousness, and with the mouth confession is made unto salvation." (NKJV) The revelation is this: The confession is not: "I am a Christian!" Rather, the confession required from the heart and mouth is: "Jesus Christ is Lord!" I had confessed this all through the years! I would sit on a bar stool in a tavern and with just one drink in me, I would begin to witness that statement to others: "Jesus is Lord!"

I know *now* that Jesus was tempted severely to turn stones into bread when His fast of 40 days in the desert was almost complete. I did come to realize that temptation is not sin, but rather that the yielding to temptation is the sin. It is just that *not knowing this,* and *not knowing how to handle temptation*—by *specifically telling the Lord of all of which we are being tempted*—and being given no assurance of my salvation—based on the sure Word of the Bible—but rather being told to '*check out my fruit production*' to know whether I was a Christian or not, I had been in bondage to mental sin and this erroneous understanding that I—who had a vision of Christ the very day I first asked Him in at age of 12—was in the 'bondage of not *knowing*' that I was a Christian for 17 years!

As I have shared already, I had to see the reality of the *fact* of God's Word to understand that when I had sincerely prayed and asked God into my heart— He *had come in!* I was then a Christian! I was a baby Christian! I was a carnal Christian! But I was a Christian! I had to see that when Jesus said in Revelation 3:20, "Look! Here I stand at the door and knock. If you hear me calling and open the door, I will come in, and we will share a meal as friends." (NLT) This invitation did not have a lot of 'do's' and 'don'ts' included! There was just a wonderful invitation to sit down with Jesus and have a meal with Him and converse and learn of Him! This is the beginning of our Salvation! It spoke of a door—which we understand is the door to our heart—Jesus—who is the door to Salvation—said that He would come in! I now understand this as His declaration of coming into a heart—which is the essence and the beginning of Salvation! And yes, we must work out this salvation with fear and trembling which speaks of seriousness and application on our part, and growth. But I really could not begin to grow until I *knew according to God's Word*—that I was His—that He was not just with me, or 'out there somewhere', but *in* me. This is the fact and the awareness that makes all of the difference in the world. This is the mystery of God, and *knowing* this mystery opens all of the other doors to growth in the Spirit!

The battle between the flesh and the spirit are the reason that we must die daily to the pull of the flesh. The Bible tells us that the flesh—even though it is weak—battles against our own spirits daily. Here is Phillips translation, again, in 'Letters to Young Churches': Galatians 5: 16–17, "Here is my advice. Live your whole life in the Spirit and you will not satisfy the desires of your lower nature. For the whole energy of the lower nature *is set against the Spirit,* while the whole power of the Spirit *is contrary to the lower nature.* Here is the conflict, and that is why you are not free to do what you want to do. But if you follow the leading of the Spirit, you stand clear of the Law."

I am not suggesting that one still has to battle in those areas where a victory has been won. I know that I have not been tempted to smoke—I only had the dreams that I have told you of concerning smoking before the spirit of nicotine was cast out—but even in that, there was no temptation rather only disgust at the thought of returning to the cigarette—the spirit of nicotine was trying to get back into my life in explicit action, but this failed when I learned of this satanic tactic and cast it out! Nor have I desired to drink alcohol since 1963. And the evil imaginings disappeared as I was strengthened more and more, growing stronger and stronger in the Lord as I ran to Him for deliverance. The evil one stopped that temptation. He doesn't continue to do anything when he sees that it is only going to cause us to run to Jesus. Thank God for the victories!

As we grow in the Lord and live free of the temptations of our old life in the flesh, the daily dying to self has to do with the changing of the temptations. Rather than spending our time resting in Jesus, we are tempted to rest on the couch to watch too much television. Being freed of using our speech of old, speaking words of perhaps profanity, we are tempted to speak negatively or critically. Using our imaginations to think within, thoughts of condemnation concerning others, is ugly in God's sight. The only thing that we can do in the matter of willpower is to *set our will,* to *seek His Strength* and then, 'Jesus is Victor'—as Corrie Ten Boom always stated! We also must cast down, not only evil spirits attempting to destroy us, but also we are told to 'cast down evil imaginations'! We need to much more often use the Authority that Jesus has given us. Too many times we pray and ask Jesus to do the things that He has given us the authority and command to do!

Do you understand? Denying our weaknesses with: "Well, if I only tried harder, I could overcome!" keeps us in the bondage of leaning upon our own strength rather than His! Again, the key *Scripture of my* life became: II Corinthians 12:9, "And he said to me, My Grace is sufficient for you, for My Strength is made perfect in weakness." (NKJV) Jesus is saying: "All that I AM is enough, for My Strength will be shown to you in *your* weakness"

Again, the prayer of speedy deliverance is: "Lord Jesus, I am weak just now, and am being tempted." "Show me your strength." "Be my Strength!" The Holy Spirit will rush in to answer this prayer and before you realize it you are no longer being tempted but rather are thinking pleasant thoughts. This is the victory! It all begins in the heart or *thought life* of an individual and when the battle is won here, it is a *major victory* for the *whole* man!

I am remembering just now an experience that has helped me in these areas of Christian growth. It is a story of Reese Howells. He was a wonderful man of God, who had so many victories through prayer. One day he was told of some shortcomings of a fellow pastor, and was asked to pray for him as the congregation of his Church was dwindling because of these shortcomings. Reese began his prayer: "Oh God, this pastor has been lack in his duties", suddenly he felt a finger press upon his lips and heard within: "If anything be lovely, or of good report, think on these things!" And the Lord gave him to know that he should speak of the good things *about this* pastor. Reese began again and prayed with words of blessing concerning this man. Within weeks of this prayer, the pastor was 'turned around' in his dealings and doings and the Congregation was blessed and grew and prospered.

Always before I read of this testimony, when realizing that I was thinking any unchristian thoughts about a person or situation, I would remember this scripture, and would try to follow it by beginning to meditate upon the beauty of the flowers or some other thing that took my mind off of the previous thought. Now I came to realize that I had to *apply kind, lovely thoughts* to this *very person or situation.* It made a world of difference in my thought life. And now that I have shared these testimonies with you dear reader, won't you, who may presently be in bondage to any of these life threatening habits, use the same methods of escape as I have testified of? Find this new thrilling joyous way of deliverance and a new life of growing maturity and of overcoming temptation—through *running* to our Lord and Savior, with—*Specific Prayer and the wonderful privilege of leaning on His Strength!*

I will close this section with the little poem He gave me concerning this subject!

'Leaning'!

Many have called Christianity a 'crutch'.
Of the truth in that statement, there's much!
When I leaned on myself, I fell flat on my face.
When I leaned on a drink, I just couldn't keep pace.
When I leaned on education, I found spiritual emaciation.
If I'd leaned on drugs, I'd have seen hallucinations and bugs.
When I leaned on a friend, I found pity the end.
I discovered that everyone is on a 90 degree angle,
And trying to deny it, ourselves we entangle.
Now since we're all leaning, try Jesus my friend.
He's the only one whom under, our weight, won't bend!

Now for a 'bit of humorous advice!'

My first published poem printed in the American Automobile Association paper! It is of my first auto, a 1937 'Chevy'.

'Driver Survivor!

She polished her car and viewed it with pride.
Then put it away 'til she wanted to ride.
Next day out it came and she started for school,
With a flat spare in the trunk and not even one tool!
Oh this girl she was 'cocky' therefore hadn't much sense
And on the way to the schoolhouse she did something dense!
She tooted and yelled and waved to her friend
Next thing she knew she had a damaged front-end.
The grill it was maimed, the fenders were pleated,
The bumper was ruined and she felt defeated.
Oh woe to the girl who learned the hard way
That lack of concentration on the road doesn't pay!

'A Call to Sanity'

'The Birthright of Ishmael'
(An excerpt from my booklet)

While reading this, my friend Rev. Marilyn Govender had a vision of a new cover. She saw the map of Israel being pulled in opposite directions by two fists!

One was the hand of an Israeli; the other the hand of an Arab!

'A Solution for Peace between Brothers'

'Questions begging an answer'

Did the 'Double Portion' promise for the 'First-Born' go to Ishmael? Was Ishmael the first child in the Bible to be named *before* he was born? Was Hagar, mother of Ishmael the first women in the Bible to be visited by the Angel of the Lord? Was the promise to Ishmael of being blessed with many children fulfilled? Whose were the sons that were promised the title of: Duke and King and Prince? Many lands were promised to Ishmael. Were the promises fulfilled? Are the oil-rich lands of the Middle East part of the promised inheritance? Did this inheritance go to the proper sons? Is it possible that a Root of Bitterness was planted in Ishmael—by his own father? Read on!

The Beginning of the Heritage of Abraham!

Genesis 12:1–7, "Now the Lord had said unto Abram, Get you out of your country, and from your kindred, and from your father's house, unto a land that I will show you. And I will make of you a great nation, and I will bless you, and make your name great; and you shall be a blessing: And I will bless them that bless you, and curse him that curses you; and in you shall all families of the earth be blessed." So Abram departed, as the Lord had spoken unto him; and Lot went with him; and Abram was seventy and five years old when he departed out of Haran. And Abram took Sarai his wife, and Lot his brother's son, and all their substance that they had gathered, and the souls that they had gotten in Haran; and they went forth to go into the land of Canaan; and in the land of Canaan they came. And Abram passed through the land unto the place of Sichem, unto the plain of Moreh. And the Canaanite was then in the land. And the Lord appeared unto Abram, and said, "Unto your seed, will I give this land." And there built he an altar unto the Lord, who appeared unto him." (NAS)

The Birth of Ishmael: The Story!

Genesis 16:1, *"Now Sarai, Abram's wife bare him no children: and she had a handmaid, an Egyptian, whose name was Hagar."*

Sarai's Plan!

Genesis 16:2–4, *"And Sarai said unto Abram, "Behold now, the Lord has restrained me from bearing: I pray you, go in unto my maid: it may be that I may obtain children by her." And Abram hearkened to the voice of Sarai. And after Abram had lived ten years in the land of Canaan, Abram's wife Sarai took Hagar the Egyptian, her maid, and gave her to her husband Abram as his wife. And he went in to Hagar, and she conceived; and when she saw that she had conceived, her mistress was despised in her sight!"*

Sarai's Anger!

Genesis 16:5–6, *"And Sarai said to Abram, "May the wrong done me be upon you. I gave my maid unto your arms; but when she saw that she had conceived, I was despised in her sight. May the Lord judge between you and me." But Abram said to Sarai, "Behold, your maid is in your power; do to her what is good in your sight." So Sarai treated her harshly, and she fled from her presence."* (Was Abram taking the 'easy-way' out, avoiding confrontation?)

The Angel of the Lord appears for the First time, in Scripture—to a woman!

Genesis 16:7–9, *"Now the Angel of the Lord found her by a spring of water in the wilderness, by the spring on the way to Shur. And he said, "Hagar, Sarai's maid where have you come from and where are you going?" And she said: "I am fleeing from my mistress Sarai." Then the angel of the Lord said to her, "Return to your mistress, and submit yourself to her authority."* Return and submit—these are always the steps to restored peace and joy. A blessing is given to Hagar, and a promise is made concerning her son, Ishmael whose Name means: *'God Hears'!*

Directed by the Angel, to call his name, ISHMAEL!

Genesis 16:10–12, *"Moreover, the Angel of the Lord said to her, "I will greatly multiply your descendants so that they shall be too many to count." The angel of the Lord said to her further, "Behold, you are with child, And you shall bear a son; And you shall call his name Ishmael, Because the Lord has given heed to your affliction. And he will be a wild donkey of a man, His hand will be against everyone, And everyone's hand will be against him; And he will live to the East of all his brothers."*

Note: Some say: "The wild ass of the Arabian deserts was a noble creature and was thus a fine symbol of the free-roving life of the Arab." Also: Presently: "From the Hebrew 'al pene' literally, "upon or against the face of". This more particularly means "in defiance of, or in disregard of," and the context denotes hostility on the part of Ishmael and his descendants against his brethren—Isaac and his descendants.

Note: This prophesy was not spoken to cause Ishmael and his descendants to react in this way, but rather, knowing all future things, God knew that this would be their reaction. Was not one of the bitter root causes of this ongoing hostility throughout the ages the *bitter root of rejection?* This thought is enlarged upon a little later in this treatise.

Another Bitter Root is the sinful emotion called: jealousy! This is the same ugly sin that caused Lucifer the created Angel, to be cast out of heaven and become Satan—the Evil one! This is the same sin that caused the first born son on earth, Cain to kill his brother Abel, thus becoming the first murderer on earth. Repentance for our sins and forgiving all those who have 'aught' against us, and the giving of thanks for the blessings that God would give and is giving, is the cure! Let us read further to realize and understand and appreciate what God has done!

'The Birth'

Genesis 16:13–16, *"Then she (Hagar) called the name of the Lord who spoke to her: "El Roi", "Thou art a God who sees", for she said, "Have I even remained alive here after seeing Him?"* Therefore the well was called Beer-lahai-roi; behold, it is between Kadesh and Bered. So Hagar bore Abram a son; and Abram called the name of his son, whom Hagar bore, *Ishmael!"*

This name was given by the Angel of the Lord before he was even born! Is this not the first time mentioned in the Bible that a child was given a name while still in his mother's womb? *Yes, it is!* Consider and see Ishmael! The Lord

God of Israel favored your forbear, even before he was born! Wake up! And glorify this Lord God of Israel who is also *your Creator!*

This first child—baby boy Ishmael—brought Abram much joy!

Abram was eighty-six years old when Hagar bore Ishmael to him. (Abram had heard from God before this incident, but was never to hear from God again for thirteen years!) Ishmael was conceived and brought forth in the natural way, of natural parents, Hagar and Abram. There is nothing wrong in having a natural normal birth. It was just not the 'Miraculous Birth' planned by God! That birth was to take place later, in parents *too old to bear* in the natural. But Ishmael was the very *First-Born* Son of Abram! Imagine how deeply Abram loved this son. Think how much, during this time, he pampered and enjoyed and instructed and played with and cared for his *'First Born' son, Ishmael!* His heart went out to him. He must have reasoned that this was the *promised Heir!*

The Command of the 'Double Blessing' concerning the 'First Born'!

This is found in Deuteronomy 21:15–17, "If a man have two wives, the one loved and the other unloved, and both the loved and the unloved have borne him sons, if the *first born son* belongs to the unloved, then it shall be in the day that he makes to inherit what he has to his sons, *he cannot* make the son of the loved, the first-born—before the son of the unloved, who *is* the first-born. "But he shall acknowledge the first-born, the son of the unloved, by giving him *a double portion of all that he has,* for he is the beginning of his strength*; to* him *belongs the right of the first-born.*" We see here the Righteous judgments of God Almighty, the Highest God, and Yahweh EL ROI—as mother Hagar the Egyptian called Him—*the God I have seen and still live!*

Now, that Hagar was not hated by Abram is obvious. She had given him Ishmael! Did God honor His Word and give Ishmael a Double Portion? We will observe this later on.

'The Covenant of Circumcision'

In Genesis 17:9–14, God established a Covenant of Circumcision with Abraham, that all of his descendants *should be circumcised* in the foreskin of their flesh; even the servants born in his house and bought with his money. Everyone who would not be circumcised *should be cut off* from his people for *he has broken* God's Covenant! Thought: "Should not Ishmael and his descendants have continued on in this Covenant plan of God?" Evidently they did not! Could this be the *basic* Scriptural reason *for the breach* between Isaac and Ishmael?

Genesis 17:18–22, "Abraham said unto God, "Oh that Ishmael might live before Thee!" And God said, "Sarah thy wife shall bear thee a son indeed: and thou shalt call his name *Isaac,* and I will establish my covenant with him for an everlasting covenant and with his seed after him. And as for *Ishmael,* I have heard thee: Behold, I have blessed him. And will *make him fruitful,* and will *multiply him exceedingly; twelve princes shall he beget, and I will make him a great nation,* but My Covenant will I establish with Isaac, which Sarah shall bear unto thee at this set time in the next year." And He left off talking with him, and God went up from Abraham."

The 'Cutting'

Genesis 17:23–26, "Then Abraham took *Ishmael* his son, and all the servants who were born in his house and all who were bought with his money, every male among the men of Abraham's household, and circumcised the flesh of their foreskin in the very same day, as God had said to Him. Now Abraham was *ninety-nine years old* when he was circumcised in the flesh of his foreskin. And Ishmael his son was *thirteen years,* when he was circumcised in the flesh of his foreskin. *In the very same day Abraham was circumcised and Ishmael his son.* And all the men of his household, who were born in the house or bought with money from a foreigner, were circumcised with him."

Abraham and Ishmael both had the circumcision of the flesh, the cutting away of the flesh that speaks of the *doing away with the old, and the beginning of the new!* The foreskin of the male covers the most important organ in his body for the bringing forth of new life. Later we see that God speaks of circumcising the foreskin of the heart—that covering of 'self-life' similar to the hardness of stone—that needs to be removed for the bringing forth of *spiritual birth!*

An example of God's Judgment: 'Sodom and Gomorrah are destroyed!'

Genesis 18:20–33, God then told Abraham of His disgust with the very grievous sin of Sodom and Gomorrah and His plan to destroy the city. Chapter 19 speaks of its destruction. *Was God putting the Sodomites out of commission that they might not influence or harm Ishmael as God knew that he and Hagar were soon to be sent away?*

Issac is Born

Genesis 21:1–7, And the Lord visited Sarah as He had said, and the Lord did for Sarah as He had spoken. For Sarah conceived and bore Abraham a son in his old age, at the set time of which God had spoken to him. And Abraham called the name of his son who was born to him—whom Sarah bore to him—Issac. Then Abraham circumcised his son Issac when he was eight days old, as God had commanded him. Now Abraham was one hundred years old when his son Issac was born to him. And Sarah said, "God has made me laugh, and all who hear will laugh with me." She also said, "Who would have said to Abraham that Sarah would nurse children? For I have borne him a son in his old age."

Hagar and Ishmael Depart

Genesis 21:8–13, So the child grew and was weaned. And Abraham made a great feast on the same day that Issac was weaned. And Sarah saw the son of Hagar the Egyptian, whom she had borne to Abraham, scoffing. Therefore she said to Abraham, "Cast out this bondwoman and her son; for the son of this bondwoman shall not be heir with my son, namely with Issac." And the matter was very displeasing in Abraham's sight because of his son. But God said to Abraham, "Do not let it be displeasing in your sight because of the lad of because of your bondwoman. Whatever Sarah has said to you, listen to her voice; for in Issac your seed shall be called. Yet I will also make a nation of the son of the bondwoman, because he is your seed."

'The Dismissal of Mother and Child'

Genesis 21:14, "So Abraham rose up early in the morning, and took bread, and a skin of water, and gave them to Hagar, putting it on her shoulder, and gave her the boy and sent her away. And she departed, and wandered in the wilderness of Beer-Sheba."

"What did we just read?"

Some bread and a bottle of water! From this father and husband—from this man of great wealth! Should he not have prepared a caravan? Should he not have given camels loaded down with goods and foodstuff, some sheep and goats for milk and butter and a way to begin to have a livelihood? What was he thinking, sending off his child and second wife with some bread and a bottle of water into the Negev, the dry, burning desert without tent or covering from exposure. Was not this method of departure unthinkable? Oh my, again our senses are assaulted and we have very little understanding. But we do have the audacity and the liberty to question!

Was this, on Abraham's part, the action of a man so grieved that he wasn't thinking straight? Wanting to obey, did he get the two out of his sight quickly less he falter? Or was he selfishly thinking to end his own pain, and not properly executing the departure? Unless the Holy Spirit teaches us, we shall not know.

We do know that previously, Abraham had deceitfully used Sarah a few times in an effort to 'save his own neck'! Oh God, Your Word is so clear to truthfully show us, even in Your choicest saints, Your chosen ones, the condition and weaknesses in the flesh that can only be corrected and avoided by leaning on Your Strength alone!

'A Root of Bitterness'

Could not the memory of this difficult deed, caused indirectly by the birth of Isaac, be repeated and handed down verbally throughout the generations and become one of the 'Roots of Bitterness' buried in the heart of the Arab descendants of Ishmael? The Word of God tells us that a Root of Bitterness can cause the whole body to be defiled! Hebrews 12:14–17, "Pursue peace with all men, and the sanctification without which no one will see the Lord. See to it that no one comes short of the grace of God; *that no root of bitterness springing up causes trouble,* and *by it* many *be defiled;* that there be no immoral or godless person like Esau, who sold his own birthright for a single meal. For you know that even afterwards, when he desired to inherit the blessing, he was rejected, for he found no place for repentance, though he sought for it with tears."

'Hagar is filled with distress!'

Genesis 21:15–16, "And the water in the skin was used up and she placed the boy under one of the shrubs. And she went, and she sat her down across from him at a distance of about a bow shot; for she said to herself: "Let me not see the death of the boy." So she sat opposite him, and lifted up her voice, and wept". (NKJV)

'An Angel is sent in response to the voice of Ishmael!'

Genesis 21:17,19, "And God heard the voice of the lad; and the Angel of God called to Hagar out of heaven, and said unto her, "What aileth thee, Hagar? Fear not; for God hath heard the voice of the lad where he is. Arise, lift up the lad, and hold him in thine hand; *for I will make him a Great Nation!*" And God opened her eyes, and she saw a well of water; and she went, and filled the bottle with water, and gave the lad drink."

Genesis 21:20–21, "And God was with the lad; and he grew, and dwelt in the wilderness, and became an archer. And he lived in the wilderness of Paran; and his mother took him a wife out of the land of Egypt."

'Now for the Promised 'Double-Blessing' of God'

We spoke of the double blessing to the First Born promised in the Word of God established in Deuteronomy 21:15–17. Having examined this Word, let us see if God, Hagar's EL ROI, fulfilled this promise!

Genesis 25:12–16, "Now these are the generations of Ishmael, Abraham's son, whom Hagar, the Egyptian, Sarah's handmaid bore unto Abraham: and these are the names of the sons of Ishmael, by their names in order of their birth: "Nebaioth, the first-born of Ishmael, and Kedar and Adbeel and Mibsam and Mishma and Dumah and Massa, Hadad and Tema, Jetur, Naphish and Kedemah!" "These are the sons of Ishmael and these are their names by their villages and by their camps *or castles;* twelve princes, according to their *peoples, or tribes* or Nations!" (These are also found listed in: I Chronicles 1:29–31.) *So important to God are these sons of Ishmael that they are listed in His Holy written Word, the Bible! Think of this Ishmael, are your descendants listed in the book you call Holy?*

'Sons, daughters, lands, Princely Titles—are these not plentiful blessings?'

Were these not more than double blessings? Twelve sons and daughters also! So many blessings were given to Ishmael, his wife and Grandmother Hagar! Not only children, but lands, towns, castles—and these sons were called *Princes* and *Dukes* and *Kings!* These are Titles of Honor and Royalty! "Oh Most Holy God Almighty, what blessings you have bestowed upon Ishmael!" In the Holy Bible we read in Proverbs 10:22, "The blessing of the Lord makes one rich and He adds no sorrow with it!"

We have just read how this whole affair of longing for children caused rivalry and upheaval in the lives of Abraham, Sarah, Hagar and Ishmael. Therefore, this multiple number of children and blessings of much land and wealth given by Almighty God to Ishmael and his descendents should have caused them a great sense of self-respect and confidence! It should have resulted in wholeness and happiness and thankfulness—with mind-set of success and prestige! Has this been the response? Why not? Has ingratitude, or a distorted sense of who he is in the eyes of God, or the teachings of a later religion blinded the eyes and understanding of Ishmael? Ishmael, why not rejoice to be called and to be known as an *Ishmaelite!* That precious name was given to you by an Angel, who was under direct orders from the Lord God Almighty—the One who created our Universe!

'A problem of mistaken loyalties'

And are these nations not blessed with oil in abundance which, through the years has created *great* wealth? If only that wealth had been distributed fairly and indiscriminately to Ishmael's entire heritage by those blessed to be in authority! If only God Almighty had been honored as the giver of these blessings! Rather—the one who came on the scene centuries afterward is known as Ishmael's god. But there is only one true God! If only Ishmael would honor *the God of his mother Hagar and his father Abraham,* rather than a god whom neither of his parents ever knew nor ever heard of!

Now what of the Blessings to Isaac?

Most Holy Father God, how many sons and land did you give to Isaac?

Genesis 25:19–26, "And these are the records of the generations of Isaac, Abraham's son: Abraham became the father of Isaac. And Isaac was forty years old when he took Rebekah to wife, the daughter of Bethuel the Syrian of Padan-Aram, the sister to Laban the Syrian. (Rebekah had been living in the city of Nahor in Mesopotamia.) And Isaac prayed to the Lord on behalf of his wife, because *she was barren;* and the Lord answered him, and Rebekah his wife conceived. And the children struggled together within her; and she said, "If it be so, why then am I this way?" So she went to enquire of the Lord. And the Lord said unto her: "*Two nations* are in thy womb, and two peoples shall be separated from your body; and one people shall be stronger than the other; and the elder shall serve the younger." (This is not *predestination,* but rather, the Lord God knew before they were born what their choices would be and therefore their destination!) "And when her days to be delivered were fulfilled, behold, there were twins in her womb. And the first came out red, all over like a hairy garment; and they called his name Esau. And after that came his brother out, and his hand took hold on Esau's heel; and his name was called Jacob; and Isaac was sixty years old when she bare them." (*Isaac had to wait* 20 *years for just two sons and no more!*) On down the family line from that beginning, there was upheaval. No sweet family 'get-togethers' for the grandparents, for these sons were separated through mutual sins, (One stole the birth-right blessing; the other despised such.) all of this, even before they bore children.

'Two sons for Jacob—Twelve sons for Ishmael'

The Lord God gave unto Isaac, *two sons!* God gave Ishmael *twelve sons!* What blessings of the Land were given?

Genesis 26:12–14, "Then Isaac sowed in that land and received in the same year a hundred fold: and the Lord blessed him." (Lands are not mentioned but rather—the Harvest!) "And the man waxed great (rather than the land) and went forward and grew until he became very great: For he had possession of flocks and possession of herds, and great store of servants! And the Philistines envied him." *Here, jealousy is seen again, sadness and upheaval and discontent, because of the blessings of others. This is such a self-defeating emotion. It causes internal un-rest and dis-ease in the body of the one who harbors jealousy.* How much better to forgive all wrongs and to rejoice in the personal blessings that God gives to each!

So, whereas *Ishmael and his wife were prolific in bringing forth sons,* (even as the Arabs of today seem to have this same ability and blessing) Isaac had to wait 20 years before having the blessing of fatherhood with the birth of twins! This means that only *one time* did his wife become pregnant and bring forth the fruit of the womb which is God's wonderful blessing!

Ishmael's Inheritance:

Presently the 21 Arab states of Mauritania, Morocco, Algeria, Tunisia, Libya, Egypt, Sudan, Lebanon, Syria, Jordan, Iraq, Iran, Kuwait, Bahrain, Oatar, Saudi Arabia, United Arab Emirates, Oman, Yemen, Djibouti, and Somalia, cover Five Million, Three Hundred Thousand Square Miles of Planet Earth! (Did we read that right, 5,300,000 square miles?)

This is almost *double* the size of the United States! *These are great birthright blessings promised and given by the Lord God Almighty—El Roi—the Lord who sees—to Ishmael and his descendants!* (Of course, these include some lands 'gained through the sword', and presently encroached upon!) And the Jewish Nation does not want any of this land—other than that portion of Land promised to them by this same God! The Great I AM, Creator of Heaven and Earth, Jehovah, El Shaddai, and Eloheem is His Name!

The Death of Sarah and burial in the Cave of Machpelah!

Genesis 23:1–2, "And Sarah was an hundred and twenty seven years old: these were the years of the life of Sarah. And Sarah died in Kiriatharba (that is, Hebron) in the land of Canaan; and Abraham went in to mourn for Sarah and to weep for her."

Genesis 23:17–20, "So Ephron's field, which was in Machpelah, which faced Mamre, the field and cave which was in it, and all the trees which were in the field, that were within all the confines of its border, *were deeded over to Abraham for a possession* in the presence of the sons of Heth, before all who went in at the gate of his city. And after this, Abraham buried Sarah his wife in the cave of the field at Machpelah facing Mamre (that is, Hebron) in the land of Canaan. So the field, and the cave that is in it, were deeded over to Abraham for a burial site by the sons of Heth."

The Seed of Aram, Father of Nations and Abraham, Father of a Multitude!

This is the same man, with a name change!

Genesis 25:1–2, "Now Abraham took another wife, whose name was Keturah. And she bore him Zimran and Jokshan and Medan and Midian* and Ishbak and Shuah." Six more sons were born from Abraham! (Evidently when God rejuvenated Abraham to bring forth Isaac, this ability for procreation was strong!) *Midian: The area of the land of Midian is the best known name in the list ranging from the head of the Gulf of Aqaba to Moab and even Gilead!

Produced out of Abrahams loins were eight sons! Their names again, are: Ishmael, by Hagar, while he was called Abram, Isaac by Sarah, after his name was changed to Abraham: and then the six sons by Keturah just mentioned!

Ishmael and Midian being half-brothers, their descendants became closely allied. The Word of God states that one day they will all dwell side by side, and among one another, in PEACE!

The Burial of Abraham by Isaac and Ishmael

Genesis 25:7–10, "And these are the days of the years of Abraham's life which he lived, one hundred and seventy-five years. Then Abraham gave up the ghost, and died in a good old age, an old man, full of years, and was gathered to his people. And his *sons Isaac and Ishmael* buried him in the cave of Machpelah, in the field of Ephron, the son of Zoar the Hittite, which is before Mamre." (This may indicate that these half-brothers were reconciled.)

Ishmael is not buried in the Cave of Machpelah! Neither his sons nor his wives are buried there! Never-the-less, the Moslems have built a Mosque over this burial cave in which reside only Jewish bodies! Supposedly, it is because of the presence of the remains of Abraham. But do the Arabs realize that they are honoring the burying place of the remains of Isaac and Rebekah, Sarah and Jacob, the Father of the Jewish Nation, and his wife Leah? (A notable exception is Rachel. She is buried in Bethlehem, Genesis 35:19.) Again, the Modern day name of this city of burial is Hebron.

How Jacob who died in Egypt got into this Cave!

Genesis 49:29–32, gives the Scriptural evidence of Jacob's burial! While living in Goshen, in Egypt, Jacob charged his sons to bury him in the same Cave wherein lay his grandfather Abraham and his grandmother Sarah; his father and mother, Isaac and Rebekah and one of his wives, Leah. Also Chapter 50: verses 1–13, "Joseph mourned and afterward he and his brothers took Jacob and buried him in the land of Canaan in the cave of Machpelah." See verse 13 especially for a reiteration of the ownership of this burial ground.

The Death of Ishmael

Genesis 25:17–18, "These were the years of the life of Ishmael: one hundred thirty-seven years, and he breathed his last and died, and was gathered to his people. He died in the presence of all his brethren." (They dwelt from Havilah—where there is much fine gold—as far as Shur, which is east of Egypt as you go toward Assyria.)

Oh Ishmael, do you not see how God has blessed you throughout your life. Your birth was prophesied and you were given your name by an Angel! You spent your childhood as the only son of the Wealthy Patriarch Abraham. You had an angel once more visit you and your mother in the first adverse experience of your young life. You have been blessed with children and vast lands containing oil and the prestige that goes along with your great wealth. You are blessed to be Princes and Oil Barons! Why would you not be thankful to the Lord God of Mother Hagar and rejoice in being an Ishmaelite? Why continue on generation after generation in the awful hatred of Isaac and your nephew Jacob and your great and grand nephews, and nieces, who are his heritage?

Be thankful Ishmael that you are not the
Covenant Race that must bear much!

Oh please see how that compared to the temporal blessings of Isaac, you have not been left behind in any good thing, but rather have been blessed much more than him! Ishmael, see how much you have been blessed in that you have *not been hounded by Satan*—because that you are not of the *Chosen Covenant Race* that was to bring forth the Messiah? You and the *Gentile races* have been blessed to be reasonably *free from the constant hounding and badgering and devious scheming to destroy and end your lineage* in the way that the Jewish Race has had to bear. Why continue to bend the knee to one whom your ancestors knew not? One who's religious commands and ideals continually 'stir you up' to harbor harmful emotions of hatred and strife? Rather, go to, find and cling to the God of Love, who has bestowed you with continual blessingsof health and abundance!

A New Path to Freedom!

Ishmael, need you continue on in a way of life that demands *blind submission?* Does the blind submission to laws, and rules, and regulations and tenants that, if not followed will bring fearful consequences, give you a sense of joy and of well-being? Does such, fill you with peace, with an awareness of being loved? Does this blind submission that is demanded fill you with love for your fellow man; for your family and friends or for yourself? Most probably rather, this way fills you with a sense of failure and dread; a sense of not ever being: 'good enough' a feeling of being rejected. How much better to follow a God who *rewards* Obedience? And this obedience is to be given out of love for a God of Love. A God *who wants to have communion with you!* How much better to have the awareness, that true obedience—which is better than sacrifice—speaks of understanding and following that which God Almighty is wanting to accomplish in you! And this ability is given through the leading of the Holy Spirit—Ha Ruach Ha Kodosh. The Spirit of the Righteous One is given by our Father God, our Heavenly Father. Through the reading and hearing and receiving of the Holy Word of God given in the Holy Bible—we can learn to follow such leading in an attitude of thanksgiving and love and true submission to His Will.

This submission then is borne out of the awareness of His Love for us. We will learn to desire to please the Heart of the One who loved us so much that He came in the form of the Body of His Son, Yeshua to sacrifice Himself on a cruel cross! Thereby dying in our place, the Perfect Sacrifice! He died in this manner that our sins be nailed upon Him! Galatians 3:13, in the New Testament—the New Covenant, cut and written through the shedding of His Blood, tells us that: Messiah has redeemed us from the curse of the law, being made a curse for us: for it is written: cursed is everyone that hangs upon a tree. *The curse was the effect of sin separating us* from God

Isaiah Chapter 53

Isaiah 53:1–12, "Who has believed our message and to whom has the arm of the Lord been revealed? 2 He grew up before Him like a tender shoot, and like a root, out of dry ground. He had no beauty or majesty to attract us to him, nothing in his appearance that we should desire him. 3 He was despised and rejected by men, a man of sorrows, and familiar with suffering. Like one from whom men hide their faces he was despised, and we esteemed him not.

4 Surely he took up our infirmities and carried our sorrows, yet we considered him stricken by God, smitten by him, and afflicted. 5 But he was pierced for our transgressions, he was crushed for our iniquities; the punishment that brought us peace was upon him, and by his wounds we are healed. 6 We all, like sheep, have gone astray, each of us has turned to his own way; and the Lord has laid on him the iniquity of us all. 7He was oppressed and afflicted, yet he did not open his mouth; he was led like a lamb to the slaughter, and as a sheep before her shearers is silent, so he did not open his mouth. 8 By oppression and judgment he was taken away. And who can speak of his descendants? For he was cut off from the land of the living; for the transgression of my people he was stricken. 9 He was assigned a grave with the wicked and with the rich in his death, though he had done no violence, nor was any deceit in his mouth. 10 Yet it was the Lord's will to crush him and cause him to suffer, and though the Lord makes his life a guilt offering, he will see his offspring and prolong his days, and the will of the Lord will prosper in his hand. 11 After the suffering of his soul, he will see the light of life and be satisfied; by his knowledge my righteous servant will justify many, and he will bear their iniquities. 12 Therefore I will give him a portion among the great, and he will divide the spoils with the strong, because he poured out his life unto death, and was numbered with the transgressors. For he bore the sin of many, and made intercession for the transgressors."(NIV)

The Narrow Way! The Only Way!

The Word of God tells us that no man or woman can come to the Father except through the Son, Jesus. (Is this intolerant? Absolutely! The first law of Eloheem—El Roi—is to have *no gods* before *Him!* And His only begotten Son said: "No man comes to the Father but by *ME!*") We who have discovered this Peace by being born again of the Holy Spirit know this sounds narrow—and it is—but it was spoken by the Author of Truth, Jesus. You must seek forgiveness of the only One who can forgive all of the years and centuries of animosity. You must do this *before there will be lasting peace between you two brothers, the sons of Abraham!*

The Lord God, is the Creator of the Universe

He is waiting to hear your hearts cry, directed unto Him through the Only Name given unto men whereby they must be saved, and that Name is Jesus Christ Anointed One, Messiah!

Ishmael, the wrath of God was taken out upon His Son Jesus and God the Father was pleased to bruise Him. Not at all because He was pleased to see the horrible beating and *every sin of mankind* being placed upon Him, but because

God loves you Ishmael and knows that His Son Jesus had to pay the full price for you to be redeemed—and He did so! This means that you can be forgiven your sins and 'Come Home' to our Heavenly Father! What a gracious invitation to you—and this is Truth! Believe it!

A Personal Word to the Israelis—Isaac,

The Word in your Bible, which so many Christians are quoting today and trying to follow, was written to you first! II Chronicles 7:13–14 says, "When I shut up the heaven and there is no rain, or command locusts to devour the land or send pestilence among My people, "if My people who are called by My Name will humble themselves, and pray and seek My face, and turn from their wicked ways, then will I hear from heaven, and will forgive their sin, and heal their land." He will heal your land, which is His Land!

Pray just now to: Peleh, Yoatz, Avi-Ad, Sar Shalom, El Gibbor! Wonderful, Counselor, Mighty God, Prince of Peace, Everlasting Father, Jesus, Yeshua Ha Messiach!

A Message for Fools:

The fool says in his heart, there is no God—Scripture! For all of the heathen and atheists and agnostics and those bound in false religions and spirits of religion who happen upon this book by Devine appointment, as long as you have breath in your body, realize who it is who can cause to come about, all of the things written in verse 13 above! Plus many more of curses, as well as the blessings, for He is the Lord Almighty God of the Universe. Turn to Him now! Today is the day of Salvation! Today, if you hear His Word, harden not your heart as they did in the day of adversity and were lost in the final 'waters of adversity,' the Red Sea, which speaks of Death. His arms are wide open to you just now in this Day of Grace. Run to Him for deliverance - before it is too late!

'An After-Word—the fundamental reason—for the writing of this book'

This an attempt to help the Arab people to understand and appreciate the 'Double-Blessing' of the 'Birth-right of the First-Born'! This was given them by the Almighty God of Israel—El Roi—the Name of God spoken by Ishmael's mother Hagar which means: 'The God who sees'! A tremendous abundance of land and blessings has been given to them! This is the answer to the cry of their Father Abraham: "Oh that Ishmael might live before Thee!" May this little booklet, birth in Ishmael a desire to search and to see and to learn of the grandeur and the beauty and the truth of this Awesome One! And then may they receive this God of Eternal Love and Peace! We who know Him and have become His Family members by receiving His Son, call him "Our Father who art in Heaven"! May Ishmael be re-born and restored in this truth!

While living among Arabs and Muslims in Bethany for a year, I volunteered as an Activity Director in the 'Four Homes of Mercy'. This is an Orthodox Christian Home for the Handicapped and infirm. I enjoyed being with the residents who taught me just enough Arabic to 'get by' daily. After those in the town received my friendship and dropped their shields of fear and indifference, I learned of their customs and many times was a partaker of the kindness of their hospitality. I was also *shocked almost into disbelief* upon learning of many of their family customs; especially concerning their women-folk and how they handle the problems that they feel are a disgrace to family honor.

In 2001, during a Retreat with a group of her Branch Leaders of the End-Time Handmaidens and Servants, Sister Gwen Shaw repeated a Prophecy that the Lord had previously spoken out of her mouth. She quoted: "I Am going to 'crack' 'crack' 'crack' 'crack' 'crack' 'crack' 'crack'—(this was repeated seven times—God's number of perfection)—the 'Wall of Islam' that Ishmael may come to Me!" Suddenly she stood up and pointed to me and said: "Gracie, you have a great work in Islam—a *great work!*" Sister Gwen never called me Gracie before. I think that she was distinguishing in a room full of people, the difference between Grace (the Grace of God) and myself as the recipient of this prophecy!

Later, I was led to write: 'A Call to Sanity—The Birthright of Ishmael!'

While I was writing this, I remembered the Prophecy given over me. My prayer is that this book will draw the Muslim Arabs to a new understanding and a new love for the Lord God of Israel, who has blessed them so outrageously!

This is a reminder to the Nations, of the Blessings of God that have been poured out upon Ishmael and his heritage, from the beginning! It is time for the brothers to come together in unity. It is time for them to reconcile and begin building together—for a marvelous future!

A song for the ascent to Jerusalem; A psalm of David!

Psalm 133:13 (NLT), "How wonderful it is, how pleasant, when brothers live together in harmony! For harmony is as precious as the fragrant anointing oil that was poured over Aaron's head, that ran down his beard and onto the border of his robe. Harmony is as refreshing as the dew from Mount Hermon that falls on the mountains of Zion. And the Lord has pronounced his blessing, even life forevermore." And the Lord God Almighty, maker of Heaven and Earth declares that this brotherhood will take place! "Oh Lord God, may it begin now!"

'Autumn Glory'

How beautiful, that the Handiwork of Thy Fingers have gloriously burst forth in one last expression of high praise, before falling at Your feet spent; awaiting a white garment of Your covering! The leaves of the trees are outdoing one another, in showing forth the magnificence of their Creator.

You could have made the living things around us so dull; all one color, pink, perchance, uniform in size and shape, six inch squares. A lovely color this—and shape, but if repeated endlessly would result in monotonous boredom. Instead, you reveal to us glimpses of Your Nature, through that which Your Word has spoken into being!

Creation is filled with beauty of color; infinite variety of shape and size—every tree differing from one another. There is not one exactly identical, and even within the realms of just one species, lies such a variety throughout the world. Who could be expert in naming them, much less knowing their life cycles? You alone, Creator of the Heavens and Earth—and all that is within know the life of each, from beginning to end.

Red, gold, burgundies, orange, yellow, brown and green, the pinks and scarlet, flow into a tapestry—a 'Joseph's Coat Garment of Praise' unto You who made them. In their expression unto You they bear witness to man of Your Glory! The leaves begin in virgin birth showing forth a fresh bright color—with perfection and symmetry of size and shape, that speaks of the perfection of their Maker. They spend their lives feeding and nourishing, taking in the poison of carbon monoxide. Then breathing out life-giving oxygen—the brilliant chemistry ordained by their Creator.

As the heat of summer, the ravages of wind, rain and insect—earth's reception committee—take their toll, causing those little tree appendages to be, weather-worn, weary and aged, they never-the-less fill up with sweetness—as they near the end of their lives and are hit with a wintry blast. They remember the many bright warm sun-shiny days of perfection sent by You. They recall all the times they have lifted their hands to praise You—as the sweet breath of Your Spirit lifted and refreshed them.

In a final anthem of praise they join one with another in putting on royal robes—and dance a silent pageant of adoration unto Thee before falling exhausted at Your Feet. In the laying down of self, they form a carpet of nourishment—to replenish the earth from which they have fed. They await a soft covering of white—to nestle and warm themselves in their sleep. They make room for another generation continuing on in the marvelous cycle of life.

"O God, grant that we—Thy noblest Creation—made in Thy very Image—may live a life—as yielded to Your Spirit—as submissive to Thy Will—as useful in life and as glorifying unto Thee even in death—as the simple leaves of the trees. Father—grant that we may be as leaves of that Tree—the 'The Tree of Life Jesus'—for the healing of the Nations!" Amen.

'Echoes from Heaven' by Grace McGonigle

#8 Hill Top Drive Finleyville PA 15332

gilah2000@yahoo.com

echoesfromheaven@netscape.net

If you have enjoyed or been blessed by my writing, feel free to drop me a line! Thank you.

Alternate Ministry addresses:

Living Waters, the Fountain of ISRAEL

P.O. B # 111 N. Apollo, PA 15332

or:

Sister Carly and Max Cheney's address

#9 Parkvue Drive Finleyville, PA 15332